The Spatial Organization of Society

Richard L. Morrill
University of Washington

Wadsworth Publishing Company, Inc.
Belmont, California

L. C. Cat. Card No.: 72–115009
Printed in the United States of America

1 2 3 4 5 6 7 8 9 10—74 73 72 71 70

Preface

Differences in the human and physical world are great, exciting, and sometimes troubling. The traveler to distant places is struck by the differences he observes between the familiar and the new. Descriptions of the neighboring city as well as tales about exotic lands focus on the unexpected, the unlikely, and the peculiar.

Spatial Organization of Society proceeds, nonetheless, from the premise that in one respect—its use of territory—human society is surprisingly alike from place to place. The similarity is not one of physical resemblance but rather appears in the predictable, organized pattern of locations and interrelations. This structure results from the operation of a few simple principles of human behavior and not from a unique man-to-space relationship in a particular location. Essentially, this structure derives from the necessity to use space efficiently; specific features of particular areas can be viewed as modifiers of the basic structure rather than as the fundamental controls over our use of the earth. Perhaps, after all, local physical and human variation will prove more significant than the ordering principle I stress. Even so, I feel that it is valuable to seek out the commonality in seemingly disparate landscapes.

For their helpful comments and suggestions, I would like to thank Brian J. L. Berry, University of Chicago; Warren E. Hultquist, Sacramento State College; Edward J. Taafe, Ohio State University; John D. Nystuen, University of Michigan; Forrest R. Pitts, University of Hawaii; William L. Thomas, Jr., California State College, Hayward; and Phillip Wagner, Simon Frazer University. Of course, I alone am responsible for any possible errors or omissions.

Contents

The Spatial Organization of Society

Part One

Geography: Spatial Behavior, Process, and Structure

1

Location Factors
and Principles

INTRODUCTION

In *Spatial Organization of Society* we intend to formulate and elaborate the broad outlines of a theory of spatial organization and behavior in human society and to present current theoretical research within this general structure.

Spatial organization is the outcome of man's attempt to use space efficiently. The wide variety of observed patterns of location and interaction and the many theories constructed to account for these patterns can be unified by common principles of behavior in space. Contrary to usual practice, in this book the environment, or quality of space, is given only a secondary role, as a modifier of the ideal spatial patterns that are a function of space alone.

Neither the specific theories presented in this book nor the general concept of spatial behavior is original. Still, we felt that a broad statement was urgently needed in order to take stock of past progress and, hopefully, to present a framework

of goals and problems for present and future research in human geography.

THE SCIENCE OF GEOGRAPHY

Geography may be approached in at least three distinct ways: to understand the uniqueness of a place or region; to discover the relation of man and environment; or to systematically explain location and spatial interaction (see Figure 1.01). The title of this book, *Spatial Organization of Society,* commits us to the last viewpoint—not because the others have less validity, but because this view represents the direction in which greater contributions are likely to be made to the growth of geography itself and to that of other disciplines.

Space, spatial relations, and change in space—how physical space is structured, how men relate through space, how man has organized his society in space, and how our conception and use of space change—are the core elements of the science of geography. While the traditional emphasis

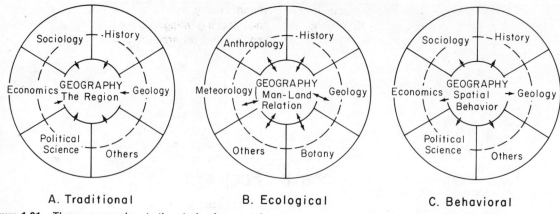

Figure 1.01 Three approaches to the study of geography.

on the distinctive character of a region (Figure 1.01A) has built up our knowledge of places, the systematic aspects of location have been insufficiently studied; and while an ecological approach (Figure 1.01B) is concerned with general relations, it neglects the significant role of space as such.

There is thus great need to develop general explanations of the role of space and spatial characteristics in nature and their effect on man, of the patterns of human occupance and location, and of the structure of human interrelations in space. An emphasis on principles of spatial behavior, according to the third view, makes possible a more unified geography; the same patterns of location and movement appear common to a wide variety of meteorological, geologic, economic, social, political, and other phenomena (Figure 1.01C). This contrasts with the first view of geography, in which the fields of sociology, history, and so forth provide facts and patterns that can be used to understand distinct regions.

Thus, in this book geography is the study of location and the spatial relations that word implies. The initial portion of the book discusses the role of spatial influences on location and interaction, and later sections stress theories of location and interaction and pay more limited attention to specific distributions of phenomena.

A location is an area, commonly recognized and defined, in which human activities take place; it may be a field of corn, a physician's office, or a bridge. It is generally a small area, but, depending on the scale of observation, can range in size from an office within a building to a large city. Interest may center on a set of locations—a crop rotation pattern, for example. A set of locations of similar or related character may be defined as a region: an area too large to be called a location, but possessing significant unity.

Interconnections between locations, such as paths, railways, other permanent fixtures and movements of goods and people, may be considered linear locations. It is more convenient and realistic, however, to regard the interactions in geography as a consequence of locational decisions.

We know that man and nature occupy space; that such space differs in quality, use, and potential; and that space separates man and the activities he wishes to relate to. Our goal is to describe, classify, and compare the use and character of space across the earth's surface; to describe and distinguish general patterns of land use, towns, transport networks, and levels of development; and to derive and test theories of the observed patterns of location, interaction among locations,

4

and locational change. Our basic thesis is that space is not just something to be filled, but that its very existence and dimensions induce both predictable individual behavior and collective order in location and interaction.

PATTERNS OF LOCATION AND SPATIAL STRUCTURE

In this section we introduce some of the general patterns of human location and behavior in space that will later be treated more extensively: the distribution of population; the distribution of development; the spatial organization of society; and patterns of spatial change, such as the spread and growth of settlement and development.

Population is distributed very unevenly on both a large scale—over the entire world—and on a small scale—within an area or town. The pattern of world population distribution consists of a very few areas, occupying only a fraction of the earth's land surface, that contain the bulk of the world's population; several smaller nodes of population concentration; and vast, scarcely inhabited areas (see Figure 1.02). Patterns of rural and urban occupance are perhaps even more irregular. There are extreme differences in wealth, industrialization, and interdependence from area to area, as well (see Figure 1.03); only a few areas have reached a relatively high level of economic development.

SPATIAL EXPERIENCE

Societies differ in the extent of their spatial awareness (knowledge of the space around them) and spatial interdependence. In technologically "primitive" societies the individual's awareness of space and of areas and peoples far from him is limited by his direct experience. A small organizational unit, such as a village or tribal area, can be self-sufficient for most purposes, and thus spatial interdependence—and spatial awareness—are confined mostly to the village and its lands and to neighboring villages. This local area is intimately known and differentiated in detail.

As societies develop technologies and learn about other areas, they often become more specialized and increase their relationships with other areas; the growth of towns requires extended rural-urban interaction, for example. If the countries of the world are arranged along a spectrum of spatial interdependence, the most functionally specialized and mobile industrial societies, like the United States, will be the most interdependent. In such national economies, essentially all regions depend upon one another; the search for economic efficiency in the nation has produced extreme regional specialization (concentration of given kinds of production in given regions) and thus the abandonment of regional self-sufficiency.

In nations such as these, an individual's existence is greatly affected by events in distant areas. The individual recognizes that he is greatly dependent upon others, and his awareness of other areas is considerable. At the same time, however, his understanding of his local area may be incomplete; although individual experience remains largely local, "local" means a radius of 50 miles rather than the five miles of the primitive villager (see Figures 1.04 and 1.05).

In advanced nations, communications link the individual instantly with the rest of his country and the world. Greater freedom of choice, a higher income, and high-quality transportation enhance his mobility, both in terms of length, speed, and frequency of trips and in the probability that he will change his residence. His field of acquaintance widens; some local customs may be diffused and become national. His world extends in space, and that which is far away and different no longer terrifies him.

Throughout history spatial interdependence has been gradually extended, a more intricate spatial organization has been developed, and man's spatial experience has broadened.

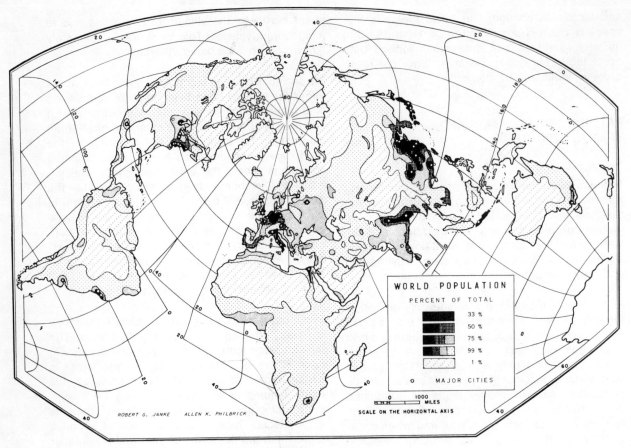

Figure 1.02 Distribution of world population. (Reprinted by permission of John Wiley & Sons, Inc., from Allen K. Philbrick, *This Human World*, 1963.)

FACTORS INFLUENCING LOCATION AND SPATIAL INTERACTION

Geography has traditionally spoken of the comparative advantages of certain locations for certain activities. What specific elements make up the comparative advantage of an area, and to what extent do they determine the area's actual development?

Two classes of factors are combined in the notion of comparative advantage. The first includes the traditional aspects of environment—the differential qualities of the earth's surface; the second contains the neglected—but fundamental—characteristics of space itself. Whether comparative advantage is realized, however, depends also on a third class of factors—economic, social, political, and other influences. The first two classes deal directly wtih geographic factors, the first with the content, the second with the dimensions of space.

The Precedent of Past Patterns of Development

Undoubtedly the greatest influence on the future location of people and activities is their present location. Most human locational decisions depend

LOCATION FACTORS AND PRINCIPLES

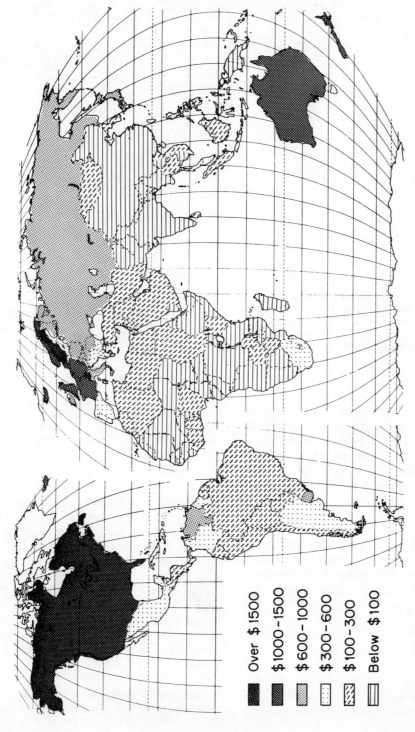

Figure 1.03   Estimated world net per capita income, 1963.

■	Over $1500
▨	$1000–1500
▤	$600–1000
▦	$300–600
▨	$100–300
▥	Below $100

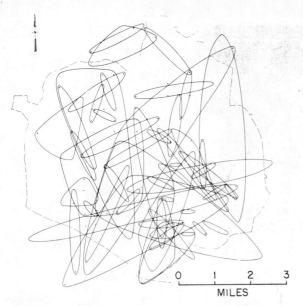

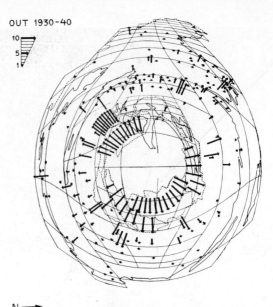

Figure 1.04 Individual travel patterns. Daily pattern of a sample of individual trip origins (+) and destinations (−) within Durham, North Carolina, in 1963. (Reprinted by permission of the University of Illinois Press, from Stuart Chapin, Jr., *Urban Land Use Planning,* 2nd ed., 1965.)

Figure 1.05 Hägerstrand's logarithmic projection closely expresses the way people perceive the space around them, greatly exaggerating the importance of nearby areas. This example shows the number (indicated by the size of the arrow) and destinations of migrants leaving a small area in central Sweden (at the center of the projection) in 1930-1940. Note that most settled in nearby regions. (Reprinted by permission of the Department of Geography, University of Lund, Sweden, from T. Hägerstrand, "Migration in Sweden," *Lund Studies in Geography,* No. 13, Series B.)

so much on previous experience that existing patterns are strongly reinforced (see Figure 1.06). Economically, the large investment in the physical structures and human resources used in existing locations militates against radically changing location. Psychologically, the individual's investment in the area, in his home, and in his associations tends to make him immobile; he would rather modify existing locations than create entirely new settlements. Thus, new investment is concentrated in existing locations; for instance, a large proportion of investment in manufacturing is devoted to modifying and modernizing existing plants rather than to constructing new ones.

The Natural Environment and Location

 Many geographers and historians have looked to the natural environment—landforms, climate, soils,

vegetation, and mineral resources—as the major key to the development of man in space. That environment is a major influence cannot be denied —but it is tempting to overvalue its importance. The natural environment of an area is significant only insofar as it is either easier or more difficult to carry on a particular activity in a particular place. The environment should be evaluated in terms of its cost to development desired by man, and in this sense, its role as a major part of the comparative advantage of a location can be measured.

Landforms Landforms partially control the cost of carrying on activities. For extensive uses such

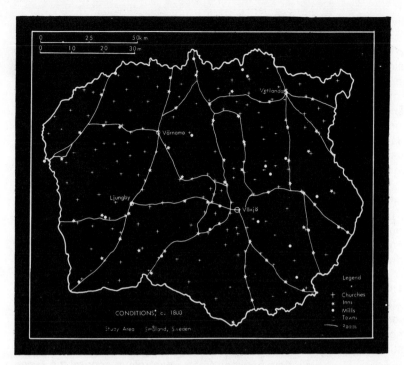

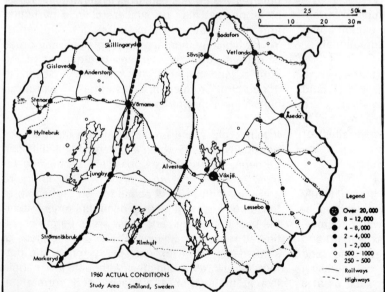

Figure 1.06 Past development as reinforcement for future development. Shown are major settlements and roads in a small area of Sweden in 1800 and 1960. The 1960 settlement pattern was much influenced by the earlier one.

as forest exploitation, but especially for crop agriculture, the slope and ruggedness of the terrain are often decisive. Farm operations are easier and far cheaper on nearly level land; sloping hills impose greater labor costs, and there is a risk of erosion. Plains and valleys thus hold most of the world's farmland. Population pressures may force hilly land to be used, but only at increased costs. Mechanized agriculture, in particular, depends on level land, and after its introduction farming has been abandoned in many rugged areas.

Transportation also depends on landform conditions; there is a direct relationship between slope and curvature and the cost of constructing and operating roads and railways. Routes are often concentrated in passes of least grade, and it is often necessary to construct costly tunnels, canals, or causeways in order to reduce transport cost and time. Transport in rough topography is so difficult that mountains may constitute effective boundaries between lowland regions and even foster cultural and economic isolation.

Urban and industrial settlement in rugged terrain is costly and normally exists only to exploit popular resources—mineral, timber, or recreational.

Water features—rivers, lakes, and estuaries—have had profound effects on location. When land transport was poor, lakes and large rivers were unifying elements and the principal means of communication; their shores were main sites for settlement. They still provide fairly cheap transport, and most major cities are on water.

Land transport frequently follows the relatively level river valleys, and river junctions and especially river mouths—focal point of water routes—are advantageous locations for exchange and processing. Points where waterways and land routes are complementary—where the crossing can be accomplished at little cost, such as at a shallow ford, a narrow, bridgeable canyon, or the first bridgeable point after an estuary—are also favored for settlement, sometimes because a change from water to land transport is required, but mainly because land routes focus toward such

crossings. Larger places show an overwhelming preference for such water locations, since transport is so vital to a city. Such positions do not inherently offer sufficient conditions for success, however; many river junctions have no towns, and some successful cities were not located on such sites because other conditions were good.

Climate, Soils, and Vegetation   Climate is most often used to explain development. The survival of agricultural man depended on the weather, and our ultimate dependence on climate is still total: agriculture is limited to locations where the climate is suitable. Rather than attempting to devise climatic explanations of human history, however, we should realistically appraise the limitations that climate imposes upon agriculture and settlement.

Temperature extremes set limits on the spatial range of a particular crop, and the normal temperature patterns affect the cost of obtaining a given output. The growing season—the length of time between frosts—controls in general the range of crops that may be successful in a particular area. Precipitation also exercises great influence. Yields typically increase with moisture, and areas of extreme drought (perhaps one-quarter of the earth's land surface) are effectively closed to agricultural production, unless there is extraordinary human interference.

If temperature and precipitation are mapped, the possibility of carrying on a variety of activities can be seen. In large areas costs are prohibitive for most crops; some areas are favorable for more activities than there is space for, so that some of these activities will have to occur under less-than-the-best conditions; and other areas permit only a limited range of activities. The actual locations of settlements, however, only partly reflect the pattern of favorable climates. Although few people live in the extremes of desert and permafrost, some of the better areas are scarcely used, and some of the mediocre areas support dense concentrations of people by applying superior technology. For example, land is used much more intensively in Japan than in comparable parts of

LOCATION FACTORS AND PRINCIPLES

the southern United States, and some Andean highlanders are attached culturally to poorer lands within their countries.

Also, man has been somewhat freed from the locational limits of climate by irrigation, drainage, erosion control, and the development of new species. Often these victories have released immense latent productivity at relatively low cost. In other cases, however, nature has been remade at high cost under difficult conditions. Many "naturally unfavorable" areas still exist that need only a small human investment—in irrigation or drainage or disease control—to become profitable, but man's desire to remain in other inherently inferior and unresponsive environments may lead to wasteful and costly efforts to remake nature.

Climate influences the location of industry in more limited ways; warmer locations, for instance, may be preferred to reduce heating costs and workdays lost because of illness. On the other hand, hot and humid conditions reduce the productivity of some people and can increase spoilage problems. The technologies of heating and air conditioning are about equally costly; they can free man from the limitations of climate, but only by increasing his costs.

Finally, climate influences location through available water supplies. In arid areas, water shortages limit agricultural and urban development. Even in humid areas, local water supplies often cannot keep up with the demands of great concentrations of people, and water must be reallocated at high cost.

Soils also vary in their productivity for various crops, stability for structures, and in their direct usefulness for construction. Areas that are poorly drained due to uneven glacial deposition or because they are on river or tidal floodplains are historically strong barriers to settlement and are settled only at high cost, probably because of population pressures.

The locational influence of natural vegetation depends greatly on the technology that exists. Men having early agricultural technologies used subhumid natural grassland for grazing and annually flooded for cultivation basins along rivers free from significant natural vegetation. Forests were considered barriers, costly to clear, but useful for game, timber and fuelwood.

When technology improved and trees could be removed, forested areas became attractive for agriculture, since their moisture supply was good and their soils were easily worked. Not until the charcoal-based iron industry and large-scale ship construction developed in the sixteenth century did forests themselves become a significant resource. Grasslands constituted a barrier to agricultural settlement until improved technology provided better plows for working the rough sod and better ways to adjust to subhumid conditions.

Natural Resources Those parts of nature that man perceives may help satisfy his needs and desires are called natural resources. A few are "free," such as climate, but these are also undependable. To use most resources human effort and capital must be expended. This cost is usually considered worthwhile, however, since the resource increases man's productivity. Thus, although it is costly to bring extra water to the land, the benefits from the resulting higher production often far exceed the cost.

What is of value and thus constitutes a resource changes. Most resources valuable today were considered valueless three centuries ago. What is a resource in one country or culture may not be in another, and what is of value in one part of a single economy may not be valuable in another part of the same economy. Through much of history the dominant resources were land and water for the production of food; wood for construction, fuel, and furniture; and metal ores, especially iron, tin, and copper. Today coal, petroleum, gas, and uranium have replaced wood, water, animals, and men as the chief sources of power, and they are also used as raw materials in production.

Many of man's recent advancements have depended highly on industrialization, which requires

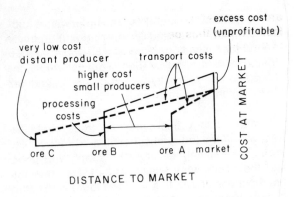

Figure 1.07 Resource use related to transport and production costs. At the market, ore A is the same price as ore C; ore B cannot be mined profitably because ores A and C cost less at the market.

A nation's resource endowment also strongly influences the cost of industrialization and the kind of economic development that is appropriate. Until fairly recently, industrialization was closely tied to the presence of raw materials and especially to the fuel coal. During this century, however, fuels are used far more efficiently, and industry has developed processes in which fuels and raw materials are much less important, thus giving nations increased freedom from the limits of their own resources.

Because resources are concentrated in specific locations, clusters of small hamlets or villages designed to exploit them are typical. But because any given resource may be depleted, these settlements are often impermanent, and sometimes decline and become extinct. In the United States there are thousands of such "ghost towns."

mineral resources, particularly the fuels. Since these resources were first utilized only in modern times, their location was random with respect to the existing patterns of agricultural settlement and land productivity. In some cases, notably northwestern Europe, high-quality coal and suitable metal ores were found not too far from areas of dense population. These fields were naturally the first ones to be used. Gradually the coal fields and, to a lesser extent, the other resource areas attracted industry and settlement, and the population shifted locally from agriculturally richer areas.

From a spatial point of view, the most significant facts about resources are that they are unevenly distributed, are often concentrated in small areas, and are depletable.

Because resources are unevenly distributed, there is striking variation in the resource endowment of different areas of the world. Since economies are contained within national boundaries, a country having a variety of internal resources has a great asset. Resources a nation lacks must be purchased at high cost and a lack of resources involves the further risk that other nations might place a military or political embargo on necessary supplies.

How much a given resource is used is a complex function of its distance to markets and the quality of the resource, which determines the cost of extraction. Naturally, the resources that cost the least, either because they are closest or of highest quality, are used first. A slight change in either factor can force a given resource out of competition (see Figure 1.07). However, the better close-in resources will be gradually depleted, and resource suppliers will probably need to use fairly remote sources before industry and population are located near them. Resource exploitation is thus a major source of growth, if an uncertain one, for regions remote from the center of the economy.

Summary The effect of environmental factors may be evaluated in terms of the cost of carrying on particular activities—whether agricultural, industrial, cultural, or military.

The environment places limits or controls on the possibilities of the development of man, governs the costs of relating to or altering natural conditions, and makes it easier or not easy to follow certain patterns in certain areas. However, environmental factors alone do not account for the differentiation of the world into developed and underdeveloped countries, for there are many

LOCATION FACTORS AND PRINCIPLES

areas with high-quality environments that are underdeveloped, and many areas with niggardly resources that are successful.

Technology allows industries in already settled areas to produce needed goods, rather than having to move to unsettled, but naturally superior, areas. It thus provides the main alternative to environmentally determined development.

The forces of the environment that are important to man change through time. Early agricultural man needed suitable land and climate to survive. Industrialization made possible the development of new mineral-rich areas poorly suited to agriculture. Today, our improved technology and ability to alter nature make it possible for the natural beauty of landforms and comfortable climate to be forces for location, not because they are necessary for life, but because they enrich it.

Spatial Characteristics and Location

Geography also exercises great influence through the more abstract qualities of space itself—its shape, size, distance, accessibility, and the relative location of parts in the whole.

Space is a fact; all economic activities, from fisheries to finance, take place in space, not at points. The demand for space for factories, fields, forests, houses, involves most of the earth—an immense territory. Space inevitably separates people who may wish to interact for their mutual benefit and products which may be profitably exchanged. Space, as territory to be efficiently used and organized, and spatial separation—or distance—are fundamental geographic factors influencing location and development.

Because man's activities require space, distance plays a role in determining the ideal pattern for these activities. Further, because activities require different amounts of space, a particular structure is given to what was originally homogeneous space; space is differentiated into a structure of areas, points, and interconnecting lines. Each location can thus be characterized by its relation to the whole—for example, according to its accessibility—and this relation tends to determine the location's future potential as much as its inherent characteristics.

Distance Distance, whether measured physically or by the time, effort, and cost required to cross the space, is the spatial dimension of separation and is important if separate objects or people want or need to be in contact. In human history, distance defined how much of the earth man could utilize. Inability to cover distance encouraged more intensive use and differentiation of the known space.

Distance has been viewed primarily as a barrier to communication, movement, and trade and is often considered in terms of the cost of overcoming that space (see Figure 1.08). Distance has represented the check on concentration of power or production at one point. Costs of marketing and material assembly limit the scale of activities; therefore, the same combinations of activities must be repeated again and again over space. Persons at a greater distance from a major center of control must pay extra costs and are placed in an unequal position. The cost of the same physical distance may vary greatly; in one direction it may be high enough to constitute an almost total barrier to travel, in another so low that it invites interaction.

Frequently, the time required to cover the distance is the most meaningful measure of spatial separation. Much of economic history concerns gradually overcoming distance by improving transport (Figure 1.08), thus cheapening spatial interaction. But this is relative change; spatial separation is still costly. It has become less of a barrier, however, because we have invested so heavily in reducing its effects.

Accessibility Since man is social and many of his activities involve coming together to exchange goods and to exercise control, an area that is accessible—or central—to customers and citizens has many advantages. An area may be central

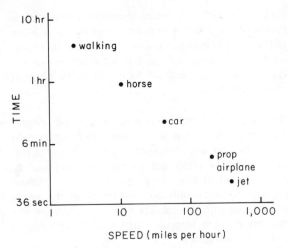

Figure 1.08 The cost in time of traveling ten miles. Distance is often measured in terms of its time cost.

because of its position within a natural basin, but more generally it is central with respect to the distribution of people or activities to which it is related.

The concept of centrality implies its opposites, isolation and location on the periphery. Location on the edge of settlement is a factor that has traditionally hindered development, weakened loyalty and unity, and lessened interaction with other areas. The periphery may be sparsely settled, culturally and materially deprived; there is often a very great contrast between the cultural capital and the provincial areas.

Agglomeration The benefits of agglomerating activities are at once economic, geographic, and psychological and are extremely important location factors. From the clusters of homes in the tribal village to the associations of shops in the newest shopping centers, one major means to improve economic efficiency and social satisfaction has been through the agglomeration of people and activities in one spot. Associations of related industries, such as the clustering of small subcontractors around large automotive and aircraft complexes, increase production efficiency. Distribution efficiency is gained by grouping the buyers

and sellers of goods and services in such places as the fair, the market town, and the shopping center. Not only does agglomeration reduce the total distance traveled, thus satisfying a geographic goal, but it makes possible the satisfaction of many goals with little effort (see Figure 1.09). The existence of additional possibilities nearby also encourages the customer to add other purposes impulsively, increasing the turnover and growth in the area. Similar benefits are experienced in information and communication.

Size The size and complexity of the units of organization, from tribe to nation, have great influence on location and development. Larger areas frequently, although not necessarily, contain different peoples and interests and may lack unity, be subject to internal dissension, and thus find it difficult to achieve rapid development and unified action. On the other hand, a larger area may also have many different resource types and qualities, which may be complementary to each other and make it possible to further specialize and hence achieve more efficiency. Also, the presence of larger internal markets and labor pools makes larger scale production possible, reduces the cost per unit of production, and thus gives larger areas greater economic potential for the same relative effort (see Figure 1.10). As will be more clearly explained later, larger size also makes possible more efficient specialization and location patterns that are more theoretically ideal.

Shape The shape of units of organization also significantly affects the costs of maintaining control, transporting goods efficiently, and communicating with other men, since these activities are obviously cheaper and easier within a compact territory. A given effort results in greater unity, and a compact shape makes it easier for one center to dominate cultural life. An irregular shape may foster regionalism, diversity, and multiplicity of control.

Relative Location Relative location has several meanings:

LOCATION FACTORS AND PRINCIPLES

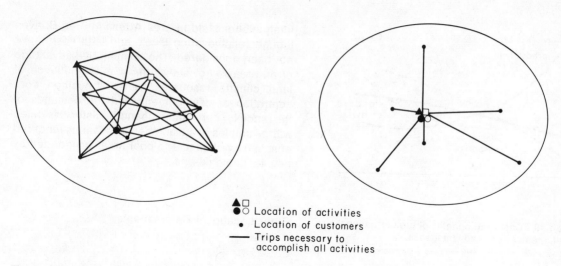

Location of activities
Location of customers
Trips necessary to accomplish all activities

Figure 1.09 Agglomeration: distance savings. Travel is reduced by nucleating activities.

1. Location relative to natural routeways, such as the location of Singapore and Gibraltar on straits, may endow a site with many communication advantages. Positions at gaps within natural barriers, such as at mountain passes and at end of large lakes (Chicago), are also advantageous to development.

2. Location on a transport net strongly influences the economic potential and viability of a place, irrespective of its own resources. For example, some junctions on the new U.S. Interstate Highway System may develop into new towns.

3. Location relative to existing centers of development is a powerful influence. Development patterns have great stability, and the potential of any site depends as much on its position with respect to more populous areas as to the natural qualities of the site.

Summary The role of space. Virtually all theory of spatial organization assumes that the structure of space is based on the principles of minimizing distance and maximizing the utility of points and areas within the structure, without taking the environment, or variable content of space, into account. Although the differential quality of areas is interesting and its effect on location and inter-

action is great, most of the observable regularity of structure in space results from the principles of efficiently using territory of uniform character. The theoretical structures for agricultural location, location of urban centers, and the internal patterns of the city are all derived from the principle of minimizing distance on a uniform plane.

Comparative Advantage

The environmental and spatial factors that we have just considered may be summed up by the concept of comparative advantage—the specific costs and returns of an activity for a given people and technology in relation to the costs in other areas. Assuming we can measure such costs and returns, an analysis would reveal two main characteristics:

1. Complementarity of location or areas: The requirements and characteristics of different activities vary so markedly that areas with the greatest advantages for some activities are poor for other activities—which might find an ideal location in yet other areas.

LOCATION FACTORS AND PRINCIPLES

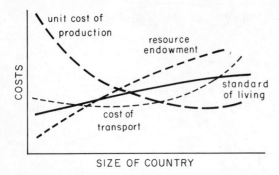

COSTS

SIZE OF COUNTRY

unit cost of production

resource endowment

standard of living

cost of transport

Figure 1.10 Costs and benefits of greater national size. Overall, greater size is advantageous.

2.   An uneven endowment of "advantages": Some areas have greater comparative advantage (and thus higher net productivity—excess of returns over costs) in scores of activities; other areas are less productive in most and even all activities. This may result in strong competition for the preferred areas and extremely intense use within them; there may be no room for activities that might be better carried on there than anywhere else, but yet cannot be done well enough to compete. Unfavorable areas, if they are to develop at all, must be satisfied with activities that will survive, even though such activities might be more profitable in more favored areas. For example, cattle grazing would be more productive on the lush prairies close to urban markets than on the western high plains, but it survives on the latter and is squeezed out on the former because more productive activities, like growing corn, preempt the better land.

Comparative advantage has been too frequently used loosely and indefinitely. It has not been recognized that advantage may be partly a result of human decisions to group activities into mutually beneficial systems, although the individual activities might not appear so advantageous. Also, the term has not been quantified, and it tends to be conceived of as absolute rather than relative. For instance, one activity is said to have an abso-

lutely higher yield in area *A* than in area *B,* even though relative price levels and land costs have not been considered. The comparative advantage of an area is not static; the relative influence of land, climate, resources, transport position, concentration of development, and the demands of the society constantly change. History is filled with examples of advantageous locations rendered obsolete by change and poor areas invigorated by new technologies.

Other Locational Determinants

Comparative advantage and past development are insufficient to explain the complexity of locational patterns and change; psychological, cultural, political, and, above all, technological and economic factors help determine how space may be used and, indeed, whether it has value to people at all. These factors may be spatially differentiated and therefore indirectly geographic.

Tradition   Cultural attitudes, beliefs, and practices influence the economic and social potential of peoples and are changed only over time. Attitudes toward work, toward eating, toward using certain foods or products, toward birth control, toward the role of the individual, family, and society, toward willingness to migrate and to change occupations—all are affected by tradition.

Level of Development   Where an activity is located is partly a function of the developmental and technological level of the economy. The skill level of workers and the level of automation exercise much control over the nature and organization of potential activities. The possibilities of substituting between labor and capital depend on their relative availability, cost, and quality. If the labor supply is great, the locational effects of power and resources may be relatively less, but, within an economy, education and skill differences in the labor force may have a stronger influence on location than differences in wage levels.

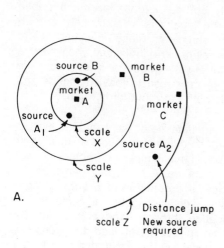

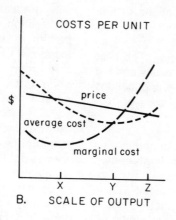

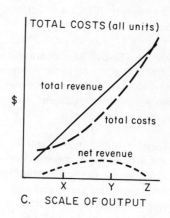

Average cost = total cost/number(n) of all units

Marginal cost = cost of the (n+1)th (next) unit

Figure 1.11 Returns to scale and spatial implications of scale. Plant is at market A. At scale X, sources A_1 and B and market A are required. At scale Y, Market B is added, but no new sources are required. At scale Z, however, a new source of material, A_2, is required in order to penetrate market C. Thus, returns decrease at Z.

The quality of internal transportation also helps govern the locational decisions that can be made. Since connections to internal transport must be available for a location to even be considered for some specialized economic activities, many locations of great potential productivity lie undeveloped, awaiting improved access to the larger economy.

Returns to Scale Scale, or volume of production, is a very powerful influence on location. Production efficiency partly depends on how much is produced. In most activities, both economic and social, larger size has resulted in lower unit cost because capital, other overhead costs, and managerial and distribution expenses are spread over more units. Machinery and plant are more fully used; labor is more specialized.

However, such advantages do not accrue indefinitely. Internal cost increases or diseconomies can result from increasing congestion, excessive

need for managers, or decline in morale. As scale increases, the lower unit production cost must also be balanced against probable increases in distribution and assembly costs, for supplies must be brought from more distant sources, and products must be sold in more distant markets (Figure 1.11 illustrates these crucial relations). The cost and time of transportation necessary to overcome distance has historically been the primary obstacle to increased scale; one of the chief benefits of improved transportation is the opportunity to realize the economies of greater scale.

The economies achieved by large-scale production strongly encourage regional specialization, but the possibilities are limited by the cost of overcoming spatial separation. However, society has moved toward realizing such economies; farm size, factory size, ship size, and truck size have all increased, and school consolidation, the growth of metropolitan areas, and the creation of common markets (such as the European Economic

Community (EEC) are further indications of this trend.

Kind of Social and Economic System The kind of social and economic system that exists and the way decisions are made have strong implications for location of activities and the process of economic development.

Tribal groups, usually small in number and in area and frequently somewhat communal in character, are typical of more primitive technology, economic organization, and spatial complexity. Decision making for location of activities is local, small-scale, and usually repetitive and traditional. Feudal economic and social organization, in which a large number of peasants support a small ruling group, provides little incentive for growth or change. So long as control is maintained and the expectations of the peasants remain low, there is little reason to increase production. Little location change occurs, but as population increases, land is further subdivided. Although this system still exists in some countries, it usually breaks down under either a need for the state to defend itself, which requires greater total wealth, or a demand for greater power, freedom, and goods by the majority of the population.

Individual capitalist economies evolve different locational patterns. Indeed, most of our theories of spatial behavior reflect such individual goals as the short-run maximization of profit. Locational decisions are made by individuals, or small groups of individuals, under conditions of risk and uncertainty. Since a small investor cannot survive years of losses in order to realize long-term profits, the optimal location for new investment tends to be near already successful enterprises and locations. The incentive of profit, however, may still be sufficient to induce acceptance of greater risks.

In a rather pure capitalist system, then, investment reinforces and only gradually extends existing patterns of settlement; economic growth in capitalist societies has traditionally originated in a fairly small region, from which development has only gradually spread. Even after much public intervention, the legacy is an extremely uneven pattern of development. Since investment and locational decisions are individual, however, a very great variety of goods and services are offered, and the response to local demands and possibilities is both easy and fairly rapid.

The greatest significance of the capitalist system is that price—of land, labor, and capital, in all their forms—provides a mechanism for achieving the efficient use of space. A monopoly can thus reduce efficiency; if production of a good is controlled by a single decision maker, he can preserve imperfect location through fixed prices. On the other hand, competition can lead to excessive numbers of enterprises. In some activities, such as electric power distribution, competing systems were chaotic and inefficient, and present milk delivery is similarly very costly. Carefully planned and regulated monopolies, where costs can be honestly calculated and excess profits prevented, can result in better patterns.

In a socialist economy, investment and prices are centrally planned and controlled, and different locational patterns may be expected. The goal of efficient use of space and resources may be identical, but since decisions are made by a few, who have greater knowledge of all areas and view the system as a whole, greater efficiency should result. Also, since the state is able and perhaps willing to sustain losses for longer periods than individual investors, it should be possible to achieve more rational and regular development and resource use. In the long run, regional differences will most likely reflect more closely the actual potential of a region rather than its developmental history, and regional income differences should be less than in capitalist societies.

However, since decision making is by a few, the potential effect for both good and ill is increased. In spite of superior information and power, no system is immune to error, and a poor decision under central planning can have far-reaching and ruinous effects. Evidence is also strong that central planning agencies are in fact, if not in theory,

LOCATION FACTORS AND PRINCIPLES

much less responsive to local demands of citizens. Finally, the monopoly power in the hands of the state makes it more difficult to use price as a test of efficiency.

Political Influences on Location and Interaction
Locational decisions are influenced by several types of political behavior and attitudes: the feeling of nationalism, the presence of boundaries, the kind of administrative structure, and the locus of power—whether central or federal.

Nationalism—the feeling of unity and loyalty usually arising from sovereignty—has an immense influence on location and development. The world consists of national economies, each with its own banking and monetary system, tax system, and other attributes of economic as well as political independence. Many nations are too small to constitute easily viable economic units; the attempt to create a fairly self-sufficient economy generally requires the imposition of protective measures that work against the utilization of comparative advantage and achievement of economic efficiency over the entire world. Tariffs and subsidies for internal industries are economic translations of the nationalistic desire for self-sufficiency.

An administrative structure inherited from an earlier era may prove inadequate to later needs; examples are the conflicts between central city and suburb and the nonviability of many counties laid out by arbitrary geometry prior to settlement.

National boundaries normally form a sharp break in political and economic authority, even though they are only rarely marked by walls or fences. Boundaries sometimes follow natural physical features; often they make a cultural and linguistic break formal and thus further hinder communication. Not infrequently, however, boundaries are imposed across natural features and economic development. For example, the U.S.–Canada border, separating almost identical natural areas, artificially imposes a $1,000 per family income differential and radically alters transport and settlement patterns (Figure 1.12). Borders are thus likely to reduce the economic strength of nearby areas. As factors determining location, boundaries foster special development: military posts, customs services, and sometimes border towns to take advantage of price, wage, product, and other differences (along the Mexico–U.S. border, for instance).

Variations in the centralization of authority may affect location and development in the economy. A nation with a strong central government may impose nationwide wage, banking, and taxation rates, tend to have a uniform economic and cultural life, and place national interests over local ones. Countries developing from several smaller ones or containing radically diverse elements tend to form federal systems in which economic power is divided among different political levels. Regional interests thus supersede national ones in many economic decisions. This diffusion of power acts to preserve regional differences in culture and development. For example, by controlling banking and local taxes, U.S. states influence the nature of industry, the quality of their schools, and the viability of their agriculture.

Changing Role of Location Factors

All the foregoing locational influences change constantly, both in character and in relative importance; for instance, the oceans were at first impenetrable barriers to man, but when the sailing ship was developed, commerce by water was easier than by land, and associations over greater distances became possible. With the railroad and the truck, land transport cheapened and development was again focused internally. Air communication today widens the area of possible interrelation, and the world shrinks as the cost and time needed to travel it decrease. Thus the nature and impact of space change. Distance remains a barrier to interaction but a less important one; improvements in transport have enabled man to go greater distances with little effort and have made possible relations that could not have existed before.

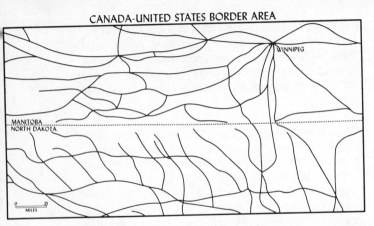

CANADA-UNITED STATES BORDER AREA

WINNIPEG

MANITOBA
NORTH DAKOTA

0   25
MILES

Figure 1.12 Broken railroad network in the Canadian-U.S. border area. Political boundaries often diminish interaction. (Reprinted by permission of Yale University Press, from August Lösch, *Economics of Location,* 1954.)

Summary: Location Factors and Predicted Patterns

In the rest of the book, the explanation of spatial structure proceeds from the deductive—what would occur under the simplest conditions—to the inductive—how local factors distort this "pure" structure. To begin with, all the local variation may introduce is a risk of missing the underlying structure. Most theory of location and spatial structure therefore stresses the spatial factors—above all, distance—which interact to bring about regular and repetitive patterns. In this book the environmental factors, the differential qualities of space, shift from playing the dominant role in the explanation of location to acting as a distorting influence on the ideal patterns that would occur on a uniform surface.

GOALS AND RESTRAINTS

Goals of Spatial Behavior

If there is an underlying order in human geography, it is that man and society try to organize space efficiently, to locate activities and use land in the "best" way. We may express man's goals as three principles:

1. To maximize the net utility of areas and places at minimum input.

2. To maximize the spatial interrelations at minimum cost.

3. To bring related activities as close together as possible.

In satisfying these aims simultaneously, substitute possibilities of course exist, but our knowledge of human behavior suggests a caveat that diminishes the force of the first three principles:

4. Some men and societies, or all men and societies some of the time, are willing to achieve a good or profitable level of satisfaction rather than the maximum. In fact, irrational and even self-destructive behavior may result from human decisions.

NOTE

The first principle implies that the sum of all parcels of land within an economy is to be used at the maximum return (or productivity) for the least possible total effort, subject to the level of technology, demands for goods and services, and distribution of resources and markets in the economy. The principle does not mean that *each* parcel is used to its absolute maximum, but that after weighing the comparative advantages of all parcels, each should be used for the best purpose that can be sustained by total demand and input capacity. For instance, land most remote from the core of settlement may not be used at all by man even if it is inherently productive, while in the center of economic and cultural control, use and value may be extremely intensified by demand.

The second corollary aim, to take advantage of the possibilities of regional specialization by maximizing trade and interaction among ideas and people at least cost, is subject to controls of technology, cost of transportation, time, and possible risks of overspecialization.

A balance exists between the possibility of reducing transport costs by developing more regional self-sufficiency and the possibility of reducing production costs by using more transport to encourage greater regional specialization. Taken together, the principles ought to insure a pattern of land use, a degree of specialization, and a volume of interaction which give the greatest return for the least effort.

The "nearness" principle is an alternative expression of the other two. It states that related activities should be as close together as possible, depending on the strength of the relation. Retail stores have the highest levels of interaction and cluster to the extreme; workplaces and residences must be within reasonable commuter time, but families are willing to substitute greater distance for site and other advantages. Farms try to be as close to consumers as possible, but the more perishable crops, for example, must be much closer than the more hardy ones.

Restraints on Spatial Behavior

Efficient location is, realistically, determined by short-run conditions and therefore subject to restraints as the economy changes. As technology continues to develop and dramatic social changes take place—for example, the reduction of social discrimination in the United States—a decision that was optimal yesterday is rendered imperfect. Yet the investment in a location, whether in plant or people or fields, is very great to the people concerned. So long as the investment continues to pay for itself, they may feel it is better to operate at less than peak profit than to abandon the investment altogether; although most locations are probably less than optimal ones (see Figure 1.13), only the really inefficient will fail. An activ-

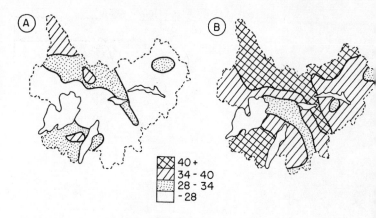

Figure 1.13 Actual and potential labor productivity. In this example from middle Sweden, indices of actual labor productivity shown on map A (in 10 Swedish kroner per hour) fall far below the maximum potential productivity shown on map B. (Reprinted by permission of the Association of American Geographers from Julian Wolpert, "The Decision Process in Spatial Context," *Annals of the Association of American Geographers* Vol. 54, 1964.

ity situated in a poor location can also alter and profitably adjust to the environment.

Some locations, however, are inefficient when an activity is first placed there. Such locations may or may not fail, depending on the degree of inefficiency. Typically, the decision maker had acted on insufficient or poor information and made an error in the location, scope, and size of his investment. However, a nonoptimal location, which is at the same time profitable or satisfactory, may be deliberately chosen. Many investors are willing to incur higher costs and accept lower profits, either because they are content with achieving satisfacotry, rather than optimum, levels of efficiency or because of overriding social or personal factors.

2

Location and Interaction
in Spatially Restricted Societies

The emphasis of this book is on societies that are technically advanced, mobile, and interdependent. Nevertheless, the majority of the world's people live in spatially restricted, largely self-sufficient, and near-subsistence societies. In such societies, barely the smallest surplus is produced for exchange, and thus spatial experience is limited; life is local and agricultural. Social and economic relations over distance are restricted, and the local area, the village, or perhaps a tribal group of villages constitutes the social space, the area in which most activities take place. Today's advanced societies evolved from such societies, and it is useful to be able to compare the characteristics of the two kinds of societies.

CHARACTERISTICS OF SPATIALLY RESTRICTED SOCIETIES

In spatially restricted societies, life is limited to a local area, reflecting both the population's close ties to the land and the poor state of its transport system. The landscape and economic and social relations seem miniaturized, with small fields, narrow roads, and a very local pattern of movement. Agriculture and handicrafts are organized on a small scale. The community usually achieves a fair degree of self-sufficiency in food and in goods that can be manufactured by hand, and trade and production of specialty goods are limited in scope, volume, and variety. Since transport is poor, distance is a strong barrier.

The pattern of life is repetitive in both time and space. The seasons enforce a rigid regime of work. A family's ties to its land are strong and partly control its spatial behavior. Any migration tends to be circular—ending back in the home village—and motivated largely by a desire to find either brides outside the village or perhaps temporary work, or because of social reasons.

In such societies regional dialects, customs, and character tend to develop—for example, note the very limited areas occupied by separate languages in New Guinea (see Figure 2.01). Individuals have an intimate understanding of and can differentiate the subtleties in the local area, in contrast to our more diffuse awareness; the environment powerfully affects the very survival of subsistence men.

Markets and Exchange

Societies are at different levels of commercialization—the degree to which they price and exchange goods and services (see Figure 2.02). The farm in western society is a business. The farmer's activities and success are governed by the national market, prices on land and labor, and exchange of goods. The peasant, however, whether intensively cultivating rice or performing traditional European agriculture, operates a small household economy. He functions as part of a larger kinship group, and his activities are governed by the needs of the group and by a strong political-economic order. Exchange exists mainly as a compulsory rent or tax; any surplus from this trade is very small. Increased productivity is compelled by his desire to improve consumption and the well-being of his household, more than by external demand. In these nonmarket economies, economic exchange cannot readily be separated from the social obligations which require it, and the change from primitive cultivator to modern farmer thus involves a radical shift from a personal concept of economics to an impersonal one.

Most less developed, near-subsistence societies do support, often by means of the small surpluses of many peasants, a small aristocracy, which obtains education, relative wealth, and a wider field of contact and experience. The system is efficient and convenient for such an aristocracy and is perhaps even a necessary stage in development; but resistance to change in such a system is very great, since the aristocracy can maintain its position only by owning extensive lands and by exploiting the labor of hundreds or thousands.

SPATIALLY EXTENSIVE ACTIVITIES

Hunting and Gathering

Some groups that are restricted to a small territory may nevertheless practice an extensive way of life —one in which the productivity per unit area is low. Few people today live under very primitive socioeconomic systems; simple hunting and gathering societies exist as fast-disappearing remnants in the areas most remote from centers of "civilization." Probably only a few million persons ever lived in such societies, since dependence upon nature to provide animals, skins, fish, and shelter can support only a few people at best.

As the better lands have been taken over by crop agriculture, the hunters have been forced into the poorest and most remote areas of the earth, even further reducing the capacity of the land to support them. A square mile or more per person is required today for such societies to exist, even though poor transport makes it hard to cross such distances. Thus, small hunting groups of 50 persons need an area with a radius of up to 10 kilometers and a food margin—ratio of potential to needed food—of as much as 40 to 1. Hunting and gathering activity survives among some Eskimos in areas too cold for farming, and also in remote hilly forests or deserts in temperate or tropical areas, where neither the technology of agriculture nor animal domestication has yet been introduced.

The social organization of hunting and gathering groups is normally tribal. Permanent settlement is limited by the large amounts of land required and by the group's poor mobility. There is great physical and cultural isolation, although the group is at least seminomadic and larger gatherings occasionally occur.

Primitive Agriculture

Forms of agriculture in which tools are limited to digging stick, hoe, and shovel still survive in fairly wide areas, although relatively few people are involved. Either because they have been forced there or because they have always existed in such remote locations, primitive agricultural societies

SPATIALLY RESTRICTED SOCIETIES

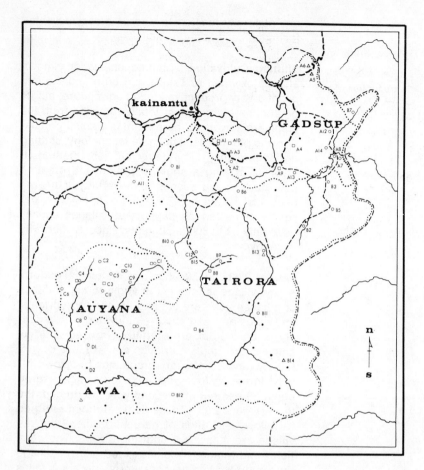

Eastern Highlands Study Area -- 1963

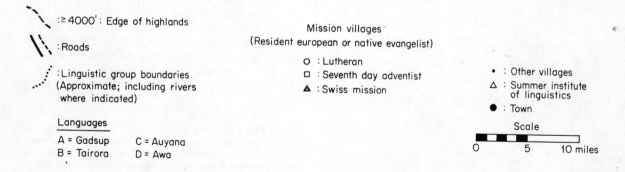

: ≥ 4000' : Edge of highlands

: Roads

: Linguistic group boundaries
(Approximate; including rivers
where indicated)

Mission villages
(Resident european or native evangelist)

○ : Lutheran
□ : Seventh day adventist
△ : Swiss mission

• : Other villages
△ : Summer institute
of linguistics
● : Town

Scale

0   5   10 miles

Languages

A = Gadsup   C = Auyana
B = Tairora   D = Awa

Figure 2.01 Language areas and village location in the New Guinea highlands. Poor transport and physical isolation partly account for the presence of the different languages in such a small area. (Reprinted courtesy of K. Pataki.)

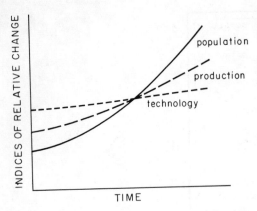

Spatially Restricted (Traditional) Society

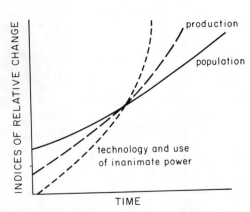

Spatially Interdependent (Commercial) Society

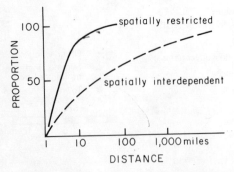

Proportion of Economic and Social Activities Conducted Within a Given Distance

are generally located in poorer areas unwanted for technically superior activities.

Shifting Cultivation Shifting cultivation, known also as *swidden* or "slash and burn" cultivation, is not a very productive kind of agriculture, but its practitioners are almost totally removed from the commercial world. Where there is a small population and plentiful land but little technology, shifting agriculture may be a fairly efficient method. It involves making a short migration and creating new gardens and villages as the fertility of an area becomes exhausted. From 5 to 25 persons per square mile can be supported; villages usually have only 30 to 300 inhabitants, since productivity is so low.

Figures 2.03 and 2.04 illustrate the typical pattern. A new village is founded in virgin forest. Patches of adjacent land are cut and burned for nutrients, and fields and gardens are cultivated with a variety of crops. Since no fertilizer is used and few animals are kept, nutrients are exhausted very rapidly, and satisfactory crops may be grown for only three or four years. Yields typically drop about 30 percent the second year, 50 percent the third (Figure 2.03). These fields are then returned to fallow, and rings of gardens farther from the village are cultivated, until the distance between fields and villages becomes excessive. The village then migrates to a new area, probably a few miles away, and the depleted land is left to recover over a long period of fallow, which may be up to 40 years. By continually shifting to more fertile land, more people can be supported at a fairly consistent level. This migration cycle also helps to maintain land fertility. Totally new villages may be founded if the old ones become too large or if internal conflict is severe.

Figure 2.02 In spatially restricted (traditional) societies, population tends to grow faster than production, while in spatially interdependent (commercial) societies, the rapid increase in technology and especially in the use of inanimate power allows production to grow faster than population. One measure of spatial interdependence is the great distance over which economic and social activities are carried out.

SPATIALLY RESTRICTED SOCIETIES

Shifting cultivation is subject to increasing restrictions. Population growth must be relieved either by migration of part of the population from the area, perhaps to settle in more intensively farmed areas, or by adoption of a sedentary and technologically improved agriculture. Often, after some contact is made with more advanced cultures, further population increase forces a group to find a permanent location for its villages and fields, since frequently no more unoccupied land exists.

Nomadism (Migratory Husbandry) Nomadic herding is also an extremely old form of occupance, first developed in Southwest Asia and Northeast Africa. Such herding is usually associated with natural grassland in arid or semiarid regions, where crop agriculture cannot be supported.

Productivity is very low relative to crop agriculture, partly because of the arid climate, partly because animals are an inefficient source of food. Such regions can support around one or two persons per square mile.

Nomadic herdsmen operate in tribal or extended-family units. Many different animals are tended and provide a wide variety of products and services: transportation; milk, cheese, and butter; meat, skin, and hides; bones for tools. In a society that must be mostly self-sufficient, such a diversity of articles available within the group is very desirable.

Given limited technology, nomadism is a remarkably efficient system of location in response to changing resources. Herds move from one pasture and water hole to another; when one area is fully grazed, the range is left to recover. Because nomadism allows fairly quick adjustment to variation in weather and grass quality, it can support a larger average herd and a greater population than can a settled livestock industry with the same technology, whose average herd size is restricted by the quality of the range in the poorest years.

Nomadic migration often exhibits a regular circular pattern (Figure 2.05), but this may be dis-

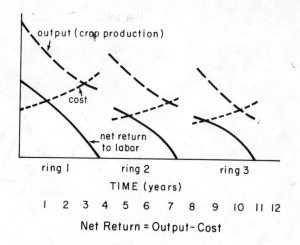

Figure 2.03 Shifting cultivation: costs and benefits. Productivity of an area falls over time and with distance of the fields from settlement.

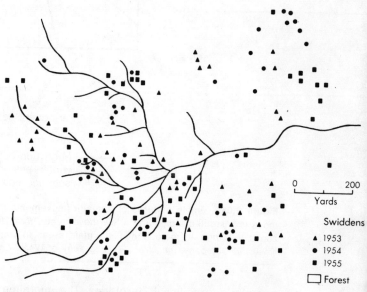

Figure 2.04 Shifting of gardens. Location and year of clearing of swiddens (gardens) among the Hanunoo, Mindoro, the Philippines. Hamlet locations are not given. In this area the cycle of reuse is about 12 years. (Reprinted by permission of the McGraw-Hill Book Company, Inc., from Donald W. Fryer, *World Economic Development,* 1965.)

torted by the randomizing effects of weather. Group paths rarely cross, since they usually

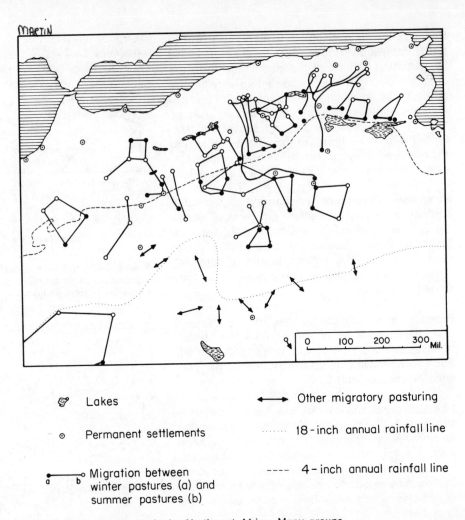

MARTIN

🝆 Lakes	←——→ Other migratory pasturing
⊙ Permanent settlements	·········· 18-inch annual rainfall line
●—○ a b Migration between winter pastures (a) and summer pastures (b)	- - - - 4-inch annual rainfall line

Scale: 0   100   200   300 Mil.

Figure 2.05 Simple patterns of nomadic movements in far Northwest Africa. Many groups move in restricted areas, and a few move rather great distances. Many move from lower arid zones in winter to more humid mountain areas in summer. (Reprinted courtesy of D. Van Nostrand Company, Inc., from *A Geography of World Economy*, Hans Boesch, 1964.)

operate in "traditional" territories. The migration may be both horizontal and vertical. In vertical migration—called transhumance—animals move to mountain pastures for the summer, lowland pastures for the winter, using pasture efficiently.

Most arid areas have a few oases, or larger water spots, supporting an area of intensive agriculture and towns and having many times the population of the larger areas of nomadic herding. Oases occasionally complement the herdsman, supplying him with vegetables, fruits, grain, tools, and water and acting as a market for his limited surpluses of animal products.

There are many restraints on nomadism. A strong national administration and boundary defense tend to eliminate cross-border movements and thus limit the free movement necessary to maintain a herd successfully. Nomadism weakens, too,

SPATIALLY RESTRICTED SOCIETIES

when a society makes an effort to commercialize agriculture and concentrate herds to produce meat for new urban markets; in these cases, settled commercial livestock ranching gradually takes over.

SPATIALLY INTENSIVE ACTIVITIES: INTENSIVE SUBSISTENCE AGRICULTURE

Today about one-half the world's population (in the past the proportion was much higher) is supported by intensive, rather self-sufficient farming. Such intensive subsistence agriculture is distinguished here from the extensive agriculture just discussed by the greater human alteration of nature, greater dependence on human labor, and the higher productivity per unit area. Most of East and South Asia and parts of Africa and Latin America are supported by intensive subsistence agriculture, and until the industrial revolution, Europe, too, was so supported. Indeed—the rise of the early civilizations depended on successful intensive farming to support greater and greater concentrations of people. Such intense agriculture both permitted and was made necessary by the growth of the population.

The village is the dominant social and economic unit in most traditional peasant societies. As a political unit it includes several small settlements, together with their surrounding fields. Villages tend to be distributed in a fairly efficient and uniform pattern. Their frequency originally was determined by the distance easily reached and returned from in a day, but new villages have been created when old ones have broken up because of population pressure, and larger consolidated and fortified villages have been created for defense.

Life on a subsistence farm was and is repetitive. Change comes only gradually, when new crops and methods are introduced that make it possible to intensify further and support a larger population. More common are gradual improvements in existing technology. Since change is so slow, however, subsistence agriculture—where the

needs of the family or village are just barely met —remains characteristic of such economies until there is a change in the political-economic organization that permits industrialization and commercialization.

Subsistence Agriculture in European History

The typical pattern of European subsistence agriculture was a mixture of communally held woodland and pasture and several hundred long, narrow strips surrounding a small village. An average family might cultivate up to 50 strips of diverse quality at various distances from the village, totaling about 5 to 15 acres. These strips were sometimes held as private property, but could still be reallocated by the village; the inner strips were generally used more intensively and frequently. A traditional fallow rotation system was employed. A strip was planted for two years, then allowed to lie fallow. Often the village lands were part of a large estate. Rents due landlords and taxes and interest often claimed half the crop, so that no surplus was available to be sold.

The population expansion of the eighteenth and nineteenth centuries led to excess land division, extreme poverty, and underemployment, and the demand for food by the growing cities could not be met by the existing farm organization. Governments and large landowners forced enclosure and consolidation of strips and communal lands into separate farms. These remained too small, however, and peasants were soon differentiated into rich and poor; the more successful often acquired the holdings of the less successful and, thus having a surplus, made the transition to a commercial economy. Those forced off the land either migrated abroad or moved into the growing cities.

East and South Asia: Dominance of Rice

East and South Asia are today the main areas where intensive, self-sufficient farming predominates. There is great variety of landscape and climate in this vast area, but the warm, moist, "tropical" rainy conditions of the long summer monsoon are most characteristic. Rice is best suited for maximum yields under just these conditions, and it has long been the staple and preferred grain of the region. In areas further inland with less moisture, or where the growing season is too short, rice is replaced by hardier grains.

The distribution of population in South and East Asia closely follows the concentration of rice in the lowlands and floodplains. Severely sloping land is not used very intensively, despite the high density of population in Asia. Floodplain locations are the most preferred, since fields can be large, and the labor needed to construct fields and supply water is reduced.

Organization of the Farm and Means of Intensification Intensity of rice production—greater productivity per acre and the ability to support a larger population—is partly achieved by paddy irrigation. The paddy represents a significant and costly human modification of nature. Carefully constructed, absolutely level rice fields are flooded at crucial times to obtain the maximum yield. Double-cropping (two crops per year) of rice is possible in near-tropical and more continuously moist areas. Rice and a small grain crop alternate in wet–dry areas, rice in the warm summer, wheat, millet, or others in the cooler winter. Efficiency of land use is further increased by using separate fields to produce seedlings while the main fields are still used for other crops.

Patterns of fields reflect minor topographic variations, ease of application of irrigation water, and the tendency of larger units to fragment into smaller ones as the population increases (see Figure 2.06). The small size of the fields makes mechanization technically difficult, and the small size of farm and surplus makes it economically impractical. Where fields are very small, even an animal cannot compete with hand labor. Where fields and farms are fairly large, however, an animal such as a water buffalo, becomes profitable; the marginal productivity, or extra output, more

than pays for the animal. In Japan, where transport is good and up to half the rice crop is typically sold, farmers have found it economic to use small hand tractors, even in rather small fields.

Heavy fertilization is a basic aid to high yields of rice and continuous land productivity. In China and especially Japan, human waste is a principal fertilizer; mud from the bottom of fish ponds and canals is also important in China. In India, however, animal dung is used more as a fuel for cooking and heating—to the detriment of crop yields. Yields are further increased by careful weeding.

All these means of intensifying rice yield depend on the use of a great deal of labor, chiefly for spring transplanting and for the fall harvest (when only a single crop is grown each year). At other seasons, farm labor is often underemployed, without enough work to keep fully occupied, and are therefore available for construction or other temporary jobs. Farms are too small; the productivity of labor and farm income would rise if a farmer were able to obtain more land. Land productivity is great at present, but productivity per man-hour is extremely low (see Figure 2.07).

All these efforts to increase productivity reflect the need to sustain the family with only a small—and possibly diminishing—farm, rather than the desire to increase cash sales. If a farmer has sufficient land, however, he will probably be eager to take advantage of commercial demand.

Problems of Subsistence Agriculture

The Problem of Land In all areas of intensive, subsistence agriculture, small-sized farms severely limit the productivity of labor. Division of land upon inheritance and transfers owing to debts and marriage result in complex ownership patterns and small farms. Such reduction in farm size tends to increase the amount of tenancy (dependence on rented land) as farmers seek to add to their holdings. Since rents may be from one-third to two-thirds of the crop, however, the marginal

SPATIALLY RESTRICTED SOCIETIES

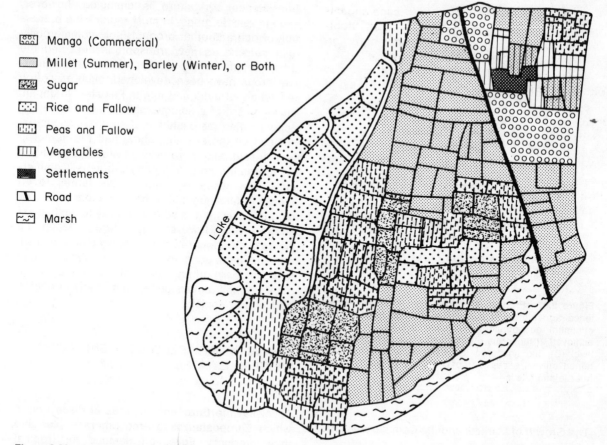

Legend:

- Mango (Commercial)
- Millet (Summer), Barley (Winter), or Both
- Sugar
- Rice and Fallow
- Peas and Fallow
- Vegetables
- Settlements
- Road
- Marsh

Figure 2.06 A village and its lands: Bauria, India (about two miles in length). Note the concentration of more intensive vegetables and mangos near the villages; rice is along the lake and canals for easiest irrigation.

return to the operator on such land is exceedingly poor.

Land division can also mean that an individual's fields are extremely fragmented—separated in space. Small fields can also result from adapting paddy fields to local topography and from the practice of allotting each family fields of each kind when village communal lands are of varying quality—for example, each family will be allotted some irrigable paddy and some upland fields. The unfortunate result is increased labor for reduced yields on a given quantity of land, since the farmer

can give less attention—especially fertilizer—to more distant fields (see Figure 2.08).

The Problem of Transport Transport is local, slow, and irregular in most regions of subsistence agriculture. Footpaths and canals are used for local travel, and rivers and major canals provide a means of long-distance transport, supplemented in Japan and India by railway systems. In general, however, local access to transport is so poor that movements beyond 20 miles are very costly, and most movements are much shorter than that.

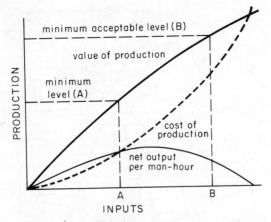

A. Low population pressure;
   moderate farm size

B. High population pressure;
   small farms

Figure 2.07 Productivity and inputs: intensive subsistence agriculture. At a lower population level (A), the minimum acceptable subsistence production level is achieved at moderate effort (cost). At a high population level (B), the necessary subsistence production is attained only at excessive cost, and the output per man-hour is much less.

The Growth of Markets and the Commercialization of Agriculture

Peasant subsistence societies have weak local or regional, rather than national, markets. Much exchange of goods, in fact, is a function of legal and social obligations.

Exchange for economic reasons is not absent, however. Although individual farm surpluses are small, there is an aggregate demand for exchange of grains, meat, vegetables, handicrafts, and outside food products and manufactures. Traveling merchants and seasonal fairs help satisfy these demands, and occasional village markets help also. Market towns also exist, perhaps one for every 200,000 people; because of the density of the rural population, such market towns may be within 5 to 10 miles of most farmers.

Subsistence agriculture is changing, however, even in remote areas. In most regions the proportion of rice and other products sold commercially is increasing as new transport is built and the urban population grows. Special export commercial crops have been developed, such as cotton in China and India and jute in Pakistan. In Japan, development of a commercialized agriculture has accompanied the evolution of an urban–industrial society; on the average, about half the rice crop is now sold, and more farmers are specializing in meat, poultry, and even dairy products. Commercialization has also permitted the farmer to increase fertilization, utilize hand tractors and other modern tools, and raise productivity to the highest known levels. However, agriculture in Japan still yields such a low return per family that a dualism remains in the economy—there is on the one hand a fully modern urban–industrial sector and, on the other, a half subsistence, half market-oriented agricultural society.

SPATIALLY INTERDEPENDENT ENCLAVES: WESTERN ESTATES

Following the European voyages of discovery, in which Europeans discovered other peoples and their products, European demand for tropical products like sugar, spices, and fruit grew rapidly. The supplies purchased from local rulers soon proved inadequate, and European companies established estates and plantations dedicated to efficient, fairly modern production of specific crops. Although these estates helped commercialize the local economy, they were at the same time part of the agricultural economy of the European mother country.

Estates, typically located in tropical environments suited for growing the desired exotic products, were subject to three restraints: location in an area in which the mother country had sufficient influence and power to protect the estate; availability of a sufficient labor supply, whether indigenous or imported; and location in coastal areas, for easy access to ocean transport. Gradually,

SPATIALLY RESTRICTED SOCIETIES

railways and roads were built, and greater advantage could be taken of better lands farther from the ocean (see Figure 2.09).

Estate Products

Major plantation products are sugar, rubber, coffee, tea, cocoa, copra, bananas, fibers (hemp, abaca, sisal, cotton, henequen), oil palm, and spices. Production of each tends to be concentrated in certain regions or districts devoted to that specialty, even though production could theoretically be located in a much greater area.

Marketing, consumption, and prices are largely controlled in Europe and the United States. Since these crops can be raised in much greater quantity than there is demand to justify, the bargaining position of suppliers is weak. In order to stabilize production and prices, the supplying and receiving countries have jointly created marketing and quota agreements setting production and trade patterns.

Estate agriculture requires considerable labor. Where local labor supplies have proved insufficient, workers have been brought great distances, either on contract (from Japan or the Philippines to Hawaii, for instance) or as slaves (Negroes to the American colonies and to the Caribbean estates). These groups radically altered the composition of the population in the areas to which they were transported. The concentration of adequate labor, local or imported, is an important reason why estates have a particular and limited distribution. Where local population pressure is great, estates must compete for land and labor with the agriculture necessary to provide local food supplies.

Mining

Western-controlled mining activities form commercial enclaves also, competing for local labor.

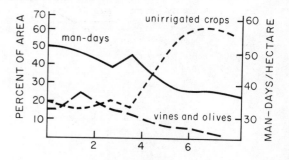

Figure 2.08 Distance to fields and farmer attention (Canicatti, Sicily). The left scale shows the percent of area devoted to vines and unirrigated crops. The right scale shows man-days per hectare (labor per unit area). Crops requiring more effort (including fertilizer) are located near the village, and labor per unit area therefore decreases with distance from the village.

Exploitation of products here begins with the discovery of a particularly rich resource, usually of such high quality that the expense of building costly transport lines, usually railroads, is warranted. Even with this expense, profits may still be higher than those received for exploiting resources in the home country. Cheap labor for mining and refining is also a factor for locating mines in a few cases, but the discovery of scarce resources is the controlling element.

Significance of Estates and Mining Enclaves

Estates and mines have brought greater commercialization to colonized countries by paying wages —no matter how low—to workers. They have also induced greater development by building the railroads and roads necessary to export goods. Secondary development, however, has generally been minimal, since investors have preferred to locate in their home country the processing operations that produce the most wealth. Also, since the railroads were built to penetrate the country and aid in exporting goods, rather than to facilitate internal circulation, the railroads create a bias

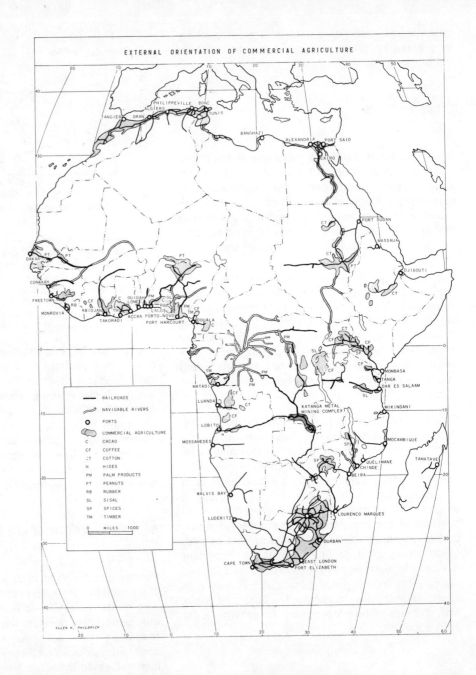

Figure 2.09 External orientation of commercial agriculture: location of western estates in Africa around 1955. Most commercial agriculture (in large part carried on by western estates) depended on foreign markets and located along coasts or railways, which provided external access rather than internal connections. (Reprinted by permission of John Wiley & Sons, Inc., from Allen K. Philbrick, *This Human World*, 1963.)

SPATIALLY RESTRICTED SOCIETIES

toward economic relations with—if not dependence upon—the mother country.

As well, in these colonies a colonial trading pattern was developed in which most of the cash income of the colony derived from export activities. Since power, banking, investment, and trade were largely controlled by the colonial administration, this income tended to be spent on costly consumption goods from the home country, rather than on economic development. In fact, official policy usually discouraged general industrialization, since colonies were more useful as captive markets. The contrasts between the small landed aristocracy and the large body of subsistence peasants thus became aggravated.

Nevertheless, sanitation facilities and other health measures were introduced by colonial nations, along with more formal educational systems. As a result, population in colonized nations increased spectacularly — without corresponding radical changes in the economy. Thus, more and more people have to be supported by an agriculture that uses only a limited technology, and real standards of living may have declined in the last few centuries in such areas as India, China, and the Caribbean. Estates have also helped redistribute the local population, concentrating people in coastal estate areas and associated towns. When estates have moved, because of disease, for example, severe short-run disruption has occurred.

LOCATION PRINCIPLES, GOALS OF SPATIAL BEHAVIOR, AND THE SPATIALLY RESTRICTED SOCIETY

We may summarize this discussion of less commercial societies with reference to the patterns of spatial behavior discussed earlier.

1. Repetition and diffusion in location: More than in commercial societies, spatial patterns of behavior are likely to be repetitive in noncommercial societies. Still, the more successful forms have gradually spread out from their points of origin—the diffusion of the wet-rice culture is one example.

2. Environmental control: Environment sets strong limits and channels the development of an agricultural economy. Thus, wet-rice cultures tend to be present where there is level land and plentiful water. The combination of relief, soil, and climate makes many areas useful only for nomadism and other areas useful only for shifting cultivation.

3. Role of distance: Given the limited technology and dependence on agriculture, distance is a strong barrier. Mobility and travel are limited, and both surpluses and deficits are difficult to alleviate. The local area must be self-sufficient, and regions tend to become greatly differentiated in language and custom.

4. Role of tradition: Religious and cultural traditions influence spatial behavior in several ways—by favoring repetition of past methods of organization, by favoring or disfavoring certain foods, goods, and methods, and by placing less emphasis on innovation and change than does western culture.

5. Level of technology: The less mechanized technology of spatially restricted societies is reflected in their dependence on human and animal labor, in their less well-developed transport system, and in their smaller scale of operations, from the size of fields and buildings to the distances typically traveled.

6. Scale: Inadequate transport and high population growth in these societies have prevented the realization of the benefits of larger firms and enterprises. Indeed, a reduction in size has resulted instead. Per capita productivity is very low and may even have fallen in the last two centuries.

7. Socioeconomic system: The presence of semifeudal forms of organization has tended to stifle change. The high degree of tenancy and land fragmentation associated with semifeudal society reduce productivity.

8. Goals and restraints: (a) Maximizing the productivity of each area. This goal has been avidly pursued, and somewhat successfully, since output per acre is fairly high. The effect of intensifying production has been to support more people performing the same activities rather than to free part of the population to pursue different activities or to raise the level of living. Whereas in a commercial society productivity is achieved by specializing and differentiating land use and labor, in a subsistence society greater productivity is dependent on intensifying local production.

(b) Maximizing interaction with minimum travel. As a result of pursuing this goal, settlements are efficiently sized and spaced, subject to the problems of land fragmentation and tenancy. But interaction (interchange of people and goods) is often limited to the area of the village and its fields. Even if trade is highly valued, poor transport and low farm productivity stifle exchange of goods.

In summary, the landscape resulting from an agricultural society with a low technology and the desire to be self-sufficient is a repetitive and miniaturized pattern—a structure consisting of independent but look-alike cells. The patterns of village organization are similar over much of the world. Still, there is little interrelation between areas, and language and culture differentiation is great. In contrast, while the commercial economy is extremely differentiated in specialized land use, the same transport system that sustains the economy fosters greater cultural unity.

Part Two

Structure of Land Use: Extensive Space

3

Commercial Agriculture

THE ROLE OF AGRICULTURE IN SPATIALLY INTERDEPENDENT SOCIETIES

Agriculture is man's most fundamental economic activity and has had the most dramatic impact on the natural landscape. Although in the most advanced countries its role has been eclipsed by the urban activities that support much of the population, it is no less important as a supplier both of food and of raw materials for industry. Agricultural production itself is under one-fifth of the economy in these advanced countries, but it provides the raw materials needed by about one-fifth of industry. Indirectly, as much as half of most advanced economies depends on agriculture. In advanced commercial societies, also, farming is more a business than a way of life—as opposed to the subsistence agriculture we just studied—and is more subject to economic controls than to the special relations of a man to the land he uses.

Agriculture has not, for many reasons, responded as well as urban activities to improved, more efficient technology; many farmers are unable or unwilling to adopt mass production techniques. Farmers are also in a weak competitive position because of their lack of organization, and low and unstable prices hinder improvement. Income levels are consequently not as high for agricultural occupations as for urban ones. Nevertheless, agricultural productivity has increased dramatically over time; in a few countries, less than 10 percent of the population provides all the agricultural needs of the country.

Commercial agriculture has a fascinating geographic distribution, in response to the interplay of environmental, market, transport, and human factors. In the self-sufficient societies we examined previously, environmental and cultural preferences often dictated farm organization and land use. When transport improved and regional and national markets became concentrated in small areas, however, specialization became possible—and location with respect to major markets became a dominant factor.

FACTORS INFLUENCING THE LOCATION OF AGRICULTURAL PRODUCTION

Major controls over use of land for agriculture are:

X 1.   Environment, especially landforms, soil, temperature, moisture, and growing season, all of which influence the cost of production of various crops.

X 2.   Location relative to major markets and the resulting transport costs for different crops.

X 3.   Consumer demand for various products.

4.   Inherent characteristics of the crop—productivity and labor required, for instance.

X 5.   Productivity of the crop in response to inputs such as fertilizer or machinery.

6.   Regional differences regarding labor quality and costs, the usual form of ownership, population pressure on the land, and the presence of alternate employment opportunities.

7.   Government policies.

Environmental Influences   For most crops, the range of conditions in which survival is possible is wide, but the range where maximum productivity can be achieved—where the value of the crop harvested exceeds the costs of production—is much narrower. There is sufficient variation in preferred locations to allow much complementarity—different crops are most productive in different locations.

Unusual pressure is placed on the best quality lands; production outside of these optimal conditions means extra effort and costs for the farmer, although these will not necessarily prohibit agriculture. One model of agricultural land use could be constructed on the basis of the suitability of the environment for different crops. Figure 3.01, for instance, illustrates the notion of optimal conditions and limits for crops. If we could construct such diagrams for several crops, we would find some areas in which one crop is best, others on which several can compete.

Clear relationships can be found between the yield of crops, handling costs, and environmental factors. An increasing slope accompanied by thinner soils and thus greater erosion risk, for instance, reduces yields and increases handling

costs. Soil quality also affects yields and production costs because of variations in acidity or alkalinity, organic content, moisture and air absorption and retention, lightness for working, drainage, and so forth. Temperature, both the long-range average and the daily temperature range, also affects growth rate and quality. Moisture supply, especially at critical periods, has a clear influence on crop yields (see Figure 3.02).

Consumer Demand for Crops   Prices are partly a function of the costs of production, but consumer demands and preferences are just as important. By creating a structure of crop prices partly independent of the costs of production, the consumer modifies agricultural location. A high price on a low-yield product, for instance, permits production in a remote area.

Crop Characteristics   Crops vary in their inherent productivity—volume of output for a given effort—perishability and transportability, labor requirements, and adaptability to machinery. Under the same conditions some crops—for example, vegetables—produce a much greater usable volume and thus, given sufficient demand, have a much higher value than, say, grains. On the other hand, grain is less perishable, can be stored longer and handled more easily and roughly, and is therefore cheaper to transport than fresh vegetables, fluid milk, and fresh eggs. However, these higher valued and less transportable crops are usually able to compete for better land.

Yield in Response to Inputs   There is a crucial relationship between yield and the addition of extra inputs—investments to increase production. In Figure 3.03, a typical pattern is shown of rapidly increasing yields with initial inputs, giving way to a slower increase in yields, and finally diminishing returns with excessive inputs. The differential response of crops to inputs such as extra water, fertilizer, weeding, and spraying affects how intensively they can be raised and how well they can compete for quality land and accessible locations. So long as extra inputs raise revenues more rapidly than they raise costs, such intensification pays. Price is important also, since producers of low value crops cannot afford to add many inputs without diminishing their returns.

Mechanization and Farm Size Mechanization can dramatically raise agricultural productivity by permitting a farmer to handle much greater acreages. In addition to powerful and efficient tractors, all kinds of specialized equipment for weeding, spraying, drilling, harvesting, and picking exists for most farm specialties. However, many farmers cannot take full advantage of this machinery because their farms are too small.

Increasing farm size certainly enables the farmer to achieve greater economies by making more complete use of labor and equipment. Unfortunately, however, farmers do not have the capital or land necessary to bring production to its optimal level. The economies of scale also may not smoothly increase with size; at the point where a hired man must be employed, for example, the economies will temporarily decrease. The farmer must also consider the risk of price variation if he grows only one product. Long-run profitability may be greater with two products, even though fewer returns to scale will be realized.

✳THE THEORY OF AGRICULTURAL LOCATION

The owner of a piece of land in a commercial society presumably wishes to achieve the maximum possible productivity. The problem for the farmer is to choose the products, inputs, and markets that will best satisfy this goal. Thünen, who formulated classical agricultural location theory, recognized earliest the gradient aspect of spatial organization. Competition for access to markets, which is a joint function of inherent productivity, transportation costs, demand, and response of the crop to inputs, causes a spatial ordering of crops: As one goes out from the market center, production becomes less intense, fewer inputs are added, and returns per acre fall.

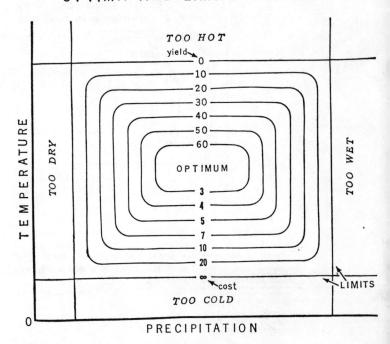

OPTIMA AND LIMITS SCHEMA

Figure 3.01 Optima and limits schema. This diagram illustrates hypothetically that for any given crop, there is an optimal combination of temperature and moisture. Non-optimal combinations reduce yields and raise costs until, at the limit, yield drops to zero and costs are prohibitive. (From Harold H. McCarty and James B. Lindberg, *A Preface to Economic Geography,* ©1966. Reprinted by permission of Prentice-Hall, Inc., Englewood Cliffs, N.J.)

Agricultural products that are unusually productive per acre, that cannot be transported easily, or that respond unusually well to inputs compete for the limited space available around a market center. Growers of crops such as these, for which the transport rate is highest in relation to net price, will bid a very high price (rent) for this land, since easily accessible land is necessary to make production feasible. Thus, because there is limited land near the market and rents are high, the farmer must employ very intensive methods.

Crops with relatively lower transport costs can use more land at a greater distance. The precise distance at which a particular crop is competitive

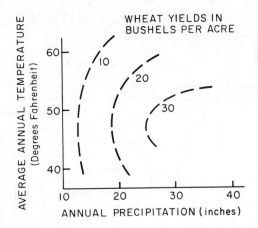

Figure 3.02 Effect of temperature and moisture on wheat yields. This figure illustrates the response of yields to temperature and moisture. Other factors, of course, may make it profitable to grow wheat under less than highest yield conditions.

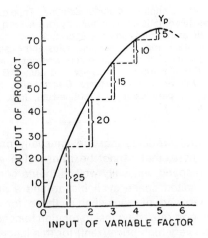

Figure 3.03 Inputs and yields. Normally, yields increase rapidly with the first inputs, then increase more slowly, and may finally decrease with additional excess inputs. (From Earl O. Heady, *Economics of Agricultural Production and Resource Use,* ©1962. Reprinted by permission of Prentice-Hall, Inc., Englewood Cliffs, N.J.)

is a function of prices, yields, and transport costs. As distance from the market increases, transport costs become greater and greater and net revenue lower and lower until the point is reached—the economic margin—where revenues equal transport costs. Figure 3.04 depicts the net return per acre for different crops with respect to distance from the market. Note that crops in zone A have a very high return initially, but that the high transport costs reduce the net return rapidly. Rather quickly, the profitable crops change. Although the crops in zone B were less profitable near the market, in B they become more profitable, since their transport costs reduce net returns less rapidly. Because they do not need easy market access, the less perishable and more transportable crops (C and D) are pushed farther from the market, where they remain profitable. The agricultural system thus extends outward until no activity exists for which transport and production costs do not exceed revenues. At its simplest, the ideal pattern of agriculture is one of concentric rings surrounding a market, with decreasing returns per acre in each ring (as in Figure 3.04).

This agricultural gradient has many effects on the pattern of farm production. Size of farm and amount of inputs will vary with the return per unit area and distance from the market. The farmer who is close to a market relies on high response to inputs to raise productivity high enough to compensate for the low transportability of his product and the high cost of his land. The distant producer, on the other hand, often finds it easier to maximize his income by cultivating more land. Land and inputs can be substituted for each other to some degree; variations in inputs can equalize income among farms of different size at a given distance (see Figure 3.05). Where land is cheap, a farmer uses more acres with a lower level of inputs; where land is expensive, more inputs make up for the smaller acreage that he can afford.

The more intensive and perishable goods can sometimes be produced at a distance from a market if an intermediate processing step improving transportability is included. A dairyman at a greater distance, for instance, transforms less

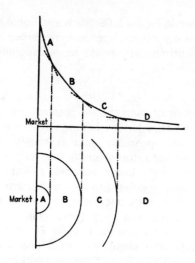

Figure 3.04 The *x*-axis indicates distance from market, the *y*-axis net return per acre. Those crops that are relatively most costly to transport bid the highest price (rent) for land and obtain the land closest to the market, in zone A. Within this zone, increasing transport costs lessen net return per acre, and the dashed line tangent to the curve between A and B indicates that at this distance, a new crop (or set of crops) becomes more profitable, creating a second crop zone, B. These have relatively lower transport costs than the A zone crops, but higher costs than those in zone C (see text). (Reprinted by permission of McGraw-Hill Book Company, Inc., from Edgar M. Hoover, *Location of Economic Activity,* 1948).

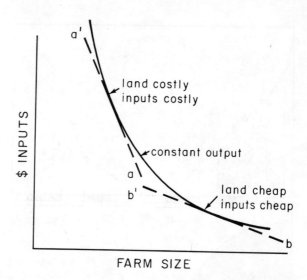

Figure 3.05 Substitution between land and other inputs. To achieve a given level of output, one may use more land at less intensity (fewer inputs per acre) or less land at greater intensity (more inputs per acre). If land is relatively costly and inputs, such as labor, also costly (dashed line *aa'*), the latter course is best; if land is cheap and inputs cheap, however (line *bb'*), the former course is best. The dashed lines indicate the ratio of land cost to input cost per unit of output.

transferable fluid milk into cheese or butter. Canning, freezing, drying, and refining in effect place distant producers of fruit, vegetables, and sugar beets a thousand miles closer to a market. Thus, greater advantage can be taken of distant but high-quality land.

Short-run stability in the location of crops is maintained from the interplay of these factors. If a farmer located near a market attempts to raise a less profitable crop, for instance, the opportunity cost (the higher price he could have received for an alternate crop) will tend to force him to shift to the more profitable crop or sell the land to someone who will. If, on the other hand, a more distant farmer attempts to raise a more productive, but less transportable crop, the higher transport

costs will reduce his net revenue. A long-term stable equilibrium is actually never reached, since ownership, technology, and demand change continuously.

The gradient is more obvious because there are crops of varying productivity and transportability, but, in theory, there should be a gradient of net returns, inputs, and farm size even if there were only one product! Very simply, a more distant producer using the same production method as one closer will have a lower net return per acre because of his higher transport costs. To obtain the same income the distant producer requires more land, but handling more land in the same way as the closer producer would increase his costs and thus decrease his revenues. However, if the more distant producer can reduce his inputs and lower his production costs more rapidly than his yields

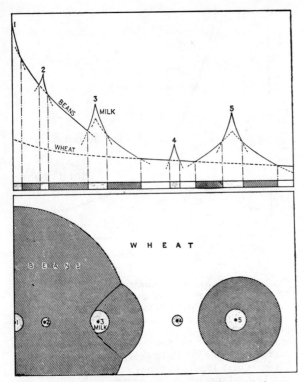

Figure 3.06 Effects of additional markets. In this hypothetical example, smaller markets 2 through 5 disrupt the pattern of land use around the main market, 1. The smallest, 2 and 4, have a demand for milk only. Markets 3 and 5 contain demand for beans as well. The demand in these smaller markets is great enough to cause nearby farmers to supply them rather than the main market. Still, the markets are incomplete; they are surrounded by farmers shipping directly to market 1. The lesser demand at smaller markets also means less competition for access to them and thus lower land prices, reduced intensity, and lower return per acre in the land immediately surrounding them. (Dollar return per acre is indicated on the *y*-axis.) (Reprinted by permission of McGraw-Hill Book Company, Inc., from Edgar M. Hoover, *Location of Economic Activity*, 1948.)

fall, so that his labor is spread over more land, he can compete with the closer farmer.

Additional Markets

Additional markets and markets for varying ranges of products create landscapes like the theoretical one shown in Figure 3.06. Such additional markets are the result of the repetitive, dispersed location of some urban centers (to be subsequently discussed).

The amount of land that is planted with a given crop is, in part, a function of the size of the market. Theoretically, products sold at smaller markets have lower net returns (partly due to higher handling costs with lower volume). Hence, smaller markets may receive produce only from a small region that is completely surrounded by a larger region supplying a very large market. Smaller markets may also be incomplete. For example, in Figure 3.06, the small markets 2 and 4 demand only milk, markets 3 and 5 demand milk and beans, and only market 1 demands all three—milk, beans, and wheat. Thus, markets 2 through 5 are incomplete.

The extent of the region serving a market increases, of course, as the demand in the market rises and as transport costs become cheaper. Historically, then, although the environment has (in general) remained unchanged, land has shifted from less intensive to more intensive crops as consumer demands have increased; the entire gradient has moved upward and outward (see Figure 3.07). The American wheat belt, for example, shifted from New York, to Ohio, to Illinois–Wisconsin, to Iowa—Minnesota, to Kansas and the Dakotas. As well, in less than 100 years the Los Angeles basin evolved from a region of livestock–hide production to one of the world's most intensive fruit–vegetable–dairy regions.

With the possible exception of the local dairy, a case of near monopoly, isolated farms of some kind of crop are rarely successful. Competitive strength seems to require the agglomeration of like producers, indirectly sharing techniques and marketing. The advantages of grouping producers of the same crop in clusters have also favored the concentration of specialties in local areas. For example, such minor crops as peppermint and

COMMERCIAL AGRICULTURE

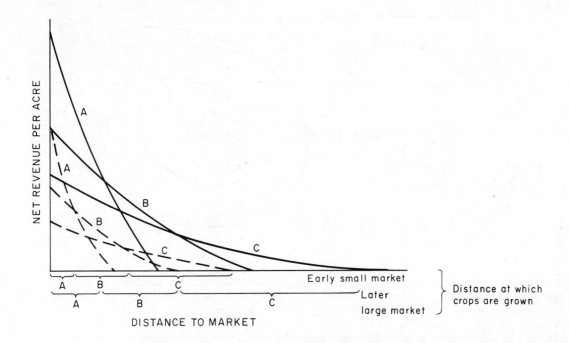

Figure 3.07 Shift of gradients over time. This figure illustrates the competition for land among three crops (A, B, and C) when a market is small (dashed lines) and later when it becomes large (solid lines). The three lines for each period indicate the decline in net return for the three crops as distance from the market increases. Where lines A and B intersect, for example, crop B becomes more profitable than crop A; even though the net return from B is not as high as for A near the market, B's net return declines more slowly.

When the market is small, producers do not need to bid as high a price for the closest land, or to use as much land, or to use it as intensively as they do later when the market is large; higher market demand requires both that more land be used for crops and that land be used more productively. Thus, land has shifted from less to more intensive crops, and the gradient has moved upward and outward.

hops are highly concentrated in small regions in the United States, and even significant crops, such as rye and potatoes, are grown in relatively small areas. Some moderate to small urban centers may thus be major markets for one or two less common products.

The Role of the Environment

The gradient theory we have just studied assumes that activities take place on a uniform plain, with the same environment, equal entrepreneurial ability, and identical level of technology at all points. The quality of real landscapes, of course, varies dramatically, even in small areas. Such variation is reflected in the costs of production and thus distorts the ideal gradient (see Figure 3.08). For instance, an enclave of above average land permits a farmer either to obtain excess profits on a crop typically grown in that zone or to cultivate a more intensive crop if the greater yield or price of the new crop can offset the increased transport costs. Thus, irrigated land in distant but exceptional environments yields up to five times as

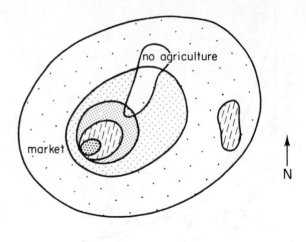

A. Effect of variation in land quality on revenue per acre

B. Distortion of ideal concentric pattern of crops due to land quality variation

Figure 3.08 A. Variation in land quality (slope, soil, climate) can cause an inversion of farm intensity and net return. B. In this figure, land quality falls much more rapidly to the southwest, and the three most intensive zones disappear. To the northeast, an island of poor quality reduces crop intensity, but farther to the east, a zone of very intensive production is possible because of superior land.

much cotton as average land and can compete successfully against much closer cotton-producing land. Similarly, in a poorer than average area relative costs are higher; the farmer on rugged land, for example, may replace wheat with livestock grazing. If cost variations due to environment are combined with the gradients around a market, an ideal crop pattern might appear as in Figure 3.09.

Improvements in transportation have radically reduced marketing costs, and the inputs and crop and animal technology available have become much better. As a result, differences in the environment are more decisive. Market influence encourages dairy farming near cities and makes low-value crops likely in peripheral locations, but as distant producers in far superior environments are able to compete against closer producers, more and more low-quality land near markets is being abandoned. At the same time, apparently poor environments can often be made highly productive with modern technology. In arid or semi-arid areas, which often have inherently rich soils, high productivity may be achieved if irrigation is possible. Great intensity of production, achieved by applying extra inputs and growing valuable crops, is usually required to compete in distant markets and to pay for the cost of water (Figure 3.10). Irrigation projects are costly, large-scale investments. The success of many such projects can be partly attributed to the secondary benefits derived from irrigating an area—crop concentration, cooperative marketing, and disease control. Some irrigation projects also have subsidies, usually from power revenues, either for the initial construction or for water costs (see Figure 3.10).

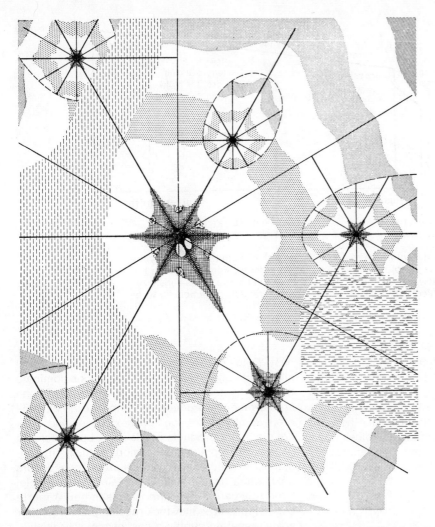

Figure 3.09 A composite agricultural landscape. An idealized picture of the land use in a region, with large zones of decreasing density and radial transport out from the major city and smaller patterns of land use and transport out from smaller cities. (Reprinted from *Location and Space Economy* by Walter Isard by permission of the M.I.T. Press, Cambridge, Mass. Copyright ©1956 by the Massachusetts Institute of Technology.)

The Decision Process

The individual farmer has many difficult decisions to make when he attempts to achieve the highest possible profits from his location. From his land, position near markets, and knowledge of crops,

he should ideally be able to determine an expected level of return and then decide on specific crops and products.

Most behavior lags far behind this ideal. Inefficiency results from lack of knowledge, uncertainty, and—often—the farmer's willingness to

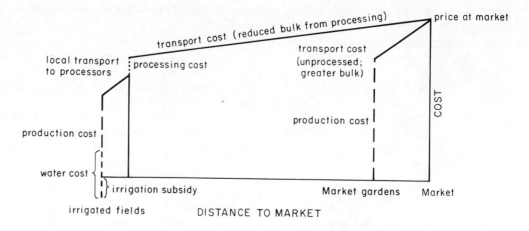

Figure 3.10 Competitiveness of distant irrigated crops. Areas distant from markets can compete in production of fruits and vegetables with nearby market gardens. For example, in this figure the irrigated fields enjoy lower production costs and have their water costs subsidized somewhat. In addition, the produce is processed locally, thereby reducing the volume to be transported.

achieve satisfactory rather than optimal levels of production. As well, uncertainty is always present in agriculture; prices and other farmers are unpredictable. A cautious response to uncertainty may reduce the farmer's long-run profits, since he will reject risky but potentially profitable choices, but it also may minimize year-to-year fluctuations.

Summary

Agricultural space consists of a pattern of crop locations and intensities that results from efforts to reduce transport costs and to maximize returns. These patterns are modified by environmental variations, such as temperature, moisture, and soil differences.

How well does the "real world" fit this scheme? The largest concentrated markets are in northwestern Europe and the northeastern United States, which are also the areas of highest productivity, highest intensity, and greatest rent—even though the areas' natural fertility is not the best. Yields decline from the market centers. Fluid milk, horticulture, and feeder operations dominate the regions near the markets. A generalized zone of intermediate productivity, emphasizing animal–crop combinations, occurs next. Beef and pork are the major products of this zone, but butter and cheese will replace them in more suitable environments. A predominantly cash-crop zone occurs next, wheat in the American plains, for example. Land rents are lower, farm size is larger. A fourth zone emphasizes livestock ranching. On a smaller scale, separate supply areas, especially for milk, can be distinguished for major regional urban markets.

TRENDS AND PROBLEMS IN AGRICULTURE

Type of Farms

The part-time farm is a common phenomenon in America and Europe (20 percent of farms in the United States). They are most prevalent in remote

COMMERCIAL AGRICULTURE

areas, such as the hilly isolated valleys of Appalachia. These small farmers can do little more than maintain their food supplies, and part-time nonfarm jobs supplement family income.

Another class of farmer, the residential farmer (15 percent of U.S. farms), works in the city but lives on a small nearby farm. He is especially common around larger cities. Contributing little to output and inefficient, he may withhold land from intensive and efficient agricultural use. Although over a third of all American farms are either residential or part-time, the value of their total output is only two percent of total American farm production.

Farm Ownership and Tenure

Because modern society is mobile and much of the rural population has migrated to the cities, ownership of farm land has become complex. Much is held as an investment by banks, businesses, and individuals located in cities. The average farm holding of individuals 50 years ago would be too small to compete in the modern economy; to secure a reasonable income a farmer must rent additional land, often again as much as he owns, which requires much additional work. Those without any land who wish to farm must rent all their land, usually for one-fourth to one-third of their crop; since holding farm land is popular, the price is bid too high and it is difficult to buy sufficient land to maintain a good income. "Tenure" as such is not inefficient; but given the prevailing low level of farm prices, the shift of farm income through rents to city owners aggravates the problems of inadequate farm income.

A recent trend in the United States and Europe is for urban investors to buy many farms and then create highly technical and specialized corporate farms. The operation of these farms conflicts with notions of traditional family farming, since workers are paid wages, but they may be a means to make farming competitive with industry.

The Effect of Government Policies

Probably no country exists in which political influence on commercial agriculture is not felt. For instance, the state usually regulates transport rates on railroads and trucks. Since accessibility to markets is a function of transport rates, any such arbitrary rate structure interferes with "ideal" location.

A more pervasive influence, though, stems from governmental attempts to stabilize production and prices and to guarantee a reasonable income to farmers. Agriculture remains more popular than is warranted by typical farm incomes. Because of family tradition, lack of other skills, and a desire to own land, too many farmers remain on the land. Too many farmers means that there is too little income per family, land value and prices are inflated, farms are too small, production costs are excessive, and there is the risk of overproduction. Government policies only add to the problem by guaranteeing the right to be a farmer and increasing arable land with irrigation projects.

Partly because farmers are spatially dispersed, they have failed to form strong organizations that might reduce competition among themselves, restrict entry, and improve their bargaining position with the larger industrial buyers. Overproduction, low prices, and low income result. The government also attempts to protect farm income by erecting barriers against foreign imports, by using guaranteed quotas, such as the quota for domestic sugar production, and by stabilizing and supporting prices. Higher support prices only encourage greater production and intensive inputs, however, so if a surplus is to be avoided, acreage must be restricted. Acreage restriction reduces the cultivated land of all farmers proportionately. Thus, the inefficient marginal producer is maintained in production. All farmers suffer—those who use their land effectively as well—and inefficient use of land results.

The government in a sense thus induces overproduction and supports inefficient location, but measures that would restrict entry to agriculture would reduce rural employment and would be politically difficult. The best solution seems to be to strengthen alternative opportunities to agriculture and to encourage farmers, by retraining them, to change their occupation.

Over the last 50 years, a massive move out of farming has occurred. However, the move has not been fast enough, even though in the United States, for example, the average farm size increased from 170 to 303 acres and the number of farms declined from 6.7 million to 3.8 million between 1939 and 1959.

Agricultural Location under Socialist Central Planning   A centrally planned economy strongly affects agricultural organization and location. Ideally, high efficiency should result from the widespread information, as well as the capital and technology, available to the state; the goal that all land be used to the best possible advantage would seem to be more easily met than under a capitalistic system.

However, centralization carries risks. Misjudgments will be applied to all the agriculture of the state and have extremely widespread effects—at least compared to an individual farmer's errors.

After the Russian revolution, the Soviet Union broke up the large estates of the aristocracy and distributed the land to the peasants. During the late 1920s and 1930s, about 200,000 collectives were created from this land. Collective lands as a whole were allocated for different uses and individuals received a share of the earnings in proportion to the work they had done. Mechanization was hastened, given the very limited supplies of machinery available, by allocating machines to specialized Machine Tractor Stations and later to collectives, rather than to individual farm families.

Soviet agriculture, like American, has subsidies. The most significant represent compromises with the past, with the traditional peasant organization of general farming. Private plots for collective farmers are tolerated; on a very small acreage they produce a high proportion of Russia's meats, poultry, and vegetables. The greater attention paid by the peasants to making these inefficiently sized plots productive represents a large indirect subsidy in time and equipment from the collective sector of the Soviet economy to the private sector.

The Soviet policy of regional self-sufficiency is reflected in a lower degree of specialization and less clear-cut zones of different types of farms than in the United States. About a third of the Soviet population works in agriculture—far too many people—and the return per man-hour is very poor. Factors reducing productivity are presently:

1.   Inadequate investment in agriculture—there is insufficient or no fertilizer, inadequate buildings, poor farm-to-town roads, lack of storage, inadequate disease control, and backward animal breeding.

2.   Lack of specialization—in poultry, vegetables, and so forth.

3.   A highly unfavorable labor force, resulting from the manpower losses of World War II.

4.   In contrast to the United States and France, for example, a less favorable environment overall.

Agriculture and Urban Use

Urban activities, including residences, are of such productive intensity and pay so well that agriculture cannot compete. Therefore, land is constantly changing from farm use to urban use in the fringes of towns and cities. Around U.S. cities there is a peculiar pattern of land use: there is some land used for intensive farming near or even inside the city limits; much land is used for "farm" residences for urban workers as far as 40 miles out; and much land is bought for speculative purposes, which raises taxes above what farmers can pay.

COMMERCIAL AGRICULTURE

EXAMPLES OF AGRICULTURAL SYSTEMS

Extensive Agricultures

Livestock Ranching   Livestock ranching is the only possible response to the physical conditions in most of the areas where it is carried out—areas of naturally short grassland with inadequate moisture for crop production and a topography too rugged for mechanized agriculture. Not all such land is so used, however. The price of livestock in markets and the costs of caring for livestock and transporting it to markets govern the maximum distance from the market at which livestock may be profitably raised. Some territory suitable for cattle may be beyond these limits and thus lie unused. Since this activity is relegated to land naturally poor in vegetation and since livestock do not convert grass to meat too efficiently, the productivity per acre is extremely low. Hence an adequate farm return requires very large ranches, averaging almost 2,000 acres in the United States and in the drier areas as much as 20,000 acres or more (over 30 square miles).

In the early days of American livestock ranching, transport was so poor that only highly concentrated and light products, such as hides and dried meats, could be shipped out. With the development of the railroad and refrigeration around 1880, long-distance livestock shipments became possible and a complementary system began to emerge. Raising the mature animals for meat greatly reduced the number of animals that could be accommodated on the range. The livestock rancher thus found it advantageous to specialize in breeding and in yearling production, shipping the cattle at a young age to the feed-grain centers near major markets for fattening. In the United States today, about one-third of all cattle are fattened through this dual ownership, and the range is thus used to fuller capacity.

Commercial Grain Farming   Since grain production is the staple of subsistence economies, it dominates a general farming agriculture in much

of the world. In advanced commercial economies, feed-grain–animal combinations have priority, and production of cash grains for human food without raising animals becomes a specialty. The grain in most demand, wheat, is the principal world commercial grain crop.

Because of wheat's extraordinary tolerance to a wide variety of natural conditions, ease of long-term storage and long-distance transport, and relatively unimpressive response to extra inputs, less tolerant crops, such as corn, oats, and hay, tend to preempt the better land closer to markets for the priority purpose of providing animal feed grains. Wheat is thus grown in locations far from markets. About one-half the world's wheat comes from specialized farms in subhumid areas. These distant lands may be profitably used so long as the better, closer-in lands are required for more intensive purposes and the demand for wheat keeps prices high enough to provide the farmer with a normal margin. The extensive wheat farm is generally profitable because the efficient but lower yield methods used have such low production costs that the low-yield wheat can compete successfully against higher yield wheat located closer to the market. This success under marginal location and environmental conditions is also a function of good farm organization; successful wheat farmers handle vast amounts of land and develop special soil and moisture conservation methods.

Grain-producing areas have been progressively pushed outward in the United States and Soviet Union into more marginal country. This became practical in the 1890s, when mechanization became a possibility. Most grain fields are closely associated with wide tracts of flat land, and large specialized farm machinery can be easily used to provide very high man-hour productivity. Even though the return per acre is rather small, the net income to farmers is unusually high for agriculture.

Labor requirements for raising wheat, however, are concentrated in the summer months. As a result, some wheat farmers—called suitcase farmers—have winter jobs in town, and care of their land is neglected. This practice is resented by farmers who must earn their entire income from farming.

Intensive Agricultures

General Farming   American and European agriculture grew out of traditional general farming, in which many different crops and animals were raised in order to assure the family's self-sufficiency. Any surplus grain, meat, eggs, or vegetables were taken to a market for sale. The development of this system, in which fodder production was part of the crop rotation, achieved an important increase in the productivity of Medieval European agriculture.

General farms are not uncommon today. In the United States and Canada perhaps one-third of the farmers live on farms of this type, producing only five percent of total farm output; in Europe the proportions are higher. The persistence of general farming reflects the isolation, conservatism, preference for traditional ways, and fear of specialization—even when specialization might mean far higher income—of many farmers. Such general farming prevails in much of Appalachia and the Ozarks and in smaller areas elsewhere where physical and cultural isolation, combined with very small farms and fields, has hindered modernization.

Commercial Dairying   In about the last 100 years, general farming has evolved into dairy farming in many areas. Dairying is an efficient response both to environmental conditions and to the influence of markets on location, given a demand for milk and related products.

In much of northwestern Europe and the northeastern United States there is a dense urban population (often over 500 persons per square mile) in an environment characterized by year-round humidity and cool summers—an environment favorable to the hay, pasture, and small grains customarily used for feeding cows. Where the land is rugged or ill-drained, it can be used for permanent pasture. Given the urban demand for milk in these areas, dairying has a comparative advantage over, for example, commercial grazing or beef or hog raising.

The spatial variation within dairying is striking. Around cities, especially larger ones, there are rather well-defined milksheds (or milk supply areas), their extent governed by the total demand of the city, the price, cost, and technology of fluid milk shipment, and the legal restrictions placed upon production. In a few areas where dairying competes strongly for very limited land (e.g., Los Angeles), the density of cows is so great that most feed must be brought in from outside.

Beyond the zones from which it is most profitable to ship fluid milk, cheese and butter are the dominant products (see Figure 3.11). As butter is a more concentrated and valuable product than cheese, it might be expected that it would be profitable to transport it further. However, it is more perishable than cheese and difficult to handle. Therefore, the precise location of butter and cheese appears to depend chiefly on local traditions and specialties.

Dairy farms in the United States have on the average been less prosperous than have wheat and beef—hog farms. This seems to reflect the smaller mean size of dairy farms (about 190 acres) and their small stock (averaging about 20 head of cattle), which make it difficult to realize scale economies on the necessary refrigerating, milking, and other equipment. Labor requirements are also heavy, and man-hour productivity is fairly low. One final problem is that rolling topography, inadequate cropland (averaging only 80 acres), and too-small fields are common on dairy farms.

Intensive Livestock–Grain Farming   The most common—and indeed the "classic"—kind of farm in Europe and America is the grain–animal farm, whose primary product is meat, especially pork and beef. It developed as the commercial, more specialized heir of the subsistence family farm

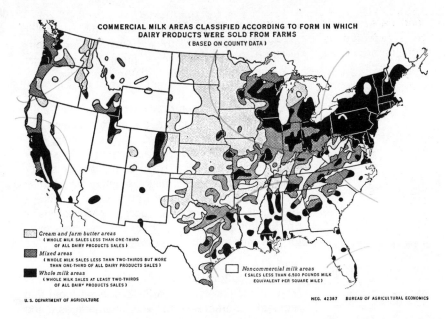

Figure 3.11   Areas farther from large markets sell more cream and butter than whole milk, since these concentrated products are relatively cheaper to transport. (From Earl O. Heady, *Economics of Agricultural Production and Resource Use,* ©1952. Reprinted by permission of Prentice-Hall, Inc., Englewood Cliffs, N.J.)

after commercial dairying and grain production specialties were established. It remains the most self-contained and self-sufficient farm system; the farmer produces the bulk of his own seed and the stock in which he specializes, and in many areas he raises enough poultry and dairy products for his personal needs as well.

The corn belt of the United States has the unequaled combination of vast stretches of level or slightly rolling land, moderate and even moisture, warm temperatures, and rich soils, and the grain–animal farm here is based on corn as the dominant feed crop. Although this system is present in southeastern Europe also, most of Europe has cooler summer temperatures and utilizes a hay and small grain combination, supplemented by intensive root crops (turnips, beets, and potatoes).

Corn has many advantages. It provides the highest volume of both protein and bulk per acre of any feed grain, and this yield can be obtained

with only reasonable effort, provided the climate is right. Hybridization has at least doubled corn yields since the 1930s. Corn therefore occupies close to one-half the cropland in many areas, dominating the entire landscape.

Corn alone, however, gradually wears down the fertility of the soil, but this can be remedied by using crop rotation systems, which provide feed variety and extra cash income and conserve the soil. Common rotations over a four-year period are corn–corn–wheat–hay, corn–hay–pasture–wheat, and corn–corn–soybeans–hay. Wheat and soybeans have a moderate yield, can be sold for high prices, and require little labor; they thus provide extra cash income. Hay, alfalfa, clover, and wheatgrass are sources of alternate feeds, and when partly plowed under improve the nitrogen and organic content, structure, and moisture retention of the soil. Soybeans have become very popular; they improve the soil and are especially valuable as a cash crop. Indeed, soybeans are today the

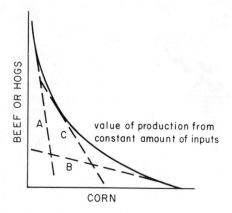

Figure 3.12 Feeder, cash corn, or balanced livestock farming. The relative importance of animals and crops varies within the corn–beef–hog farm type. Where the value of beef or pork is high compared to the value of corn (dashed line A)—very close to markets and on costly land, for instance—feeders should be emphasized. Where the relative value of corn is greater (line B)—on large, level, highly mechanized farms, and where special transport rates exist—there should be an emphasis on corn. More commonly, on moderate-sized rolling farms, a balanced mix of corn and animals is preferred (C).

major source of edible oil in the United States, especially for margarine.

The typical farm raises beef cattle and/or hogs; the combination is often preferred because income can be stabilized and feed used to its maximum. Up to one-third of the cattle produced are purchased from western ranchers as yearlings (in the United States) and fattened on the corn-belt farms. A feeder-in-transit privilege, providing a through rate even though the cattle are stopped and fattened on the way, encourages the practice. Farms average about 250 to 350 acres, and mechanization has permitted a rapid increase in farm size and income.

Feed grains, such as corn, sell for a lower price than food grains, such as wheat. Yet, the transport rate is the same for both grains, and corn is thus overwhelmingly consumed on the farm or shipped only short distances. Corn does become a cash crop in areas of very level land where a high degree of mechanization is practical, such as in

North Central Iowa and near some major feeding areas, such as Chicago and Omaha (see Figure 3.12). East Central Illinois is also a cash-corn region because of preferential transit rates.

In Europe, farms generally have greater self-sufficiency and variety; poultry are more usually a part of the farm, rather than a separate specialty. Population pressure and a tradition of subsistence agriculture have also resulted in an excessive farm population and farms too small or fragmented for efficient production (European farms average 100 acres, U.S. farms, 300 acres). More intensive production and subsidized prices are necessary for a farmer to make a reasonable living.

Other Agricultural Specialties—Horticulture Other farm specialties tend to reflect unusual local and regional characteristics and advantages, and occasionally enterpreneurial aptitude. Location of a farm near large urban markets justifies intensive production of horticultural specialties: flowers, fruits, vegetables, and berries. In the United States, for instance, the rather urbanized belt from Hartford to Washington, D.C. is an area of very specialized vegetable, flower, fruit, and seed production. Inputs are great; fertilization is over three times the national average. In Europe, this expected pattern is even more pronounced.

However, placement of horticulture in traditional locations has declined as a result of the more powerful advantages of a complementary environment. Because of their year-long growing seasons, California and Florida (in the United States) and parts of the Mediterranean basin have a winter monopoly on fruits and vegetables. This advantage has permitted these areas to specialize, increase their output, and reduce their costs. These areas have also had lower labor costs; Mexican bracero labor (temporarily imported on contract), for example, played a big role in making California and Texas competitive. Thus, even though remote from final markets, these areas have come to dominate production of fruits and vegetables. Although perishable and bulky fruits and vegetables are expensive to transport, these areas can successfully compete against local suburban producers because their production costs are so low (see Figure 3.13). The growth of canned and frozen foods has also aided this shift.

Areas with a winter growing season usually have distinct specialties, also—crops that won't grow in other parts of the country. Subtropical crop specialties such as citrus fruits and some kinds of grapes and olives are sources of cash income to farmers.

Cotton. Cotton is an inherently fairly productive crop, but it is at the same time highly transportable. If it had not traditionally developed under the plantation slave system as a labor intensive crop (one where labor costs are a high proportion of total cost), it could readily be grown on larger, more mechanized, and distant farms, comparable to wheat farms. This is in fact occurring in the western United States.

Since the land available for cotton far exceeds that required by demand for cotton, the risk of overproduction is always present. Government price supports have encouraged excessive planting and at the same time increased competition from cheaper foreign cotton for traditional American markets. In order to reduce production in the United States, acreage restrictions on cotton presently limit the farmer to as little as one-fourth of his available cotton acreage, and the spatially inefficient result is that cotton planting is dispersed among countless small fields—each farmer's best land, whether he is an efficient or inefficient producer.

Poultry. In the United States poultry has become a specialized agricultural product, displacing the poultry raised as a sideline on the general, dairy, and livestock farm. Chicken, once a Sunday luxury, has thus become one of the cheapest foods. This trend has also begun to emerge in Europe. Near large U.S. markets, eggs are the dominant commodity produced, on a rather industrial basis using imported grain. This is the most obvious example in agriculture of a response to economies possible with greater scale.

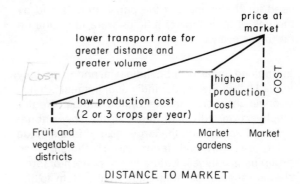

Figure 3.13 A long growing season in distant subtropical fruit and vegetable districts permits efficient, high-volume, low-cost production. Together with volume discounts on transportation, the low production cost allows such districts to successfully compete with horticulture near the market (market gardens).

In other areas (largely the southern United States), chicken raising has developed on some formerly poor, marginal, general farms on a contract basis. Feed companies supply the chickens and much of the feed and guarantee to buy the full-grown birds. There is more security for both farmer and distributor under this system, but prices remain low because of excessive competition, and the farmer typically remains poor.

Rural Life and Settlement

Although in most commercially advanced countries the rural population has declined and been surpassed by the urban population, about a third of the people in such countries remain rural dwellers. In Europe, rural settlement was and is largely village-oriented; for reasons of protection, conservation of land, and efficiency of social contact, a concentrated settlement is preferred.

The spacing and size of villages reflects the density of population, cultural preferences, and transportation available, modified by natural conditions. Village spacing was also influenced by the need for the support of the parish priests and by the risk of land neglect if fields were more than a few miles away.

In England, in parts of Scandinavia, and especially in the United States, the individual homestead has become the norm. In the United States, greater emphasis on individual freedom, the sheer abundance of space, and the larger size of farms made living on individual farms more efficient than grouping in villages. Naturally, the pattern of farmsteads reflects the adaptation of the farm to the distribution of arable land. In the American interior, however, where most of the land was arable and the land was previously uncultivated, areas were settled according to the regulations of the Homestead Act; each adult family member was given a quarter section in a square township. As a result, farmstead spacing is amazingly uniform.

Farm hamlets and villages grew up in the United States more as service centers than as centers of farm residence, although recently there has been a tendency for farmers to move to town to obtain better services, partly as the result of school consolidations.

Commercial Forestry

Forestry represents the least intensive use of farmland in humid areas. Individual land holdings are large, and net return per acre is low to moderate. However, in rugged areas, where soils are poor for crops or where forests are of especially high quality, use of land closer to markets for forests can compete with other uses. Forestry is also becoming increasingly agricultural; trees are planted, thinned, and sprayed for disease.

About 40 percent of the world's managed land is in forests. About one-third of the original forest, which covered one-quarter of the land surface of the earth, has been cleared, largely because the land is more valuable for farming—which can support many times more people on the same amount of land. The land remaining as forest land is normally more remote or more rugged than that used for agriculture.

Although wood is valuable for construction, chemicals, paper, and other purposes, the basic raw material derived from the forest, the log, is of such weight and bulk that long-distance shipment is discouraged. Because they are remote and not accessible to good transportation, large areas of good forest are left untouched, at least so long as closer-to-market forests remain sufficient for man's needs. High transport costs also encourage the development of alternate materials, especially for construction.

Production costs for lumber vary tremendously. Within the United States, for example, because logs have a large mean size, costs per board foot are low enough in the Pacific Northwest to justify transporting lumber to eastern markets. In both Europe and the United States, the nearby quality forests were exploited early until today the major forest activity is on the periphery (see Figure 3.14). The older exploited forests may be used again as trees begin to regrow, but the newer peripheral forests will probably continue to be dominant; conservation and sustained-yield methods (where new growth equals or exceeds timber removed in the long run) were adopted before the peripheral forests were destroyed. Also, in the peripheral areas there are few or no competing activities, and land ownerships are large and efficient.

In the earliest days, logs were transported to the sea on the rivers. Logging railroads soon provided access into the great interior and the virgin forests of America, Russia, and Scandinavia, and today the less costly, more adaptable logging truck has taken over. Logs are brought very short distances to forest roads by cable or tractor and are then moved a short distance to a sawmill where excess weight is removed (see Figure 3.15). In some forest areas, such as in Scandinavia and Russia, logs are still floated down rivers, and in others, floated along the coasts, as in Canada, Sweden, the United States, and Siberia.

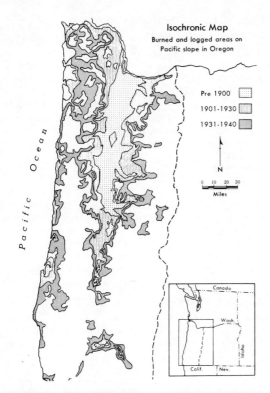

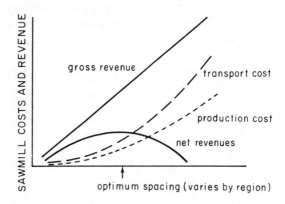

Figure 3.15 Optimum spacing of sawmills. As the volume of logs through a sawmill increases, production costs increase more slowly than gross revenues. However, because the logs must be brought in from greater distances, transport costs increase more rapidly than gross revenues, outweigh the savings in production costs, and reduce net revenues. The optimum spacing of sawmills is that which allows each sawmill the maximum net returns. Sawmills will tend to be closer together in areas of very dense and rich forests.

Figure 3.14 Use of forests over time. Resources are first taken from more accessible areas. As these resources are used up, they are taken from less accessible areas. Since this map was made, the area of active logging has shifted more into southwestern Oregon. (Reprinted by permission of the Association of Pacific Coast Geographers, from *Yearbook, of the Association of Pacific Coast Geographers* Vol. 19, by K. Erickson.)

Different patterns of logging are used. For many species (such as pines and hardwoods) selective cutting of mature trees, although fairly costly, is the most efficient method of maintaining a sustained yield. In douglas fir–hemlock regions, stands are so regular that clean cutting (removal of all trees) is most efficient. A checkerboard pattern (where alternate sections are cut) is favored for quick reseeding and minimum erosion and watershed damage, but larger cut areas are less costly and preferred by lumbermen.

To be commercially successful forestry must be able to compete with possible alternate uses of land, labor, and capital. The return is generally sufficient to be competitive if the forest is fairly close to centers of demand and the lumber is of high quality and high quantity per unit area. Thus, some forests very near major markets are not used because higher production costs in these areas outweigh the higher transport costs from more distant, but better quality, sources.

Forestry alone cannot support a dense population. However, exploitation of forests may generate sufficient capital to permit the establishment of a secondary industrial economy. Thus, early New England had few resources except trees and fish, but these yielded the capital to create textile and other industries.

Part Three

Structure of the System of Places

4

Towns as Central Places

In human organization of space, the greatest physical contrast is that between rural and urban forms. In the most advanced countries, the vast majority of the population lives in dense concentrations over small portions of territory. Such concentrations began in a very early period, when towns arose to perform certain functions: (1) To exercise control. (2) To act as a center for the exchange of goods. (3) To process resource materials. The first two constitute, in a broad sense, service or "central-place" functions—those provided from a center for a surrounding territory or hinterland. We will discuss these two central-place functions in this chapter.

THE EXISTENCE OF SERVICE CENTERS

Why do service centers exist? Even in the most primitive societies, people demand goods and services which they do not themselves produce; all people (at one time or another) desire greater material security and luxury—which are typified by the possession of products made by others. To obtain such products, a place is needed where goods can be exchanged. Human societies also require direction, military protection, and religious or ethical control. Thus, the service functions are necessary ones for all human societies.

The Agglomeration Principle

Man is a social animal, and man also attempts to accomplish tasks with the least possible effort. Early man attempted to achieve these goals by agglomerating into villages—the most efficient social and spatial forms for his semicommunal life. So long as the group had many joint activities, held some lands in common, and continually changed the plots tilled by one family, a village at the center of the group lands minimized the distance men had to walk to their fields and to meet one another.

Towns grew up later as an extension of the same principle of minimizing distance. The village had specialized in some activities, but a local village could neither provide nor support many functions; some functions might require the combined purchasing power of several villages to obtain adequate support, for instance. Each village might provide one of these functions, but since persons in all villages would want to use each of the serv-

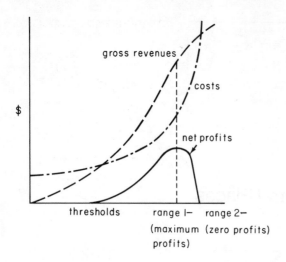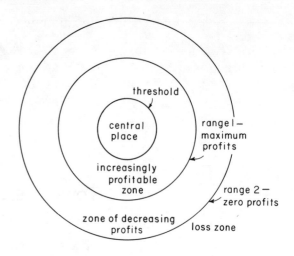

Figure 4.01 Threshold and range of a central-place activity. An activity will have greater costs than revenues until a threshold volume and market area are reached. Profits then increase so long as revenues from more distant customers exceed the costs of serving them, until at range 1 the range of maximum profits is reached. After this, profits decline until the maximum range of sales, range 2, is reached; here, costs equal revenues.

ices, villagers would have to travel to all other villages to use all the services. It is obvious that if all of the functions could be located in one village, the total distance all villagers would need to travel could be greatly reduced. In fact, that village which would minimize the traveling distance for all villagers could be found—and, ideally, given free competition and efficient behavior, such a central village will attract and hold all of the service functions. By agglomerating these services the added possible benefit of impulse buying may occur. A person coming to town for one purpose is likely, by the proximity of additional services, to use some of these services as well. Finally, the relationships between the services themselves, such as financial relationships, are enhanced by centralization.

CENTRAL-PLACE THEORY: THE SPATIAL STRUCTURE OF CENTRAL PLACES

Activities will group, for spatial efficiency, in a central place, but how many activities can be so grouped? How much territory can one center efficiently control? If more centers are needed, how will they be arranged?

Spatial Equilibrium of a Central Place

For any activity, losses are incurred until the volume of sales reaches the critical level, or threshold. Profits then increase so long as the revenues from new customers reached by extending the market area exceed the costs of serving them (assuming the store pays for the delivery costs), and this defines the optimum market size (Range 1 in Figure 4.01). However, stores may have to deliver beyond the optimum range because of competition and thus receive lower profits. If the customer pays for his own transport to the store, the optimum market size is defined by how far he is willing to travel, since there is a limit to the time and transport cost an individual is willing to spend when seeking goods or services.

TOWNS AS CENTRAL PLACES

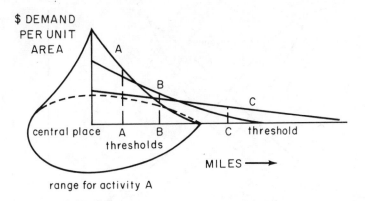

Unit Area Sales, Threshold and Range

$ DEMAND PER UNIT AREA

A

B

C

central place

A   B
thresholds

C   threshold

MILES →

range for activity A

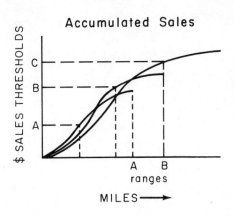

Accumulated Sales

$ SALES THRESHOLDS

C

B

A

A   B
ranges

MILES →

Figure 4.02 Demand, sales, threshold, and range. Demand for goods falls with distance from the seller, and thresholds vary for different activities A, B, and C (left-hand figure). The range (area within which customers will buy) is shown for activity A. This range is beyond the threshold area for activity B but is less than the threshold area required by activity C. In the right-hand diagram, note how sales at first increase very rapidly with distance, and then more slowly.

The time element is especially important to certain perishable central-place activities; services such as police, taxis, public transport, doctors, hospitals, and education can hardly be postponed. Families also cannot stock groceries or gas for long periods, and people demand that such activities be reasonably close. Limitations in time and cost of transport thus define the maximum range at which a good may be profitably offered.

In Figure 4.01, the increasing transport costs resulting from enlarging the market (when the store pays) gradually outweigh the additional revenues. The position of the threshold, the area of optimum profits, and the maximum range of the activity are partly a function of population density (modified by income) also, since a lower density—and hence fewer sales per unit area—increases the ratio of transport cost to net revenue. In a sparsely settled area, the minimum threshold might be farther than the maximum range of the activity, and the service could not be offered at all.

Central-place activities are essentially distributional; they are located at a point, and the customers are spatially diffuse. The problem of locating a central place is thus one of minimizing the distance traveled by customers while maximizing the profitability of the activity. The larger the sales, the larger are the potential profits, but more sales require more customers and therefore a larger territory. However, more distant customers incur greater transport costs; even if they spend the same total amount as nearby customers, they will receive fewer goods and services. As a result, demand for a service falls with distance from the service. Figure 4.02 summarizes the concepts of threshold, maximum range, and optimum level for a central-place activity.

Consider the competition between two suppliers of the same activity (Figure 4.03). Ideally, the suppliers will locate so that each can maximize profits (although there is the risk that a competitor might enter the market midway between the two sup-

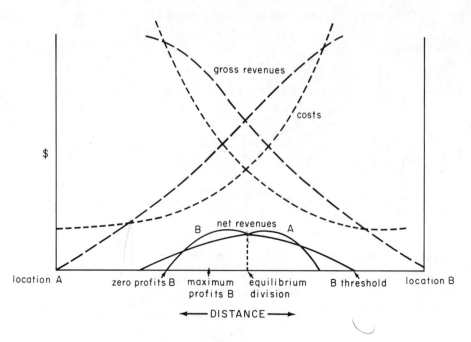

Figure 4.03 Equilibrium of two central places. Central places A and B are located far enough apart so that each achieves almost maximum profits (at the equilibrium division). They do not locate farther apart, for then a competitor might enter midway between them. See Figure 4.01 for additional explanation.

pliers, reducing all three to marginal thresholds and minimum profits).

Central-place theory could be called a theory of spatial monopoly. Each center has a competitive advantage in a given piece of territory because of the factor of distance—transport costs are significantly less for customers close to the centers. However, this spatial monopoly is strictly limited by competition; if one center raises prices, its cost advantage is eliminated, and neighboring centers can capture portions of its market and either destroy the first center or force it to return to its original price level. However, one center may offer a fairly low uniform price everywhere in order to capture more distant markets and destroy competing centers. With a uniform price, nearby customers are "discriminated against" in the sense that they are charged more than the cost of serving them, although still less than a competitor charges

(see Figure 4.04). The extra profits are used to subsidize sales to distant customers. The greater total sales and lower costs may permit further price reduction. Since all central places can use the same weapon, however, equilibrium will tend to be restored.

The market areas within which stores make a profit (threshold to maximum range) are similar for many activities. Indeed, many central-place establishments, such as variety and department stores, contain within them goods and services with varying—but overlapping—threshold requirements. The precise combination of activities that can theoretically occur together is determined by: (1) The similarity of their thresholds and ranges. (2) The population density and the average income of the region. (3) The nature of transport costs in the area. Ideally, if an activity with a given threshold is successful at a given point, all activities

TOWNS AS CENTRAL PLACES

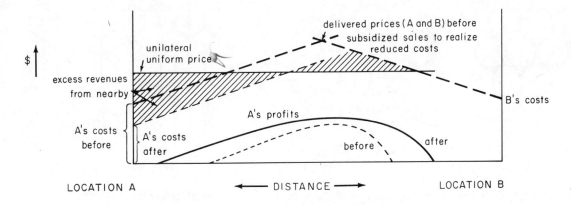

Figure 4.04 The sellers at places A and B originally divide the market between them at the point where delivered prices are equal. When A then unilaterally adopts a uniform price, distant customers are subsidized by the extra profits A receives from nearby customers. The greater sales enable A to reduce costs, and when it reintroduces delivered prices, it has increased profits and extended its market at the expense of B.

with a lesser threshold should also be successful there.

Theoretical Hexagonal Central-Place Structure

Classical central-place theory assumes: (1) A uniform plane of constant population density and purchasing power. (2) Transport costs varying linearly with distance. (3) No attenuation of demand with distance. Given these assumptions, imagine a set of these central places, each with its own spatial monopoly. It may be demonstrated that a triangular arrangement of competing centers and markets is the most efficient (Figure 4.05A); the "unserved" area is minimized, and all persons are as close to a center as is possible.

Observe that such a structure implies that no additional center will exist unless the total market for a center is at least seven times the minimum market size. In that case, six competing centers will immediately arise, because all customers of one center must be closer to that center than to any other. But unserved areas remain outside the circles. However, the circles will collapse together into a hexagonal structure, such that the overlap of the circles equals the unserved areas, and total distance from customers to centers is minimized (Figure 4.05B).

The use of the hexagon as the optimal structure is demonstrated over and over again in nature. An isolated circle is more efficient than a single hexagon, but a set of circles is not as efficient as a set of hexagons.

What activities will the smallest central places contain? Because of the benefits of agglomeration, the smallest places will include the activity with the highest threshold that does not exceed the maximum profitable range of the activity with the lowest threshold.

The Marketing, Transportation, and Administrative Principles Say one place (such as *A* in Figure 4.05B) succeeds in adding activities that require greater support than can be obtained from

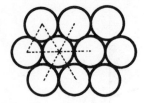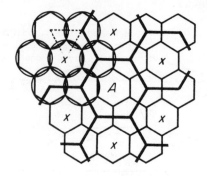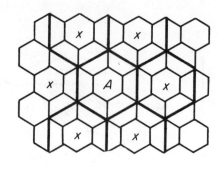

A. Triangular arrangement of circular market areas

B. Collapse of circular trade areas into hexagons; development of hierarchy according to the "marketing principle"

C. Development of hierarchy according to the "transportation principle"

Figure 4.05   Development of central-place patterns.

its basic market area. The activities will then require support from the markets of the six surrounding places in order to reach threshold levels. In this case the closest villages that can compete—that can also offer the higher threshold activities—will be the six labeled x in 4.05B, located exactly as far from the neighboring villages as is A. Now if boundaries are drawn midway between these seven more important "higher level" places, a larger set of hexagonal trade areas will be revealed. Each of the larger places serves one-third of the trade areas of its six surrounding villages as well as its own area, so that the total area and population served is three times that of the smaller places. Similarly, if one of these larger, second-level places (which could be called towns) adds additional small-city level activities requiring even larger market areas, a third level of market areas will be created in the same way.

The marketing principle at the top of Figure 4.06 illustrates this process. Here the large black dots are the towns, the thin lines depict the boundaries of their trade areas, and the small city in the center

is seen to require one-third of the trade areas of the surrounding towns for its large trade area (thicker lines). This hierarchy, in which each more important place and trade area is three times as large as the one smaller, is called the marketing principle because every customer is as close as possible to a center at every level of the hierarchy.

Observe however, that a transport system to serve such an arrangement is not efficient (see 4.06, top). The important transport links between larger places do not pass through intermediate ones. If, instead, every other village in a line (in Figure 4.05C, those labeled x) were to add the second-level town functions, the trade area of the smaller places would be equally shared by the larger places. As a result, the trade area of each larger place would be four times as large as the one smaller. In this theoretical arrangement, transport is more efficient, since routes connecting the largest places pass through the next largest (see 4.06, bottom right), although customers must travel farther to reach a center at a given level of the hierarchy.

The System of Central Places
After The
Marketing Principle

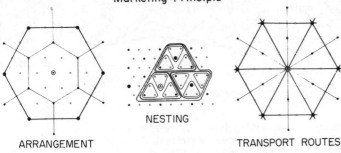

ARRANGEMENT

NESTING

TRANSPORT ROUTES

Administrative Principle

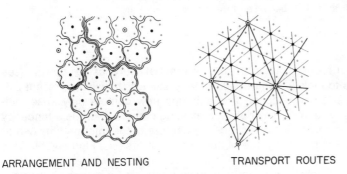

ARRANGEMENT AND NESTING

TRANSPORT ROUTES

Transportation Principle

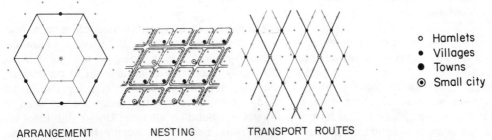

ARRANGEMENT

NESTING

TRANSPORT ROUTES

○ Hamlets
● Villages
● Towns
◉ Small city

Figure 4.06 Ideal central-place patterns. One ideal pattern for the hiearchy of central places is the marketing principle. In the figure in the upper left, the relative location of hamlets, villages, towns, and a small city are shown, and the market areas for the towns and the city are indicated. If smaller places were nested wholly within larger ones, the middle pattern might occur. The upper right diagram shows the more important (thicker lines) and less important transport routes. Patterns for the relative locations of hamlets, villages, towns, cities, and major transport routes may alternately follow the administrative principle or the transportation principle. Note that the former principle avoids dividing the market areas of smaller places, and that the latter has the most efficient transport pattern (see text for details). (Reprinted by permission of the Regional Science Association from B. J. L. Berry, "Central Place Studies," Bibliography Series No. 1, 1961, Regional Science Research Association.)

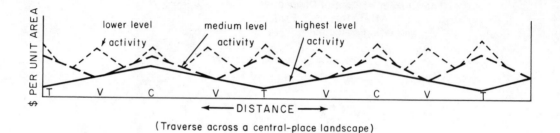

(Traverse across a central-place landscape)

Figure 4.07 Pattern of demand in space. In this cross-section through an ideal central-place landscape, one passes through this sequence of central places: T (town), V (village), C (city), V, T, V, C, V, T. The lower or village level activities are of high volume, but decline quickly with distance from a central place. Customers will travel farther for medium or town level activities, which are available in towns and cities, and farthest for city level activities. The cities have the lowest volume of sales per unit area, but, because of their great market area, have the highest total sales.

Figure 4.06 depicts patterns of places and roads as seen from the air. An alternative view is to look at what happens to the level of sales across such a landscape. In Figure 4.07 we see a cross section of sales per unit area along a main transport route according to the transportation principle. For the lower level activities (villages), sales per unit area fall rapidly from each center. From the less closely spaced towns, sales fall less rapidly, and for the highest level activities, sales fall least rapidly and extend over the widest area.

In both of these arrangements, border places and areas are split up among larger centers—among three centers in the case of the marketing principle and between two centers for the transportation principle—rather than being contained completely within the market areas of the larger places. This split may seem confusing from a planning point of view, but much evidence demonstrates the "torn loyalty" of smaller places in such a median position. For example, residents of Hartford, Connecticut, shop in both New York and Boston. Indeed, historically, new towns have frequently developed midway between existing towns. Economically, when purchasing power increases to the point where only one-third or one-fourth as much territory is needed to achieve threshold sales, competing centers may arise to take advantage of the interstitial purchasing power (see Figure 4.08). Many studies, however, present evidence that although new centers may arise midway between existing centers, there is a tendency for nesting—the capture of the intermediate center by one of the larger centers (see Figure 4.09). This suggests that the economies wholesalers, retailers, and customers achieve by having fewer main destinations outweigh the increased distances (Figure 4.09).

For purposes of administration, such as for school districts and governments, the division of smaller areas between larger ones is not convenient. Obviously, if smaller ones are not to be divided, the only logical arrangement is for the larger place (town) to serve the entire market area of the six surrounding villages. Under this ideal arrangement, called the administrative principle, each larger market area is seven times as large as the one smaller (see Figure 4.06, center). Nesting is automatic, but the transport system is not too efficient and customers travel farther than in the marketing and transport principle arrangements.

In an economy where regional self-sufficiency is a planned goal, an administrative structure would tend to develop or—at least—one where lower

TOWNS AS CENTRAL PLACES

order centers were nested under higher ones. Also, in national economies or isolated regions of a limited extent, which one large center could easily dominate, one would expect to find only a single ring of provincial satellite cities around the primary center, following the administrative principle.

These principles suggest possible ideal arrangements of service centers. During a period when economic exchange is limited but government strong, goals of administrative efficiency would be expected to affect arrangements most. As economics becomes more important, an arrangement may arise that violates political boundaries (for example, cities like Kansas City on state boundaries) and improved transport, in turn, may tend to readjust places so that they are arranged closer to the transportation principle. All three principles act together in a real landscape, and the composite patterns—not so ideal—are many (see, for an example of one urban pattern, Figure 8.02).

Modifications of Central-Place Theory

Work on central-place theory in recent years has amassed powerful evidence about the variation in the thresholds, ranges, and groupings of central-place functions; about the mutually repellent pattern of places at a similar level; and about zones of spatial monopoly and the existence of a hierarchy of places. Naturally, the confrontation of theory by empirical behavior has led to important modifications of central-place theory. Variations in theory followed these changes:

1. The assumption that an area is a uniform plane was relaxed to permit physical and cultural variation, such as varying population density or a particular settlement pattern.

2. The assumption of simultaneous development over limitless space was relaxed to allow for the development of central-place patterns in time, and from areas of early settlement.

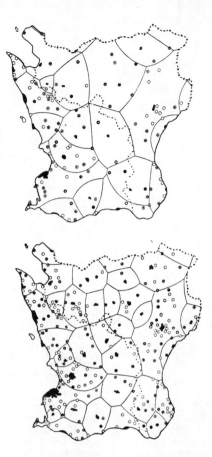

Figure 4.08 Development of new central places. This example from the southern Swedish province of Skane shows the proliferation of central places over time. The market area boundaries shown are for local bus service around towns (irregular black blobs). Note that many new centers are at the edge of the earlier market areas. (Reprinted by permission of the Department of Geography, University of Lund, Sweden, from S. Godlund, "The Function and Growth of Bus Traffic," *Lund Studies in Geography* No. 18, Series B.)

3. The assumption that people will always make a perfect response and have perfect information was relaxed.

4. It was recognized that places of greater size dominate larger areas then do smaller places, even for the same goods.

5. Central-place theory was merged with agricultural rent theory.

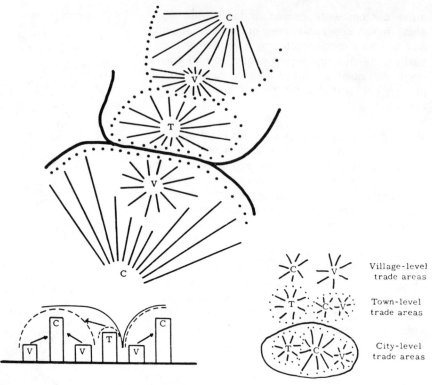

Village-level
trade areas

Town-level
trade areas

City-level
trade areas

Figure 4.09 The nesting process. The town and its trade area, midway between the two cities, are served entirely by one city rather than being divided. A cross-section is shown below it; height of bars may be interpreted as the number of central-place functions. (Reprinted by permission of the Regional Science Association, from B.J.L. Berry and R. Tennant, "Retail Location and Consumer Behavior," *Papers and Proceedings of the Regional Science Association* Vol. IX, 1962.)

6. The effect of other town-building activities was recognized.

The admission that the physical quality of space varies, and that population density therefore varies in space, had these effects on classical theory: recognition that the size of hexagonal market areas varies, and hence their shape is distorted. Locally, conditions of poor topography with irregular transport, as in Appalachia, lead to many small settlements with a very limited variety of goods and services. Because of topography, the scattered location of mines, or historical accident, dispersed cities—closely spaced small towns with limited services, rather than one larger one—some-

times occur. This arrangement is inefficient and results in increased travel, decreased consumption, and reduced demand for higher level activities.

It has been observed, too, that even if land quality is constant, transport quality is superior between large places. As a result, corridors of greater development are induced, producing sectors of greater and lesser population and settlement density (the city-rich sectors of Figure 4.10). In much of the United States development of a central-place system occurred in the context of a rectilinear land survey system. Transport routes thus tend to be north-south and east-west, settlement to be in a square pattern, and trade areas to be more square than round or hexagonal.

Viewing central-place development as a process in time as well as in space introduces two main complications:

1. Changes occur in the nature and price of goods and services, in population and in purchasing power, and in the quality and cost of transportation; that is, the parameters determining threshold, range, and profitability change, and

2. There is the possibility that the entire central-place system develops as settlement itself spreads across a territory.

Experimental studies have illustrated both that the hierarchical pattern of places gradually develops as purchasing power increases and—more recently—that smallest settlements decline as transport improves. Theoretically, changes in parameters such as an improved transport system will render the existing settlement pattern non-optimal. For instance, with improved transport, older places that are too close together will lose some importance as central places. Where settlement spreads gradually, as in the United States, places beginning in a later period should, because of improved transport, be theoretically farther apart and also more dependent on the transport system. Thus, the passage of time has an important effect on the arrangement of settlements.

People do not possess enough information or care enough about costs and profits to behave in a truly optimal fashion. Building a theory as if people did or could behave in such a way is valuable, however, because it depicts the state toward which people are moving, even though imperfectly. Including nonoptimal behavior and uncertainty in central-place theory has these effects:

1. There is variation around the optimal position for a place in the hexagonal structure.

2. There is variability in the mix of goods and services offered by places at a given level; some places will not take advantage of their opportuni-

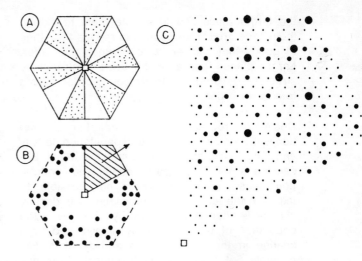

Figure 4.10 City-rich and city-poor sectors around a metropolis. Sectors of denser population and larger places (stippled areas in A, dots in B, detail in C) tend to develop. In C, note the concentration of the largest places along the lines connecting the vertices of the sector. (Reprinted by permission of the Yale University Press, from August Lösch, *Economics of Location,* 1954.)

ties, others will try to offer goods with a threshold that is too high.

3. Customers will either not be able to distinguish between short-distance differences or other personal considerations will at times be more important. The result is that theoretically clear-cut market areas will become overlapping fields (see Figure 4.11).

Central-place theory uses a strict geometric approach to the delineation of market areas. Thus, with respect to a given level (say, towns), the trade areas are all considered to be identically sized hexagons—despite the fact that some of the trade areas will contain centers (small cities, perhaps) offering higher level goods and service areas. Studies of actual shopping behavior indicate that larger places having greater quantities of the same goods (due to their larger internal populations) will have a competitive advantage over neighboring smaller places offering the same goods. Even setting aside the fact that larger places are better known, the benefits of greater scale for sellers in the larger place should enable them to extend their trade area. The result is to reduce the range of goods that smaller surrounding places offer. Larger places thus alter the basic central-place structure by dropping intermediate-order places to a lower order.

One major problem with the uniform-plain assumption is the existence of the rural population density and land-rent gradients from major markets. Because a larger trade area is needed when population density decreases, it is not possible to maintain the ideal hexagonal shape. This density change is often accompanied by a change in the population of places at a given level and by a change in the mix of goods and services. For example, Salt Lake City, in a low density area, has a much smaller population than cities in high density areas with a comparable variety of activities.

An attempt to preserve hexagonal market-area shape while adjusting to the declining density away from metropolitan areas produces a rather different central-place pattern. Figure 9.01 on page 178 illustrates a possible surface combining rent gradient and central-place theory.

Finally, everyone should be aware that central-place theory explicitly excludes other town-building activities that are of an "export" rather than a "central" character. These activities—most typically processing — directly affect central-place theory, however; if there is an initial growth of, say, processing towns, these towns will develop a demand for services. Since the industrial population is not diffuse, but concentrated in clusters of settlements, the central-place pattern will have a rather different spatial appearance than the theoretical arrangement that occurs with uniform population density.

Central-Place Theory and Reality

Central-place theory has been widely criticized because neither research nor maps show the "pure" patterns of development. But searches for such patterns are naive. Central-place theory as developed is, of course, incomplete. Many functions give rise to and help support towns. The real contribution of central-place theory lies in its description of spatial behavior. The crucial test of the usefulness of central-place theory is not the strict geometric forms that might be observed, but answers to these questions:

1. Do groups of entrepreneurs seek to serve the available purchasing power and to carve out somewhat monopolistic service areas? This, of course, is the basis of any shopping center decision.

2. Do places with similar activities in similar physical and cultural environments tend to be regularly spaced? Experimental research does provide evidence that the distance between places offering a certain scope of activities does not vary much.

3. Do individuals tend to minimize the distance traveled to satisfy their desires? Many researchers have observed the tendencies of individuals to behave efficiently to minimize travel, although for a variety of reasons they will often travel beyond the closest opportunity.

4. Does one individual have available and use a hierarchy of service centers—does he go to different places for different types of goods and services?

Particular debate has raged concerning the existence of an hierarchy of places and the observed continuum of city sizes. Each of us is aware, from our own shopping behavior, of the existence of a hierarchy. We go to the local store or gas station often, go less frequently to a larger town or shopping center, and travel infrequently to a bigger city or downtown (unless we live there). Yet, if we look at most larger nations and list all cities by size, we find that a continuum exists.

The fact that different sizes of places exist is explicit evidence of a hierarchy, but we cannot expect there to be a clear hierarchical division of places, since: (1) Almost half the support for cities comes from other than central-place activities, that proportion varying widely from city to city.

(2) The density and relative purchasing power of the surrounding population varies. (3) Entrepreneurs and individuals often make mistakes. The net effect of these and other factors is to cause much variation around any theoretically expected size—and thus a continuum, rather than a hierarchy, of city sizes.

A test for a hierarchy can be made only in a territory that is meaningful—that is, within a range of distances actually used by individuals. If we examine any areas within which most trips to central functions can be made, we discover that there is a fairly clear-cut hierarchical division of place sizes, despite varying industrialization and other factors.

Historical Development of Urban Patterns

In primitive and poor subsistence societies, permanent markets could not be supported because there was not enough demand. The small surpluses of individual families could be best exchanged locally and by barter. Still, there is always demand for some outside products, and the problem was how to meet such small amounts of demand scattered over such a wide territory. One mechanism to solve the problem was the itinerant peddler, who did most of the moving himself. Another was the annual or occasional fair, where people from an area having even the poorest transport could get together once a year to exchange goods.

As the demand for trade and outside goods gradually increased, fairs become more frequent and closer in space. Less spectacularly, groups of farmers together with small merchants and service people also developed the periodic market. These markets circulated among a set of nearby villages, spending perhaps a day or two in each. Gradually, the fairs of larger places become permanent, and villages favored because of better average accessibility to a wider area became permanent market towns.

With industrialization and the growth of cities, agriculture became commercial. Improved roads and railroads increased rural accessibility, and increased personal income reduced thresholds and permitted the rise of new service centers.

Commonly Recognized Levels of Settlement

The existence of a spatial hierarchy is reflected in the terminology we use to describe settlements. Increasing size and greater functional complexity of a center require a larger population for support and a wider spacing between centers. Figure 4.12 illustrates the relation between area served, population of the central place, and the entry of village-, town-, and city-level functions.

A *hamlet* may contain up to 500 persons, but more typically around 100 to 200; at present it usually serves about 2,000 persons and offers such everyday convenience goods and services as taverns, gas stations, and small grocery stores for which people do not wish to travel more than five minutes or so (about three miles). As transport has improved, by paving rural roads, for instance, more distance can be covered for the same effort, and many of the lowest order places have disappeared as more people can travel easily to larger places.

The *village,* containing from 500 to 2,500 persons (mean population about 1,000) and serving an area that may include up to 10,000 persons, offers a greater number of functions, including some which an individual may use only occasionally but for which there is constant demand: bakeries, several churches, schools, a post office, a general clothing store, a hardware store, auto repair shop, farm implements, feeds, and perhaps a doctor, dentist, or bank.

The *town* has a population that may range from 2,500 to 20,000 (mean size, 10,000) and serves 25,000 to 100,000 persons, The American town, often the county seat, is the traditional urban place; it dominates regional life and is the social and economic center which everyone knows. It is also the usual place of entertainment; it has the nearest hospital, newspaper, big high school, lawyers, and courts; it has doctors, dentists, veterinarians, large churches, it is a place where cars, farm equipment and supplies, appliances, furniture, and jewelry are usually bought; and insurance and real estate agents, cleaners, and hotels can be found here.

The town is probably no more than a half-hour to an hour, or 12 to 15 miles, away from most of the people it serves. In both Europe and the United States the large metropolis has replaced the town as the chief power in our lives; but the town heritage is still great, and, even in the city, much individual activity is focused in town-sized shopping centers.

The *small city* contains from 20,000 to 200,000 people and serves a million people; it is the district capital, whose geographic significance lies in its role as center for distribution and communication. It is at the bottom of the wholesale distribution ladder, the smallest market that can efficiently support a middle exchange between manufacturer and retailer. Here may be a college, a department store, medical specialists, much retail and service specialization (for example, stores specializing in music, sporting goods, photography)—in a sense the outpost of "metropolitan life." These cities are served by good roads, railroads, and fair air connections and are so located that in a day a family can travel to and from the center, have time to shop, and do business.

The *large city,* a regional, state, or provincial capital, includes from 200,000 to 500,000 persons and serves a population of from one to three million. These cities are more self-contained, possess a range of local manufacturers, and have perhaps a university, major department stores, specialized hospitals, and more sophisticated shopping and entertainment. Wholesale trade and finance may exceed local retail trade and banking in volume. These large cities are the highest level cities that most people need to reach; almost all necessary goods and services can be found here.

The *metropolis,* with near or over a million residents, dominates a large area containing from 5 to 30 million people. The metropolis is the controlling center of the modern economy, the place where most decisions are made, where much of a country's manufacturing is carried on, which dominates distribution, culture, education, innovation, and communication, and which generates expansion of the economy and the culture. People living up to 500 miles away may rarely or never visit the metropolis, but they feel its influence through the agricultural market, the banking structure, mail-order houses, wholesale–retail relationships, and so forth.

CENTRAL-PLACE ACTIVITIES

Retail Trade

Central-place activities are many, and their relations are complex. Retail trade is the most important and most obvious such activity; an individual spends much time and money utilizing the complex of shops that sells the goods and the related repair services that he needs and desires.

To keep in business, the retail outlet chooses a location where it can be seen and attract customers. This is accomplished in three ways:

1. A retail decision maker places a premium on central accessibility—on being at the center of a transport subsystem. For instance, lower order activities like groceries and drug stores are often located at the center crossroads of a hamlet or village or at arterial crossings in a city; higher level activities are in larger places or at intersections of more important roads.

2. Retail activities locate together in mutually beneficial groups. The activities that most seek to form such clusters include clothing, jewelry, stationery, confection, and shoe stores.

3. Each group will try to locate as far from like competing groups as possible, in order to assure each retailer a fairly secure home market.

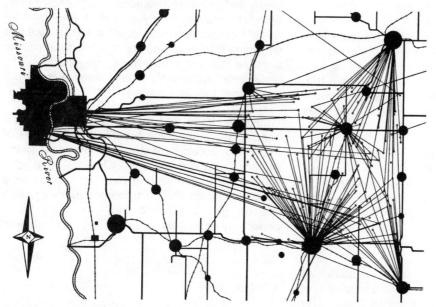

Figure 4.11 Overlap of trade areas. "Desire lines" connecting rural customers (small dots) with urban places (larger circles and Omaha, to the left) where furniture is usually bought indicate that centers do not monopolize all nearby customers, but rather that their trade areas overlap. (Reprinted by permission of the Regional Science Association, from B.J.L. Berry and R. Tennant, "Retail Location and Consumer Behavior," *Papers and Proceedings of the Regional Science Association* Vol. IX, 1962.)

While the majority of retail trade is grouped together and does best in locations where routes come together, large sectors of business are increasingly oriented toward traffic arteries and depend on traffic moving along a major road. Motels, auto, and trailer sales and service, rent-all dealers, drive-in restaurants, and most gas stations have a partly linear market—the vehicles traveling along a road. Since these facilities are automobile-oriented, they need much parking space for customers and cannot afford the rents of nucleated commercial centers.

Trade Areas   The store and the business district or shopping center to which it belongs have a trade area, defined by the shopping trips of its customers. Pure central-place theory defines these areas absolutely and geometrically. We realize, of

course, that individuals do not have perfect information and do not always behave quite optimally; they do not always go the shortest distance for a good or service. More realistically, then, we discover a field or pattern of shoppers about the store or center. Its extent is governed by the distance to competing centers of similar or larger size, and its intensity is controlled by the density of consumers in the area. Trade areas or shopping fields that are derived from asking customers the "place usually frequented for shopping" are found to overlap (see Figure 4.11).

This lack of precisely delineated trade areas reflects not only the inability of customers to distinguish small differences in distance, but also the conflict between the goals of minimizing distance and those of maximizing quality or quantity and

TOWNS AS CENTRAL PLACES

the subtle differences between supposedly identical mixes of goods and services.

Multipurpose Trips Part of an individual's efficiency in distance and time and part of the explanation for apparently inefficient overlap is that several purposes are often combined in one trip. We make short, one- or two-purpose trips more frequently, but multipurpose, longer trips may accomplish much more.

Many trips involve travel to more than one retail location, either because the shopper was frustrated at the first center or because, more usually, he perceived that each center offered some items the other lacked. A multipurpose trip to two locations will still save time and distance over two single-purpose trips to one closer center.

Multipurpose trips provide one of the theoretical bases for the agglomeration of functions at few, larger centers. Agglomeration makes it easier for a business to maximize the availability of its service to the most people. Not only do shopping centers make possible the satisfaction of planned multipurpose trips, but the presence of other stores can often induce greater consumption than is originally planned by the individual.

Wholesale Trade

Wholesale trade is spatially, as well as economically, an efficient and necessary intermediary between the manufacturer or farmer and the retailer (see Figure 4.13). The producer, who specializes in a few items for very wide distribution, can neither spend the time nor afford to handle countless small orders from retailers; the retailer, who stocks an immense variety of items, does not have the time to order small amounts from countless producers. As well, dividing large shipments into smaller lots would be a bookkeeping nightmare to both producers and retailers and result in extremely high distribution costs.

The spatial and economic hierarchy of central-place theory is well illustrated by wholesaling. With wholesaling, costly long-haul shipments of small lots are avoided; long-haul, large-volume movements from producers to wholesalers make possible the scale benefits of transport. At the same time, the retailer enjoys much quicker delivery from regional centers.

Wholesale trade is concentrated in the largest central places, although not only the size, but also the relative location, of a place is important. In the United States, for example, wholesaling is relatively more important in those metropolises on a border between the northeastern manufacturing regions (the core) and the more agricultural periphery, as well as those in regional centers of the periphery.

Transportation

Transportation facilities within towns are central-place activities, since they make possible distribution and exchange. Warehousing (temporary storage), especially associated with wholesale trade and marketing of local produce, constitutes a "time cushion" between producer and consumer—if a month's goods are stocked, producers do not have to adjust to day-by-day changes in consumption, and consumers do not have to wait long for goods.

A special problem of warehousing and exchange is queuing—finding the best coordination of activities to simultaneously minimize waiting, costs and time of storage, and taxes on inventories. The merchant or wholesaler wishes to meet all requests, but he has a limited storage capacity and finds it impossible to have enough stock to meet every contingency. Queuing theory permits minimum levels of stock to be estimated that will meet all but the most peculiar and, therefore, expendable demands. The spatial implications are great. Part of the cost of having to turn away customers is the ill will caused by having to send and wait for

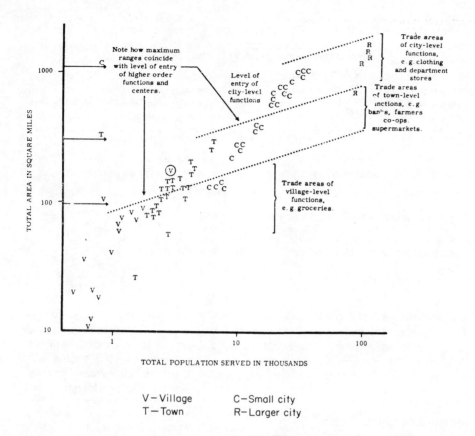

Note how maximum ranges coincide with level of entry of higher order functions and centers.

Level of entry of city-level functions

Trade areas of city-level functions, e. g. clothing and department stores

Trade areas of town-level functions, e. g. banks, farmers co-ops. supermarkets.

Trade areas of village-level functions, e. g. groceries.

V — Village   C — Small city
T — Town   R — Larger city

Figure 4.12 Relationship between population, area, and the functional level of central places. Note that the maximum population (range) served by villages is about the same as the minimum population (threshold) supporting a town. Because of variation in population density, however, there is much overlap in the area served by villages and towns, towns and small cities, and so forth. (Reprinted by permission of the Regional Science Association from B.J.L. Berry and R. Tennant, "Retail Location and Consumer Behavior," *Papers and Proceedings of The Regional Science Association* Vol. IX, 1962.)

goods, and part is the likelihood that the customer will shift to a new dealer at a new location.

Other Central-Place Activities

Financial and related services—banking, real estate, and insurance—are especially vital control services. They are often associated with other medium-threshold goods in multipurpose trips and hence are found in all towns and district shopping centers. However, there are higher level components of such services, such as commercial–industrial banking and investment services, that seek large-city and downtown locations for the convenience of the most important customers and to ease interoffice transactions.

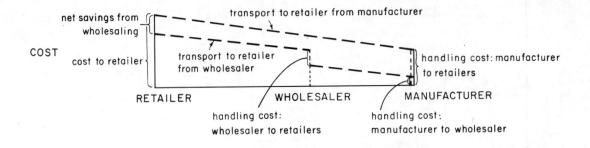

Figure 4.13 The spatial efficiency of wholesaling. If the manufacturer sells directly to retailers, his handling and distribution costs are very high because of the many retailers and the small size of his shipments. However, handling and distribution costs are small when manufacturers sell to only a few wholesalers, and retailers save by dealing with a few wholesalers rather than many manufacturers.

Real-estate and local insurance offices have low thresholds and find it relatively easy to enter a market. Since they depend on advertising and selling in the home, their locational preferences are not very strong, and they are frequent tenants of low-rent stores on lesser arterials.

Schools are central-place activities which follow administrative principles of spacing — that is, higher level schools include a few schools from the next lower level in their entirety. Schools need to be located centrally for their pupils, but a policy conflict arises out of the desire for close accessibility and the economies in teaching, facilities, and materials that can be realized if schools are larger and more widely spaced. This conflict is seen in the constant battle between the proponents of the one-room schoolhouse and the effort at providing consolidated schools in order to permit access to better equipment, more specialization in teaching, and the like. Some towns have experimented with consolidating all schools on one central campus so that all are used to their maximum, and students can be exposed to advanced teaching and equipment. This involves costly busing and some time loss, and, for the elementary grades, such concentration may well be uneconomic.

Summary

Central places are important—and increasingly so —for the support of the economy. Since they exist to serve a local population, they are so located that a regular structure of markets is formed. Since the demand for goods varies, this spatial structure becomes a hierarchical one as well. Distortion of the ideal spatial patterns is due to many factors, not the least of which is the location of resources and of processing activities, to which we now turn.

5

Industrialization: Towns as Processing Centers

INDUSTRIALIZATION

Although increased commercialization, international trade, and internal exchange encouraged the development of market towns and ports, the town-building impact of industrialization — the growth of manufacturing—may have been even greater. Societies gradually began to demand more products than individuals could make at home and came to appreciate the efficiency of specializing in the conversion of raw materials into more finished products. Greater profits required greater productivity, and industrialization was thus accompanied by rapid mechanization and a shift to inanimate sources of power, vastly increasing production. The demand for resources, which were both converted into other goods and used as fuels, also grew rapidly.

The spatial impact of industrialization was enormous. Metal ores, wood, and fuels became the resources most emphasized, instead of agricultural land, and the location of the two kinds of resources hardly coincided. Thus, towns frequently developed in areas of low agricultural productivity in order to exploit valuable resources. Since industrial towns did not depend on a spatial monopoly over scattered farm customers, they often grouped in clusters rather than dispersed, as did market towns. This new basis for towns effected also a large-scale redistribution of population from the rural areas of rich farming to areas with rich resources. However, not all industry exploited these new resources. Processers of agricultural products and makers of goods demanding high craftsmanship tended to locate in the older market towns.

Industrial activities typically utilized first the new resources closest to areas of existing development, but when these resources were depleted, often because of wasteful and inefficient procedures, more distant sources had to be used.

In the early stages of industrialization, primary industries—making the simplest conversions of raw materials—tended to be dominant. In more affluent economies, secondary industries—manufacturing that builds more complex products (appliances, computers) out of primary products (steel, paint)—are dominant. The primary base of production is no less necessary in advanced economies, but a high standard of living depends on the willingness of the consumer to pay for more and more elaborated products—clothes, for instance, not cloth.

General Significance of Industrialization

Although some manufacturing can be done in the home, industrialization is significant, first, because a firm may specialize in a limited range of products with specifically trained labor and management. Because of specialization, per capita productivity is vastly increased. The second significant aspect of industrialization is the substitution of inanimate energy for animate energy, a step which increases per capita production far more than does specialization alone. Although in the very short run the substitution of machines for men may cause "technological unemployment," the long-term effect is to increase production and wealth. It is this ability to produce goods with only a fraction of the labor force that permits a higher standard of living for all to develop; mechanized industrial production is 50 to 100 times more productive than is handicraft production. For instance, it might seem cheaper for an American family to buy flour and make its own bread, but it is far more efficient for society and saves time for the family if the bread is bought ready-made. The apparent savings are illusory, because the economy—and the standard of living—grow only by increasing specialization and thus raising productivity per worker. In sum, industrialization makes per-unit production much cheaper.

Spatial Significance of Industrialization

Industrialization led to these major geographic effects:

1. Previously unvalued mineral resources became as important as land, climate, and animal resources.

2. The population became generally concentrated in cities.

3. Areas with clusters of urban settlements were created.

4. Sharper distinctions became evident between prosperous and poor areas.

5. Goods were moved increasingly long distances between regions.

We will briefly discuss each of these effects.

Mineral resources, more than agricultural ones, are the basis for our present industrial and service structures. Mineral resources have attracted industries, and cities have been built around them, whatever the surrounding agricultural potential. Since mineral resources are concentrated in small areas and large-scale production is most economic, cities and population have become concentrated in a few favored industrial areas. Industrial settlements have taken new forms different from market towns, such as clusters of mining settlements and large clusters of textile, steel, and other industrial towns.

Another major spatial effect has been the weakening of regional and local self-sufficiency by the great demand for long-distance movement of raw materials, fuels, and foods; because resources are located in particular places and industrial enterprises are large-scale, industrialization requires great spatial interdependence. Industrialization has also made available both better mining equipment to permit lower quality ores, previously considered valueless, to be mined, and larger and faster farm machinery to permit previously marginal lands to be cultivated.

FACTORS DETERMINING INDUSTRIAL LOCATION

Processing (manufacturing) activities are the main alternative to central-place activities for support of towns and cities. Processing typically provides about one-fourth to three-fifths of the employment and value of products in a town. The total value of processing activities—manufacturing and construction—is about one-third to one-half an advanced nation's gross national product.

A higher level of spatial complexity is involved with processing activities. Central-place activities involve mainly distributing goods to local consumers, and efficient location thus depends on having the best access to customers. Processing has different constraints on location: distribution is to consumers who may be distant and large, rather than local, small, and dispersed. Materials must be collected from specific points within a wide area; many processing costs vary in space; and variation in costs with size (scale) of operations has a very great influence. The manufacturer's desire to maximize his profit—the difference between revenues and total costs—means that he must be located to minimize total costs of obtaining materials, processing them, marketing output to customers, and be located favorably with respect to other producers of the same goods. Also, while regional variations in labor costs, taxes, and the like affect only slightly central-place locations, which are controlled chiefly by distance, they strongly influence processing locations, often changing the optimum site for a plant away from a more central location.

Industrial location, even in theory, is also a more complicated problem than central-place location because variation in the quality of space—the location of specific resources, for example—is an explicit part of theory. Decisions are also more complex—and more interesting—because it is possible to substitute among all these elements; outlays for machinery may be substituted for labor, for example.

Before attempting to summarize the theory of industrial location, we review the elements included in the theory.

Location of Resources and Markets Resources and markets do not exist in all places, but rather at sporadic, specific sites. They are spatially separated, and a successful manufacturer must overcome these distances.

Transport Costs and the Transport System Assembling, or collecting, raw materials and distributing the finished goods to markets is subject to specific transport charges and costs in time. Even where the dollar cost of transport is not great, the presence of a quality transport system is essential.

Spatial Variation in Processing Costs Another factor complicating the ideal processing location is considerable variation in space of labor productivity—price and quality—land, corporate and inventory taxes, costs of construction, and maintenance, heating, and cooling costs. However, the cost of labor is a function of the expenditure per unit of product, not of the wage rate, and many companies are thus willing to pay high wages for highly productive workers. Variations in labor costs are also a function of the degree of economic development and of relative labor supply.

Demand For a new industry to be created and existing ones to survive, an unfilled consumer demand must exist willing to pay a price that will more than cover manufacturing costs. Demand changes fairly rapidly, and industries must learn to adapt their technical processes and spatial behavior in order to survive.

Technology A feasible process to produce a good must exist if costs are to remain below prices. Internal production efficiency results from standardization of products, mechanization, labor–management cooperation, and reduced turnover. Extreme specialization in production reduces costs, simplifies both assembly and distribution (in other words, the problem of finding the right location for the firm), but also increases the short-run risks caused by price fluctuation, change in consumer demand, and increased competition for supplies and markets. Thus, although a firm may standardize its products, it also usually finds it beneficial to diversify and manufacture a small set of products; diversification may complicate manufacturing, but it reduces the economic and geographic risks of the firm.

Capital Processing industries usually require large outlays of capital, but are somewhat less risky than service activities; new plants typically require at least $100,000, and may run to $10 million or more, but a new shop can be opened for a few thousand dollars. Hence, lending agencies for processing activities are large and rather cautious. Since capital is generated in the largest amounts in already successful industrial locations, the most available capital is within large financial–industrial centers. Such capital may theoretically be mobile, but lenders are inclined to be more willing to invest in known areas in accepted lines of activities. Also, in an economy that is predominantly private, the lender and the prospective manufacturer must seek fairly short-run profitability, reducing the likelihood of either developing radically new processes and products or of placing manufacturing plants in totally new locations.

Agglomeration Economies The economic relationships that have the strongest spatial element are the economies of agglomeration and returns to scale. The benefits of agglomeration have already been discussed with reference to central-place activities (refer to Figure 1.10). For industries, agglomeration—clustering of industries in a given location—is spatially and economically efficient when the industries share identical resources or markets or have strong interindustry linkages (many sales to each other). As with central-place activities, however, even unrelated activities may enjoy indirect benefits when located together. These benefits may be due to the availability of better transport, more capital, or a larger labor pool, or to the use of a common technology. Also, where heavy industries employing mostly men (such as steel) are dominant, light industries employing women (such as candy) are attracted.

If transport costs are low and brand loyalty is high, competing producers of the same good frequently are located in a cluster. Here, they may take advantage of a common skilled labor force, spin off ideas and personnel from competitors, and, above all, make easy comparison purchasing for customers.

Industrial Interrelations: Input-Output A valuable short-term description of the linkages between industries is given by an account of input-output flows—the dollar amount that each industry purchases from each other industry (see Figure 5.01). It is also possible to construct a similar table for the interindustry flow of goods. Analysis of such tables reveals that industrial complexes exist, in the sense that industries within a complex have more relations with each other than with industries outside the group; but the existence of such a complex does not necessarily imply spatial agglomeration of these industries. If a set of related plants, for example oil fields, refineries, synthetic fibers, and perhaps clothing or tire manufacturers, is isolated, the structure of the location of all the plants taken together will be more optimal than the location of any one type of plant considered separately.

One typical industrial complex consists of integrated iron and steel, by-product chemicals, fabricated metals, and machinery; another includes sawmills, pulp mills, and so forth. When these industries are adjacent in space, transport costs are reduced, and less handling is required for raw materials (Figure 5.02A). Detroit, for example, is the most rapidly growing steel producer because of the huge consumption of steel by the auto industry.

Textile and clothing manufacturers also form an industrial complex. However, textile plants are typically separate from apparel plants because the labor requirements are very different (Figure 5.02B). Also, alumina processing (smelting of bauxite ore to aluminum dioxide), which doesn't use electricity, tends to be separate from aluminum refining if savings from cheap electric power for refining more than offset increasing the transport costs for raw materials and the finished aluminum.

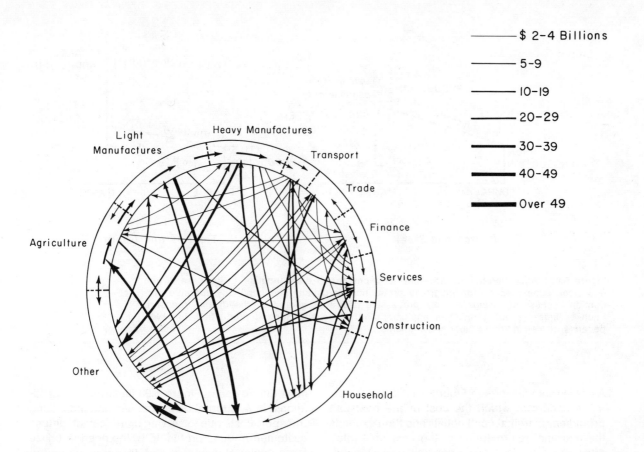

Figure 5.01 Input-Output: interindustry flows of goods and services (after Isard). Shown is the value of goods and services flowing between and within major economic sectors in the United States, about 1955. (The chart is partly hypothetical.) Flows to households represent retail consumption; flows from households represent labor costs and family savings. Such a diagram reveals the significant linkages between sectors of the economy.

In general, the spatial concentration of related activities increases the total distance required for assembling basic materials and for shipping the final products, but it is justified so long as savings in the shipments between activities and in other relations between industries more than offset the increases (Figure 5.02).

Returns to Scale Returns to scale refer simply to the expected reduction in average unit cost when more units of the same product are manu-

factured, but the spatial relations of scale may not be so well understood. As scale increases, the costs of development, new machinery, plant, and overhead are spread out over more units; labor productivity is raised; more internal specialization is possible; the large quantities of inputs needed can be obtained at a reduced price and shipped at a lower rate; the large shipments of the goods produced receive lower transport rates; machinery and specialized personnel are more fully utilized; and inventories of raw materials and products can be relatively lower.

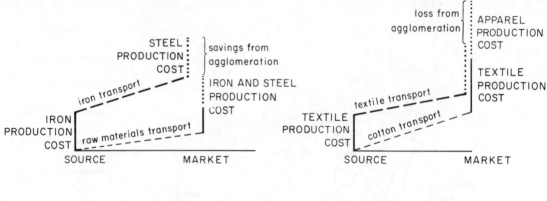

A. Iron and Steel

B. Textiles and Apparel

Figure 5.02 Agglomeration of industries—economies and diseconomies. In the case of iron and steel, agglomeration (or integrated production) is usually cheaper than separated production because of savings on both processing (less fuel, shared overhead) and transport. Such savings are not a result of agglomerating textile and apparel production, however, because of their different labor requirements.

As scale increases (see Figure 1.11) a point normally occurs at which the cost of the next unit produced (marginal cost) equals and then exceeds the marginal return (price of the next unit sold), after which average costs per unit rise. Depending on the behavior of prices, another point occurs at which total profit is maximum and then declines. Costs rise internally (within the plant) and profits fall; plant reconstruction, labor shortages, internal transport inefficiency, congestion, and managerial confusion raise production costs; and externally (outside the firm) the necessity to seek more distant resources and markets raises transfer costs excessively.

However, if internal processing inefficiencies do not occur, average costs will decline with increasing scale while a firm remains within a spatially restricted market. Since most markets are in fact located at points and spatially separated (in cities), increased scale will sooner or later force a firm to use more distant markets or suppliers a discrete jump in space away. The accompanying jump in transfer costs may more than offset any econo-

mies due to scale. Figure 5.03 illustrates two situations. In A, internal diseconomies and increasing transport costs due to serving more distant, diffuse customers reduce profits. In B, the need to utilize large material sources and to serve large but sporadic markets gives more than one fairly profitable level of output, but also an eventual decline in profits.

Industries for which transport costs are high and scale of output is limited tend to seek protected market areas, either monopolies or oligopolies (where only a few producers control supply and demand). There are other industries for which transport costs play only a small role in determining optimal scale (see Figure 5.04). The aircraft and machinery industries are typical examples. For these industries no significant spatial monopoly is possible; firms must share virtually the entire market. Scale is usually limited by the firm's share of the market, rather than by diseconomies. As a result, prices are likely to be rather uniform, and plants will be located in places that minimize spatially varying processing costs.

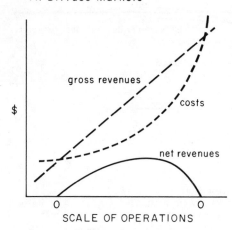

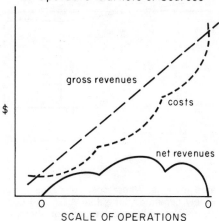

Figure 5.03 Returns to scale and market and source location. Where customers are everywhere small and diffuse, profits gradually increase and later decrease. Where customers or material sources are few, large, and sporadically located, several levels of output may be relatively profitable.

These industries are likely also to benefit from the processing-cost benefits of agglomeration discussed earlier in the chapter.

Substitution in Manufacturing   Even one kind of manufacturing involves a complex variety of inputs, and there are perhaps many different processes for a number of specific products. Many possibilities for substitution are thus available to the firm when finding an optimum location or attempting to maximize profits.

Substitution among inputs is common—for example, coal, oil, gas, or nuclear material can all be used to produce electric power, and both plastics and wood can be used for containers. Figure 5.05 for example, illustrates a substitution between pig iron and scrap; which one is used largely depends on the relative price and available supply. When substitution is made between two inputs, one located in a remote region and the other near major markets, the significance of location is most important. Thus steel, paper, and other industries

exhibit a dual spatial orientation, locating either at resources or at markets.

Substitution between processes is closely tied to substitution between inputs—for example, the kind of wood used tends to dictate which pulping process can be used to make paper—but even using the same inputs and making the same outputs, some variety may be possible; for example, steel is made in electric, Bessemer, open hearth, basic oxygen, and other furnaces.

Substitution among outputs involves either finding the optimum combination of products or varying details in a single product. Product substitution is especially important in adapting behavior in the existing location when consumer demand changes. It is a limited method, however, because industrial machinery can do only specific tasks.

Capital and labor may also be substituted for one another, to some extent; an investment in machinery, for instance, reduces labor requirements and labor costs, and where labor is scarce or expen-

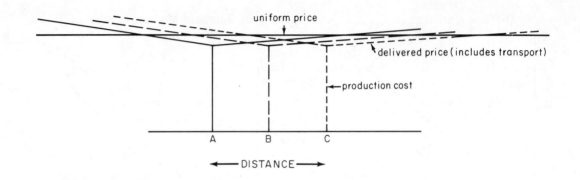

Figure 5.04 Shared markets. Where costs of delivery are low and delivered prices virtually the same, even widely separated firms like A, B, and C can compete over a wide area. The firms will prefer to quote a uniform price and not attempt to capture a local market.

sive, such capital investment is indicated. Where labor is cheap, however, there is less pressure for automation. If machinery cannot be substituted for labor, an industry is limited to locations where labor is sufficiently cheap.

Substitutions between revenues and costs are common because of spatial variations in prices and the importance of transport costs. Areas where higher prices can be obtained for goods may also entail higher costs, so that profits are often equal in areas having widely varying price levels. Substitutions between transport outlays and other outlays are also of great interest geographically. Aluminum producers, for instance, may substitute higher transport charges for power costs, in order to take advantage of the savings in electrical power usually available only far from major markets. Petroleum refineries can choose between transport charges for crude petroleum and those for the finished products. In general, when savings are made in processing costs, whether power, labor, or taxes, increased transport costs must be accepted.

One other fairly common substitution is between returns to scale and transport outlays. A large-

scale producer can substitute his cost savings for higher transport costs and greater market penetration (greater distance at which he can profitably sell), but smaller producers may also successfully compete by accepting a smaller market, especially if their plant is physically separate from any others.

THEORY OF INDUSTRIAL LOCATION

Industrial location theory, because of the greater number of variables, lacks the simple geometric elegance of central-place theory—but, for the same reason, it is more challenging. The theory has developed from two directions: first, from concern with the optimal location of a single plant and, second, from the study of the equilibrium among a set of related firms.

Location of the Single Plant

As with any choice of location, the optimal site for a firm is that which is central, minimizes the costs

TOWNS AS PROCESSING CENTERS

of the necessary spatial relations, and, if selling prices vary for the product, maximizes the difference between costs and revenues. A classical theory of firm location was formulated by A. Weber in 1909. Optimum location was seen primarily as the point where the transport costs of bringing the necessary raw materials and of supplying goods to the necessary market were at a minimum. Because of transport costs, orientation to resources or markets was considered the normal case. However, if variations in other costs, particularly labor, were sufficiently great, a location determined solely by transport costs might not be the optimal one.

In its simplest form, the transport-cost approach compares the weight of a unit of output with the weight of the raw materials necessary to produce that output. Transport costs are a simple linear function of weight and distance. In the trivial case where there is just one product, one market, and one raw material, if the product is heavier and thus incurs higher costs, location will be at the market. If the raw material is heavier and incurs higher assembly costs, location will be at the material source. With multiple sources and markets, if the weight of one product or resource exceeds the sum of the weights of all the others, usually a case where one is extremely heavy or has much bulk gain or loss in processing, location is easily determined.

In Figure 5.06, the weight and hence transport cost of raw material 1 exceeds that of the other raw material and of the product. If different transport rates are considered for different raw materials and finished products, it is necessary to compare the per-mile transport inputs—that is, weight times transport rate per mile—in order to compare costs.

Most often, no one cost determines location alone. Since, in this formulation, transport costs are strictly proportional to distance, the optimum site must be somewhere within the space bounded by the sources and markets For two sources and one market or one source and two markets, the location triangle technique provides a graphic solution. Location shifts from an end point but remains

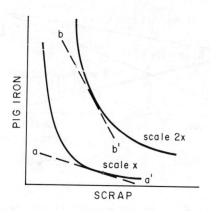

At scale x, cheaper scrap is substituted for pig iron

At scale 2x, limited scrap supply alters price ratio bb' in favor of pig iron

Figure 5.05 An example of input substitution: steel production. In this example, the solid lines indicate the combinations of pig iron and scrap that will produce a constant amount of steel. The slope of the dashed lines indicates the ratio of pig iron price to scrap price. Line aa', for instance, shows that scrap is cheap if not too much is needed and the scale of steel production is limited, while bb' shows that if more is needed, pig iron is cheaper.

closest to the point from which transport is most expensive (see Figure 5.07).

Since this simple model assumes that the transport surface is the same at all points—that is, there is no existing transport network—finding the ideal location is equivalent to finding the bivariate median or "point of minimum aggregate travel"— the point where ton-miles for all the products is the least.

Our theory so far, then, is that the optimal location of a plant is at the point where transport costs to

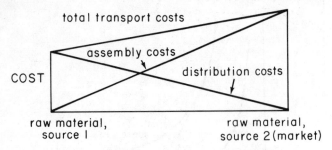

DISTANCE BETWEEN SOURCES

Figure 5.06 Simple raw material transport orientation. The line labeled "assembly costs" shows the cost of obtaining raw material from source 1; the line "distribution costs" shows the combined cost of obtaining material 2 away from its source and of delivering the product to the market. Total transport costs (assembly plus distribution costs) are lowest at source 1 because the transport cost of raw material from source 1 exceeds the combined costs of transporting raw material to source 2 and the finished product.

and from its necessary resources and markets are at the minimum.

Isodapanes Fairly complex location problems can be handled graphically by the isodapane method, as suggested by Weber and developed by others. The goal is the same—to seek the ideal location for production, given a set of necessary sources and markets. In this method, one draws isolines (or isotims), where the cost of transportation for a raw material or a finished product is constant at every point on a line surrounding each source and market (see Figure 5.08). At any point on the map we can then calculate total transportation costs for both materials and products. Lines showing constant total costs, called isodapanes, can then be drawn, and the optimum, where costs are lowest, can be found (Figure 5.08).

The isodapane technique makes it possible to include variations in processing costs, whether occurring at single points or varying systematically over the surface (Figure 5.08). Indeed, this is

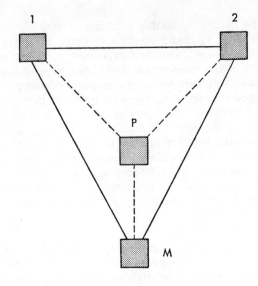

M — Market

1 — Localized gross raw material

2 — Localized gross raw material

P — Production center

– – – Transportation route followed

Figure 5.07 The location triangle. In the simple case of a triangular arrangement of two material sources and one market (1, 2, and M), the ideal location for production (P), minimizing total costs, will be within the triangle bounded by the sources and markets and closest to the location that involves the highest transport cost (here M, since shipping the finished product is costliest). (Reprinted by permission of the Houghton Mifflin Company, from R.J. Sampson and M.T. Farris, *Domestic Transportation*, 1966.)

the use for which Weber originally intended it. Thus, lower labor costs may more than offset an increase in transport costs associated with shifting a firm from the optimal transportation position. Although variations in processing costs are traditionally seen as deviations from transport optima, it is more realistic to seek from the beginning the point where *total* costs are minimum, since in fact

TOWNS AS PROCESSING CENTERS

transport costs are not always the controlling ones.

Even with this elaboration, Weberian theory is still partial and in a sense unnecessarily complicated. It does not consider the serious questions of scale —whether there should be more than one plant, for instance—the possibility that alternate or multiple sources of raw materials might be used, and, especially, it considers neither the presence of a transport net, which limits to a network, the real possibilities for an industrial location, nor realistic transport rate patterns, which strongly militate against intermediate plant locations in favor of end points or nodes. Since transport rates are lower and connections better at nodes (towns or intersections) of a transport network, the problem of the best location is reduced to deciding among a finite set of points, rather than points on an extended area. Realistic rate structures are illustrated in Figure 5.09. The economies in rates for travel of longer distances and the steep initial rates favor end points for industrial locations. For example, in the triangle case (Figure 5.07), even if the finished product were only a little costlier to ship than the raw materials, the market location would be optimal; that is, it is advantageous to eliminate one of the hauls completely.

For the case where there is one market and one resource, Hoover illustrates the role of realistic rates and transshipment costs (costs incurred from shifting carrier or transport mode). Terminal handling charges (loading, unloading, etc.), reflected in high transport rates near origins, clearly favor location at markets or sources; one long haul at a lower rate per mile is cheaper than two shorter hauls at higher rates per mile. The classical cases of industrial orientation, to either the market, often because there are higher rates on finished products, or to needed resources, often because great bulk or weight is lost if the raw materials are processed at the source, are illustrated in Figure 5.10. Similar diagrams can be used to study the possible orientation of plant location toward cheaper labor (Figure 5.11). Processing costs do not usually vary gradually in space, but rather change more sporadically.

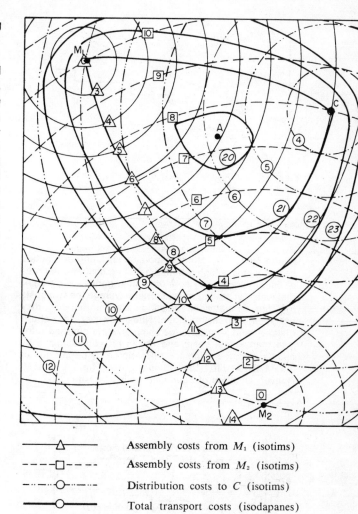

—————△—————	Assembly costs from M_1 (isotims)
- - - -□- - - -	Assembly costs from M_2 (isotims)
—·—·—○—·—·—	Distribution costs to C (isotims)
—————○—————	Total transport costs (isodapanes)

Figure 5.08 Lines of constant transport cost (isolines or isotims) are shown for assembly of material 1 away from its site (M_1); for material 2 away from its site (M_2); and for distribution of the product to the market (C). The italic numerals show the total of the three transport costs. Point A is the optimum location, where total cost is less than 20. (Reprinted from *Regional Development and Planning* by John Friedmann and William Alonso, eds., by permission of the M.I.T. Press, Cambridge, Mass. Copyright ©1964 by The Massachusetts Institute of Technology.)

Transshipment costs are sufficiently important to help explain the presence of industry in many port and river cities. A transshipment or break-of-bulk

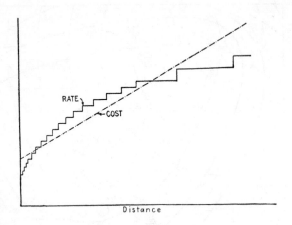

Figure 5.09 Realistic transport rates. A carrier's actual costs include a high terminal handling cost and perhaps a linearly increasing cost of hauling goods over greater distances. In setting rates, carriers average the two costs together, so that while rates increase over distance, they rise at a decreasing slope. Note, however, that short-distance and long-distance shipments are charged rates less than actual costs and are in effect subsidized by middle-distance shipments. (Reprinted by permission of the McGraw-Hill Book Company, Inc., from Edgar M. Hoover, *Location of Economic Activity,* 1948.)

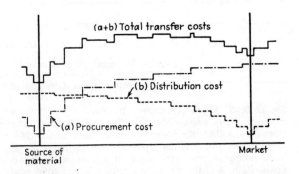

Figure 5.10 Realistic orientation to market or material end point. As in Figure 5.06, assembly (procurement) costs are greater than distribution costs to the market, but, because of the structure of transport costs, a market location is better than any intermediate location beyond the immediate vicinity of the material. (Reprinted by permission of the McGraw-Hill Book Company, Inc., from Edgar M. Hoover, *Location of Economic Activity,* 1948.)

point may be an optimal site because often either the distribution costs of a firm include shipments to several markets, or materials are assembled from several sources. Thus, we may view Figures 5.10 and 5.11 as generalizations, where "material location" stands for a point central to all the necessary suppliers and "market location" for a point central to all markets. Either or both may be at transshipment rather than resource or market locations. The greater the number of suppliers and markets, the less dominant any one supplier or market becomes and the more likely it is that the optimum point will be a centrally located node, whether or not the node is itself a source or market of consequence. Between a single source and a single market, a transshipment point is less likely to be the best location, unless a processor's in-transit privilege* is available or a shift from ocean to land transport is required.

The isodapane technique can be used to show locations on transport networks and realistic rate structures. As is evident from Figure 5.12, it is primarily the nodal points (markets, sources, junctions) that need to be evaluated. The isodapane technique can also show fairly easily the cost of multiple sources of the same material so that each source can be evaluated at every point of the surface at which it is cheapest. Such problems can soon become graphically messy and arithmetically tedious, but a computer may evaluate costs for a finite system of places fairly readily.

The modified Weberian theory we have developed may now be summarized: the optimal location for an industry is the point where transport and processing costs are at a minimum. This point is most likely to be an end point if there are very few markets and sources, and a central transportation node if there are many sources and markets.

---

*A through transport rate from source to market is quoted, even though the materials are stopped and processed somewhere between.

TOWNS AS PROCESSING CENTERS

Spatial Behavior of the Firm: Returns to Scale

The Weberian approach is most appropriate to large material sources and urban markets and determines the location of industries from their transport and processing costs. The effects of scale are ignored. Two examples of scale relations were given in Figure 5.03, one the relations of a plant whose customers were small and diffuse (everywhere) and another those of a plant whose customers were large and sporadic. In the first case, the scale of the plant may increase continuously as the market expands to a greater distance and more customers become available. However, if the firm pays for delivery, transport costs increase as a result and gradually outweigh the savings on processing costs, and the optimal scale and market size are thus found. If the customers pay a delivered price (price at plant plus transport), then consumer demand falls with distance from the plant. In this case, the number of potential customers falls off rapidly with distance, and then delivered prices will yield maximum profits because distant customers can be ignored. However, if the number of potential customers increases with distance, then it will clearly pay the firm to quote a uniform delivered price to all its customers; even though nearby customers will be penalized, in this way the firm can attract the largest number of customers and it can realize greater returns to scale. The plant in these examples acts like a central place; it expands to encompass as large a market as distribution costs will permit.

Cases of More than One Plant

Restricting the manufacture of a product to one firm or plant is unjustified; admitting more than one plant into our landscape may greatly reduce transport costs and thus raise profitability, despite possible scale benefits when there is only one large producer. However, as soon as we allow more than one plant, we are forced to estimate

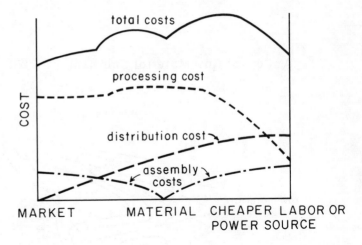

Figure 5.11 Processing or market orientation. In this example, a cheaper labor or power source, despite fairly high assembly and distribution costs, enjoys almost as low total costs as a close-to-market location (distribution cost steps smoothed for simplicity).

how many, their size, and their relative competitive position in space.

In the earlier example of the isodapane approach to problems of several markets and sources, a possible alternative would have been to establish more than one plant, whether branches of a firm or competitive plants. An infinite number of combinations of locations and sizes is of course theoretically possible, but a study of scale relations will yield a smaller range of profitable plant sizes. Thus, the approximately ideal number of producing units can be found for a given region. The problem can be reduced further by evaluating only a manageable set of locations of lowest cost and testing the appropriate scales and numbers of plants. For example, if the lowest cost locations were all markets and the optimal scale of production were fairly low, a plant could be established at each market proportional to the size of the market; total costs could then be compared with those found with the one-plant solution.

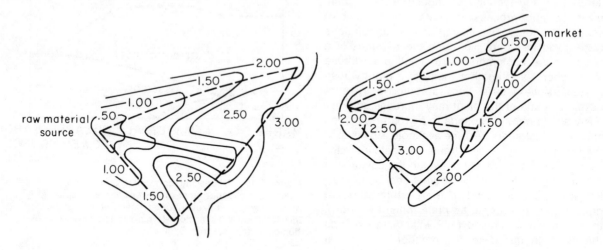

A. Cost of Raw Material Shipment

B. Cost of Product Distribution

C. Variations in Labor Costs

D. Total Cost Surface

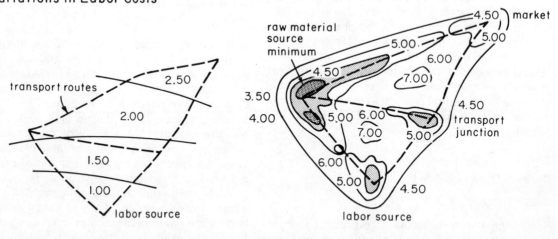

Figure 5.12 Cost surfaces and optimum location as modified by presence of transport routes. Isolines of cost are shown separately for raw material shipments, product distribution, and labor. Note that transport and total costs are relatively lower at nodes (market, material source, labor source, transport junction) and along transport routes. In D, the lowest total cost areas are shaded. Note that the lowest cost location is a point, the raw material source.

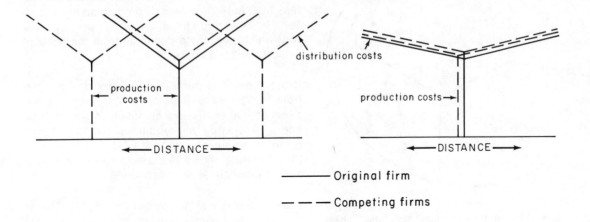

A. Transport Costs High

B. Transport Costs Low

distribution costs

production costs

production costs→

←DISTANCE→

←DISTANCE→

———— Original firm

— — — Competing firms

Figure 5.13 Entry and spacing of competitive plants. When distribution costs are high, new competitors will try to find a poorly served market and obtain a local monopoly. Thus, firms tend to disperse, A. When distribution costs are very low, however, firms tend to cluster and share a large market from one location, B.

Consider the case of customers arranged along a line. If there is only one firm, the optimum location for distribution will be at the median customer. If there are two firms, Hotelling's equilibrium solution may apply: both will be located at the center; each may dominate the customers on its own side or the two may share the whole market. The truly optimum—although unstable—solution is at the two points one-quarter of the total distance from the two ends, where distance traveled by customers would be less. However, this solution will not last long; the firms are likely to move toward each other in an attempt to acquire a larger share of the market. The risk here, of course, is that the distant customer may be lost altogether, and more competition will develop on the edges. Also, one competitor may be content with a smaller, protected share of the market; in that case, the larger competitor should locate so as to minimize distance traveled for the remaining customers.

For industries where the costs of transporting the final product are much greater than the costs of transporting raw materials or where either customers or suppliers are spatially diffuse, plant location tends to follow the central-place spatial-monopoly principle because customers will not travel far for products and plants cannot afford to ship products very far (Figure 5.13A). Within a firm, the number and size of the plants are determined by the balance between economies achieved by having more customers and the costs of farther transport. Also, the spatial penetration (the market or supply area) of one plant is checked by the ability of the plant's competitors to collect materials, process them, and distribute products to closer markets at a lower delivered price. This pattern is most obvious on a local or regional scale—dairies, newspapers, and bakeries, for example.

On a national scale, the territorial size of the national economy is so great that there are many markets and material sources for virtually every industry. For many industries, transport costs become significant only on a national scale. In indus-

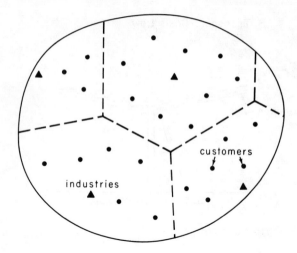

Figure 5.14 The spatially monopolistic firm: market areas. Where customers are small and diffuse, a central-place pattern for industries tends to develop. Although each location has a monopoly over each area, there may be more than one plant in each location (see text).

tries such as machine tools, however, regional markets are large enough and transport costs great enough from any one location to bring some dispersal of plants and at least a limited degree of spatial monopoly.

Figure 5.13A illustrates a typical dispersed central-place location pattern. Each center of production may have plants from several firms, which together dominate the market area. This is an oligopolistic structure and often occurs when customers demand a variety of brands (television and cars, for instance).

As transport costs become relatively less high, locating at specific resource clusters may become less favorable, or, alternatively, spatial monopolies —which are based on least distance—may weaken and firms may seek the points of minimum costs over a wide territory. This frequently results in clusters of similar plants sharing large regional or national markets (Figures 5.14 and 5.15). Moderate transports costs do not inhibit the scale of production until great distances are reached.

However, other constraints, such as internal processing diseconomies or, especially, division of the market by customer preference for various brands, may limit feasible scales of production much earlier. Hence, several firms may locate within a territory which one could dominate from the point of view of transport costs.

If the firms in a particular industry do not gain from agglomeration (see page 82), they will disperse so that each has a monopoly in a small area and a wider area where markets overlap (Figure 5.15A). If agglomeration yields extra savings, then the clustering shown in Figure 5.15B occurs, and spatial monopolies are abandoned.

Weber illustrated this by means of his critical isodapanes. Assume production occurs at a set of low-cost sites. If the savings incurred by carrying out all production at one location—that is, by agglomerating—exceed the additional transport costs, then all plants should be located at the point of minimum transport costs within the region. In Figure 5.16, the circles represent the distance at which transport costs equal the savings gained by agglomeration. If these circles intersect, then the savings of agglomeration will exceed the additional transport costs.

Frequently, the ideal point location is not obvious. Many places within a region may have almost equal expected profitability, so that the ultimate location decision within the set of places must be considered random from an economic–geographic point of view.

Summary: Location of Related Sets of Firms
The location of the firm represents an individual adjustment to the existing pattern of the industry, but we may also analyze the spatial pattern of the industrial system as such. Plants in a single industry exist in a dynamic equilibrium with each other and with important sources and markets. If plants have identical inputs and outputs and significant transport costs, a spatial equilibrium may be determined in which plants and the areas in which they have a spatial monopoly are optimally located, scale is optimal, and total profits are maximized.

TOWNS AS PROCESSING CENTERS

A. Partially Shared Markets

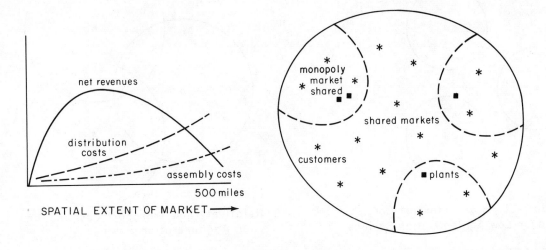

B. Totally Shared Markets: Clustered Production

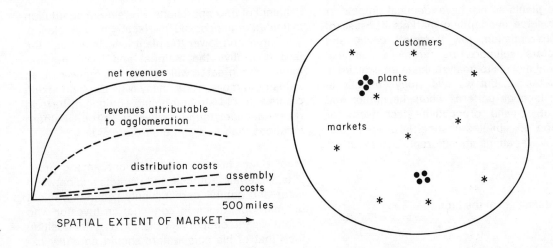

Figure 5.15 A. When transport costs are moderate and agglomeration benefits limited, plants may be either dispersed or clustered, but the area monopolized by a plant (or plants) is very limited. Most of the market customers must be shared. B. When transport costs are low and agglomeration benefits are great, plants tend to be highly clustered and share the entire market.

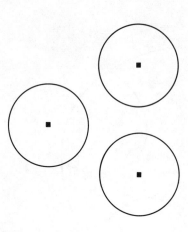

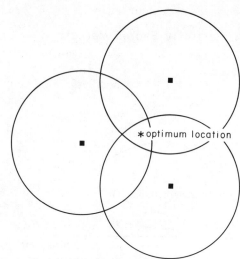

A. Relatively High Transport Cost
and/or Low Agglomeration Savings

B. Relatively Low Transport Cost and/or
High Agglomeration Savings

Figure 5.16 Agglomeration determined by critical isodapanes. The circles are isodapanes showing transport cost equivalents of savings obtained from agglomeration. They are critical because if they intersect, the savings to each firm obtained by agglomerating will exceed the additional transport costs incurred from serving the more distant customers.

But if the plants do not have identical outputs or inputs or serve overlapping markets because of brand differentiation, low transport costs, and other factors, solutions are far more complex. Operational models to analyze these interrelations do not yet exist, but we can study changes in industrial location patterns when the nature and location of demand, productivity, technology, or substitution possibilities change, in order to discover how variations in different factors affect location.

Spatial Adjustment of the Firm

Every firm has a huge investment in its existing plants, but changes in demand, technology, transport routes, and rates may render existing locations nonoptimal or even unprofitable if the plant fails to adapt. In fact, major behavior changes at existing plants are far more common than estab-

lishment of new operations. However, if adaptation is limited or impossible, the factory may be closed. The older and lower the plant investment and the less restrictive the material and labor requirements, the greater will be the willingness of an industry to move. Thus, many New England textile plants with old structures and equipment have in recent decades found it easier to shift to southern locations than to adapt their old plants.

More often, however, substitutions among products, materials, sources, and markets and between labor and capital permit highly profitable, if not optimal, operations to continue; an investor who might wish to open a new plant in a better position than that of his competitors should carefully examine how far they might be able to adapt to the additional competition. As a result, a new plant is most likely to be located in areas where new demand has developed as a consequence of population shifts (for example, this is the main reason for the growth of industry in the Los Angeles area) or

TOWNS AS PROCESSING CENTERS

in areas of new supplies (such as a new petroleum field). New plants are nevertheless often located in areas of existing competition, especially if the product offered is somewhat new or different or if the demand for the product has increased beyond the capacity of competitors to meet.

It is hard to adapt to changes in the location of demand. Price manipulation of nearby customers in favor of more distant customers (such as with uniform delivered prices) can work for a while, but either relocation or a change in the product mix may be necessary. Changes in the nature of demand may require costly retooling, a shift in the location of markets, or manufacture of a higher quality product. Thus, textile makers who have successfully survived in New England have often shifted to new goods that require more highly skilled labor or more machinery.

Changes in the source and assembly cost of industrial raw materials are common, and are usually met by shifting to new sources, such as foreign materials of higher quality, or by using substitute raw materials, such as replacing pig iron with scrap (see Figure 5.17). Increases in the relative cost of labor typically result in increased automation, if it is feasible. Changes in technology requiring a radical shift in the manufacturing process may force a plant to be abandoned, unless the location remains excellent for the new process. Reductions in transport rates, with an attendant rise in the optimal scale of the plant, have often weakened the position of many smaller producers; many survive, however, by shifting to custom production and by providing special services, such as quick delivery.

Interregional Input-Output A valuable tool for estimating the regional impact of expected changes in production or demand among industries is the input-output or interindustry flows table introduced above (see p. 82). If such a table were available for major regions to show the purchases each industry makes from every industry in every other region, it would be possible to estimate the regional consequence of changes in regional shares of demand or production. No such break-

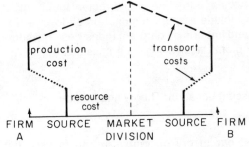

1. Before Depletion

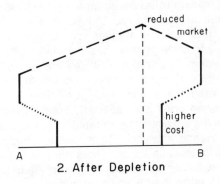

2. After Depletion

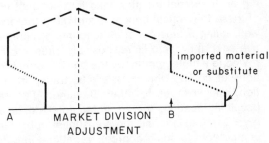

3. After Adjustment

Figure 5.17 Adaptation of individual firms to change: depletion of natural resources as an example. Before depletion, firms A and B use nearby resources at equivalent costs and they divide the market almost equally at the point where delivered costs are equal. When B's source becomes depleted, however, its costs rise and its share of the market is reduced. To survive, firm B finds a cheaper imported resource or a substitute. This lowers its costs so much that it can expand its share of the market at the expense of A.

down exists, but some single-region input-output tables include a slight regional breakdown of exports and imports by different industries, and some interregional analysis is thus possible.

Processing Location: Theory and Reality

Even if our theory encompassed all factors that might make an optimal location, we know that real locations would not be expected to coincide with the theoretically best ones. As has already been stressed, information is at times scanty, or misunderstood, and some people have more information than do others. In addition, decision makers willingly accept varying degrees of "irrationality" so long as profitability continues. Obviously, too, manufacturing firms are especially subject, even more than are service firms, to rapid technological changes. Hence, the problem of long-run imperfection in its location always faces the plant, and adaptive behavior is hence very important for owners to realize their investment in a plant.

Practical Plant Location   In practice, men choosing an industrial location take into account most of these theoretical concerns and other factors as well, using a time-honored accounting, comparative-cost approach. Here, possible sites are narrowed to a finite number by the general considerations of competition for markets, transport position, and linkages to other industries. For each possible location, the expected total costs and revenues (considering the adjustment behavior of competitors to some degree), variations in output and input mix, and so on are compared in detail. While less mathematically sophisticated than some industrial theory, these practical methods, even though based on accounting computations, are behaviorally highly complex in that reactions of competitors are estimated. Also, practical industrial location can and does take into account more personal and psychological constraints than are appropriate to a general location theory, such as preference of owners for a location because of historical ties.

Centrally Planned Economies

Industrial location under centrally planned economies is subject to the same factors of costs, profitability, productivity, and opportunity costs. In practice, too, methods for choosing locations are probably nearly identical to those used by private individual firms. Yet, theoretically at least, a planned society might be expected to show some differences in the choice of an industrial location. For instance, if the state is the general owner of all industries, it might be willing to accept a longer period of loss before a new unit becomes established. A tendency for more rapid and extensive development in peripheral areas on egalitarian grounds—so that money is more evenly invested across the territory—should also result. Soviet experience supports these predictions at least partially. Also, an approach that maximizes benefits to society as a whole, rather than a single firm, could result in more efficient location patterns.

On the other hand, however, the impact of centrally planned errors may be far more disruptive. For example, the "Great Leap Forward," China's industrialization program, attempted to apply the technology and organization used for handicraft production to the manufacture of major industrial goods like steel. As a result, disastrous problems of lack of uniformity, waste of raw materials, transport congestion, and low productivity limited the plan's achievements.

Summary

Two very general theoretical statements about industrial location may be offered:

1.   Manufacturing is so responsive to the benefits of increased scale of production that the minimum size of an industrial plant will tend to create small urban settlements around it.

2.   Manufacturing will be more concentrated in an economy than will population—that is, it will seek the largest, densest markets—because of scale

benefits, because of the gradient in density of settlement, and because industry has spread historically from an early point of origin. Further, manufacturers will tend to be concentrated in larger places; except for cases where resources are available only in sparsely settled areas, most industries find that in isolated areas they cannot achieve sufficient scale economies without incurring excessive distribution costs. A much larger producer in denser urban areas can supply these additional peripheral customers because of his low costs.

Industrial location theory is frustrating because it does not result in a consistent kind of spatial pattern. Central-place theory argues that a regular pattern of dispersed urban settlements is the most efficient and profitable way to provide almost all service, exchange, and collection activities. If the raw materials for industry were dispersed evenly and processing costs were invariate, industrial location theory could be reduced to central-place theory. But precisely because space does vary in quality, because needed raw materials do exist only sporadically and are often costly to transport, and because labor and other processing costs do vary, industrial location patterns are inconsistent.

One could argue, then, that industrial production is also carried out most efficiently within a central-place structure, unless savings on processing costs or on transport costs for raw materials or semimanufactures outweigh the savings in distribution costs obtained from locating at markets. Locating near resources in the situation where assembly costs are high is, actually, exactly analogous in purpose to the central-place type of location at markets, except that here a spatial monopoly over a supply area—instead of over a market—is the most efficient solution, and the resulting spatial pattern is very different—more sporadic or randomly clustered than is a central-place pattern—reflecting the more random location of resources. This resource type of supply area structure is most efficient only when other costs—processing costs and/or transport costs on finished products—are less than savings on transport obtained from location at the resource. These two kinds of central-place industrial patterns rep-

resent the polar forms of plant location, in which transport costs for either resources or finished product are dominant, yielding a sporadic pattern of towns in the case of resources and a regular pattern in the case of markets.

It is easiest to view the other major industrial spatial location patterns by reference to these possible conditions:

1. Both assembly and distribution may be dominant, rather than one or the other.

2. Transport costs may be balanced or outweighed by other costs, such as labor or power.

3. Labor of sufficient quality, skill, and price may be sporadically located, like resources, and rather immobile.

4. A profitable enterprise may have few, a moderate number of, or many suppliers and markets.

5. The industry may need to be located near more powerful firms, for which a specific location is more important.

Perhaps four different spatial patterns result when industries seek an optimal location. Similar or identical patterns may occur for otherwise rather unlike industries. The first two polar types, as discussed above, are the regular lattice pattern of central-place theory—call it Type A (refer to Figure 5.14)—and the cluster pattern of plants with small monopolistic resource supply areas—Type B (Figure 5.18).

If production requires, as in condition (3) above, a highly skilled and talented labor force, the industry will seek to locate in large places at the upper levels of the central-place hierarchy, which attract such skilled labor. This condition results in a spatial pattern like Type A, but because of labor immobility rather than high transport costs.

Because cheap labor, power, and taxes are sporadically located, like resources, location determined by any one of them will likewise result in a Type B spatial pattern. Here, minimization of processing costs, rather than transport costs, is the key to optimal location.

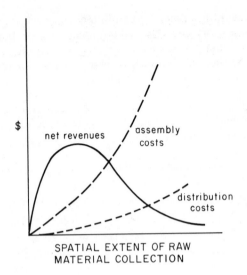

SPATIAL EXTENT OF RAW
MATERIAL COLLECTION

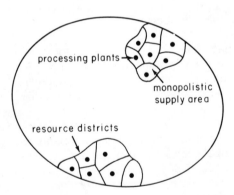

Figure 5.18 When assembly costs are very high, the zones from which plants can collect materials are limited, and each plant attempts to obtain a local monopoly supply area. On a national scale, the plants appear to be clustered because of the concentration of the resource in certain regions.

If condition (1) holds, the industry may attempt to attain a spatial monopoly for both market and supplies—as did the steel industry in Birmingham, Alabama, for example—or it may seek control over just markets or just supplies. In this case, a point

of transshipment may be desirable. This third type of pattern (Type *C*) is a kind of combination of Types *A* and *B* (see Figure 5.15A).

Finally, where processing and transport costs are somewhat balanced, where skill requirements are moderate, and, especially, where there are many suppliers and many markets—that is, where none of the polar conditions exist—then there is greater freedom in determining location, and, spatially, industries locate at random within any region rich in suppliers and markets (Type *D;* see Figure 5.15B).

EXAMPLES OF MANUFACTURING SYSTEMS

We intend here to classify and analyze the various manufacturing systems with respect to the general principles of location and not to examine in much detail the precise nature of any one industry. Looking generally at manufacturing location, we can recognize these spatial orientations:

1. Location determined by a spatially restricted and/or relatively immobile material resource with high transport costs.

2. Location of market-oriented manufacturing in accordance with the pattern of central places because of high distribution costs.

3. Location in relation to a spatial complex of specific resources and markets with both high assembly and high distribution costs.

4. Location determined by a spatially restricted and relatively immobile human resource with moderate to high labor costs.

5. Secondary location determined by less-free supplying or receiving industries.

6. Location in relation to the agglomerative advantages of the largest markets.

7. Location conditioned by spatially limited, but diffuse, sources and markets, with moderate transport and labor costs.

8. Relative freedom of location.

TOWNS AS PROCESSING CENTERS

Resource Orientation   Location near a spatially restricted material resource (1) may be alternately thought of as transport orientation, since it is the high cost of transportation that requires production at the source; this high transport cost is in turn a function of the low value per unit or high proportion of waste per unit of the raw material. Possible processing locations are dictated by the locations of such resources, but whether it is feasible to use such a resource depends on the spatial relationship among all of these resource locations.

Mining. Mining operations are a special class of this type of orientation, where the only process may be extraction of ores. The resource is typically a very impure ore, interspersed with valueless material. Extraction of the ore alone may occur, but more often some simple processing is necessary to separate the valuable from the nonvaluable material.

Processing at the mine is typically for the purpose of reducing bulk to a point where it is possible to transfer the ore. Whether this point can be reached depends on processing costs (which are partly a function of the quality of the resource), transfer rate, distance to markets and to competing sources, and overall demand and price. Those mines succeed that can operate within these restraints. In Figure 1.07 (page 12), for example, ores C and A can be sold at the market price; C is of high quality and has low processing costs, although more distant, while A is of low quality but is close to the market. Ore B, however, cannot compete because it is of such low quality that processing costs are excessive, even though its mine is moderately close. An increase in demand (price) or depletion of the sources of A and C might well change the situation, of course.

Smelting. The poorer the ore, the lower the metal content and the greater the likelihood that processing will be necessary at the mine. When metal content approaches half the ore, such as with iron ore and some bauxite, little treatment is necessary, but many ores have proportions of metal as low as one percent, and the shipping of such raw ore is not feasible. Smelting—heat processing using coal, petroleum, or gas—is indicated whenever transfer costs for the ore exceed the combined cost of smelting, fuel transport, and metal transport. Smelting is the case of extreme orientation to resources and is the kind of manufacturing most likely to be found in remote, sparsely populated, perhaps rather inhospitable regions, which, despite all this, possess the coveted ore.

Food and Wood Processing. The largest group of resource-oriented manufacturers are those who process biotic raw materials, especially agricultural and forest products. For historical and other reasons, the best forest sources are usually distant from major population centers, and much agricultural production, too, because of its space requirements, is well away from more concentrated markets. Such raw materials are also normally characterized by low transferability. They are bulky and perishable and are therefore costly to handle and ship. Often they lose much bulk or weight and become much less perishable during processing, hence increasing their transferability.

Canning and freezing plants, which frequently use riper, less transportable products, tend to be located as close as possible to the raw materials. Output per plant is rather low because each plant cannot assemble much material at the high cost of transport. Hence, processors of fruits, vegetables, sugar beets, and fish are also likely to be found in otherwise remote and less-populated areas.

Another group of food processors—meat packers, creameries, flour and feed mills—locate to a large degree in response to resources, but also must consider their ultimate markets. To reconcile these interests, the agricultural resources themselves are located as close to markets as competition permits, and processing locations are intermediate between resources and markets. In the United States, for example, the most favored locations for these processors are the "gateway"

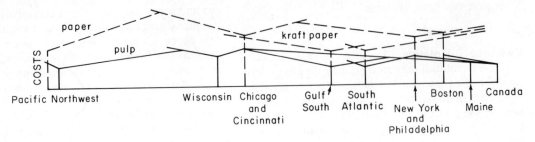

Major Pulp and Paper Locations and Zones

Figure 5.19 Spatial equilibrium of pulp and paper. This is a diagrammatic generalization of spatial competition. Only major features are depicted. Production costs (vertical lines) and transport costs (sloping lines) are shown for major locations of pulp, kraft (brown) paper, and other paper producers. Intersections of transport lines at peaks define the zones within which given producers are most competitive. Note that Chicago and New York, major paper producers, can receive pulp supplies from several sources at similar costs: Chicago from Wisconsin, Maine, and the Gulf South; New York from the South Atlantic, Maine, and Canada. Also, the Gulf South and South Atlantic produce both pulp and kraft paper.

cities, dividing rural and urban sectors of the country.

Wood processors, including sawmills, veneer–plywood makers, shingle mills, turpentine and rosin makers, and wood pulp manufacturers, are further cases where the bulk and weight lost in processing attract manufacturers to the specific resource locations (Figure 5.19). Sawmills, for example, although not very responsive to scale benefits, are sensitive to transport costs; hence, they are small and widespread. However, depletion of local resources restricts the useful life of the sawmill, and an intermediate scale of processing with larger supply zones is becoming most profitable.

Aluminum. A special kind of orientation to a costly, relatively immobile resource occurs in the "power-intensive" industries that find the lowest cost electricity sites the optimal locations. Final aluminum, magnesium, and titanium refining requires vast amounts of electricity, which is the single largest and most variable element in costs. Locations in relatively remote areas with large hydroelectric resources, such as Quebec, Norway, the Pacific Northwest, and Ghana, are common. The high

value per unit weight of aluminum justifies the extremely long shipments of the intermediate raw materials, alumina, and finished aluminum.

Central-Place Orientation Central-place manufacturing can be considered that which is extremely market-oriented because of the very high cost of final distribution. In such cases, transferability of the final product is poor, and processing often creates greater bulk or weight, increases perishability, or makes time more important.

Typical examples of such industries are the beverage industry, particularly in the bottling of soft drinks; water is obtainable everywhere, the syrup base has only a small bulk and is highly transportable, and the final product is very bulky. Other examples are the bottling of fluid milk; freshly baked soft goods, which have greater bulk and perishability than their ingredients; manufactured ice; and newspapers dealing with local affairs, for which demand is timely and spatially restricted. Much of the construction industry, especially residential building, and production of many of the materials that go into construction, such as sand and gravel, brick, concrete, and concrete block, are similarly disposed to markets.

TOWNS AS PROCESSING CENTERS

Higher Levels of Central-Place Orientation. For many industries, distribution costs are greater than assembly costs, but not so great as to limit delivery to a small area. However, in a large economy with vast distances between markets, such as the United States, the costs of distribution are sufficient to make possible somewhat protected regional markets. Many kinds of manufacturers have thus established branch plants in major regional centers. Much of the automobile industry is highly concentrated, but there are assembly plants in the large cities of major regions. The same is true of much steel, cement, petroleum, food processing, furniture, and other industries, to be discussed below.

Orientation to a Spatial Complex of Resources and Markets   For some industries, both the raw materials and the finished products exercise some control over location, generally if the costs of transport tend to exceed possible differentials in processing costs. Use of several raw materials and many markets with significant transport costs may further complicate the location problem. In such cases, there is a complex of location possibilities: an industry may locate in response to any one of the sources or markets or even choose locations between sources and markets. Rarely are the transport costs of any one raw material or finished product so great that that alone determines location. Location thus becomes essentially the point where total transfer costs are at the minimum.

Iron and Steel. The iron and steel industry is an especially basic industry because of its linkages to the fabricated metal, machinery, transport, military, hardware, and construction sectors of the economy. The industry is complex; it uses a mix of raw materials that allows for some substitution, a variable processing technology, and has considerable product differentiation as well as the above-noted variety of markets.

Material requirements for primary pig iron production in blast furnaces include coking coal, iron ore, and limestone. In the making of steel, scrap can be partially or largely substituted for pig iron, coking coal is not strictly needed, and a variety of power sources are usable. Modern techniques have greatly reduced fuel requirements. Thus, the location of steel production is freer than that of iron, although such freedom is limited by the advantages of integrated production with iron.

Historically, coal was the dominant control over iron and steel manufacturing, since it was required in the largest volumes and there was not much scrap. The optimal location was near whichever coalfields were closest to steel markets. However, as requirements for coal have been reduced to one-third what they were in the 1830s, as demand has become elaborated into more finished goods that have higher transport costs, as scrap supplies have mounted, and as nearby iron-ore supplies have been depleted, a less simple location orientation has evolved.

In the United States, when the chief ore supplies were in the Mesabi range in Minnesota, lake ports fairly close to, but not on, coalfields—such as Cleveland, Erie, Chicago, Detroit, and the intermediate Youngstown, all major industrial markets—became profitable locations (Figure 5.20). More recently, the ever-increasing demand of concentrated metropolitan markets, their great supply of scrap, and the increasing dependence of the industry on imported ore have justified expansion of steel production into coastal markets in Philadelphia and Baltimore. Steel centers have arisen in new areas, too, when demand has grown sufficiently to permit production at a scale large enough to compete with older, distant centers.

Although integrated plants producing both pig iron and finished steel products offer advantages such as fuel and transfer savings and single administration, separate production of finished steel is often profitable, particularly in regional markets, such as Houston, Los Angeles, San Francisco, and Seattle, lacking readily available coal and at a distance from large, integrated basic producers. These regional steel mills must purchase pig iron from other producers, but they can utilize much scrap; one of their great advantages is much quicker delivery.

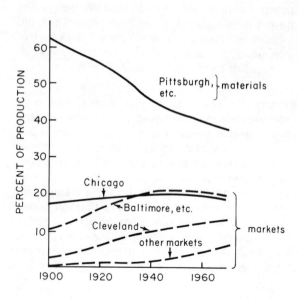

Figure 5.20 Change in location of steel production. Locations near markets have become more important for steel production over time.

petroleum. Hence, the advantages of locations near markets, while real, are not overwhelming, and with a few products of sufficiently large volume, field refineries can compete with those in markets. However, the technical development of multiproduct pipelines and tankers was necessary before oil field refinery location could become competitive.

Electric Power. Generating electricity from steam involves high costs for both transporting fuel and transmitting electricity. Transmission costs have historically been higher, and thus large plants are usually located near major markets, but technological improvements in high-voltage long-distance transmission, as well as in fuel efficiency, are beginning to permit coal, gas, and petroleum power stations to be installed up to 300 miles from the final markets. This is expected to be an important future use of much Appalachian and other coal.

In summary, the pattern of iron and steel production reflects both historical inertia in its location near coal fields and also the strong attraction of markets, which have dispersed the industry somewhat. Minimum costs can be found in many locations because distance protects markets, and there are many ways in which processing techniques and products can be substituted for each other.

Petroleum Refining. Petroleum refineries and petroleum-based chemical products are located more simply than are iron and steel mills and illustrate clearly the advantage of location at end points—the oil field, market, and certain intervening transit points. Processing of crude petroleum is efficient—there is little weight or volume loss—and the slightly higher cost of handling and shipping refined products, which are of a greater variety and more volatile, does not outweigh by too much the slightly greater bulk of the crude

Processing Cost and Amenity Orientation

Orientation to Spatially Restricted and Relatively Immobile Human Resources For industries in which the use of skilled labor constitutes a major part of the technology and adds most of the value to the products during their manufacture (4), spatial variations in the productivity and cost, skill, and scarcity of labor play a big role. Labor costs may also be important by default when transport of raw materials and products is relatively cheap. It is possible that this kind of orientation is not inherently necessary, but rather a matter of choice; some industries may choose locations with cheap labor rather than use a more automated technology that would enable them to pay higher wages.

Textile manufacturing, for example, has always been a labor-intensive industry, with a traditionally high ratio of women to men. The industry has long had some difficulty in competing for labor when other industries were present, but found it pos-

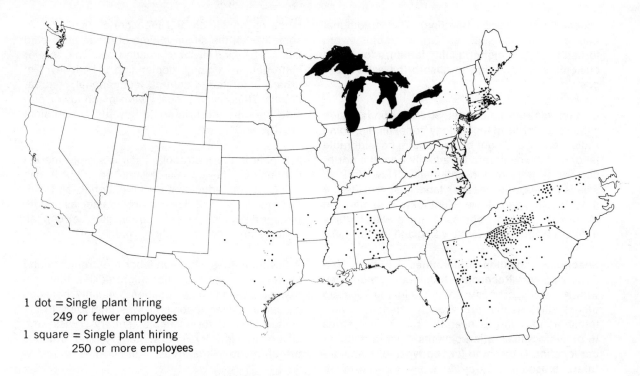

Figure 5.21 Location of textile manufacturing. An example of dispersal to clusters of small towns. (Reprinted by permission of the McGraw-Hill Book Company, Inc., from Richard S. Thoman, *Geography of Economic Activity,* 1962.)

1 dot = Single plant hiring
   249 or fewer employees

1 square = Single plant hiring
   250 or more employees

sible to survive so long as workers could be found willing to accept lower wages. Radical change in other industrial sectors thus forced radical change in the spatial pattern of textiles. In the United States, textiles were first made in New England, where capital, surplus labor, and many good water-power sites were available. Machinery, shipbuilding, and other industries began to bid up the price for labor and early welfare legislation was passed; unions developed, work stoppages were held, and many operations elected to shift their locations to clusters of small towns in the southern Piedmont, where the conditions of surplus labor were comparable to those in New England a century earlier. Other advantages of the South, especially in small towns, were lower taxes, less costly services, absence of unions, easier access to cotton supplies, no competing industries, and such factors as only moder-

ate capital and skill requirements and small necessary plant size. Certain segments of the textile industry resisted the shift, mostly those which required more highly skilled labor, which were hesitant to move, or which could continue to use immigrant and minority groups at lower wages; such segments included some finishing, finer woolens, printing, carpetry, and some knitwear (see Figure 5.21).

Furniture and luggage manufactures illustrate well the conflict between markets, sources, and locations with lower labor or processing costs, The early furniture industry was located in relation to the labor supply and the hardwoods of southern New England and the Michigan–Ohio region. As with the textile industry, competition for labor, superior southern hardwood sources, and similar factors led to a partial relocation of the industry, especially to North Carolina. The traditional northern centers, such as Grand Rapids, were forced to shift to higher quality furniture for which customers were willing to absorb the extra labor costs.

Certain mass-produced electronic goods made with a standardized technology, for example, some radios, parts, and light bulbs, require considerable labor and have migrated gradually from the northeastern centers of innovation like New York to smaller cities with cheaper labor just outside the industrial core—in Iowa, Kentucky, Virginia, and Minnesota—and to depressed areas with surplus industrial labor, such as New England in the 1950s.

Secondary Location Determined by Less-Free Supplying or Receiving Industries Industries with low transport costs and technical linkages to other industries that are strongly oriented toward transport may locate near the related industries to obtain agglomeration benefits. Such a dependent location is common for two types of manufacturers: those using by-products and those who are small suppliers to larger industries. Many chemical concerns use by-products of iron and steel mills and petroleum refineries. Tin-can and other container companies are located where they best can supply the less flexible food-processing industry. Special-machinery manufacturing tends to be located in areas where the machinery is used; for instance, drilling equipment is made in Los Angeles and Houston. Aircraft components are produced in major airframe centers, and the very large auto-parts industry locates in a wide region around Detroit.

Location Determined by the Agglomerative Advantages of the Largest Markets Many industries characterized by fairly high labor costs, high prices, and high value added during production are powerfully attracted to the largest metropolises and their satellite suburbs. Transport costs are not important in these cases, and markets may be somewhat diffuse even if located in mainly metropolitan areas. The higher labor costs are a function of higher skill and education requirements, the significance of research, the impor-

tance of innovation and managerial skill, and, in some cases, the sheer volume of moderately paid labor. The kind of labor needed also may prefer metropolitan regions, demanding a high level of urban amenities (cultural, educational, recreational). Thus, even if costs were much lower outside the city, the firm could not attract sufficient quality labor.

Not only is the metropolis itself a sizable market containing a large, flexible labor pool, but it also has superior educational, recreational, and cultural facilities, and, for the firm, easier access to transport (including more frequent service), capital, advertising, communication, and other services.

A few industries with high labor requirements and moderate wages have not migrated but have remained in traditional locations, usually because a special skilled labor pool was immobile. In the United States, for example, cutlery, brassware, silverware, jewelry, fine stationery, and watches are all made in the areas of the earliest industry.

The apparel industry traditionally consists of small-scale enterprises with limited ranges of products, usually having under 50 employees (in the United States), and showing extreme metropolitan concentration and inertia. In the United States over 40 percent of all clothes are made in New York City, notably within a small area of Manhattan; Moscow, Paris, and London are similarly dominant in their countries. The largest cities have the greatest pool of skilled workers who will accept only moderate wages—especially women and recent immigrants. In addition, the marketing and distribution advantages of a large metropolis are strong incentives for this industry, which depends much on publicity—most easily disseminated from the largest city—and fashion—a product of the concentration of the wealthiest and most important segment of society in a national capital.

The publishing and printing industries (except for local newspapers) similarly reap special benefits by locating in a cultural capital and hence also are placed in New York City, London, Paris, and Moscow. The relative immobility of printers within the apprenticeship structure of their union also plays a role, and transport privileges, such as low mailing rates for books, make great centralization possible. Thus, general book publishers and high-quality periodicals needing centralized or even cooperative distribution are concentrated in New York. Mass publishing of very high volume material, such as Bibles, telephone books, mail-order catalogs, and mass-circulation magazines, are published in more central locations such as Chicago.

Complex Orientation

Interindustry Orientation The largest group of manufacturers in the most advanced countries makes machinery, transport, and communications equipment, and other elaborated products. Using a variety of simpler manufactured inputs, especially formed steel, and shipping to a fairly wide market composed of other industries (such as machine tools) or even the entire national market (such as autos), they are not tied to one particular source or market by transport costs, time requirements, or labor cost advantages and thus possess a limited freedom of choice: they can locate within a set of sources and markets that often have the same boundaries as the urban industrial core of the economy. The quality within the region of transport position, labor pools, relationships to other industries and competitors, and benefits of agglomeration will influence the optimum site for the long run, as well as the locations chosen.

Motor Vehicles. The automobile is the single most valuable product and the largest user of steel, rubber, and glass in several advanced countries, especially the United States. As producers of a highly mobile and widely desired good, location at or near the center of the transport and industrial net would be optimal. In the United States, Chicago would probably be best if the industry did not yet exist, but Detroit and its environs, which are not too far away, was just as good a

location when the industry developed 50 years ago and the greater market was near the Atlantic seaboard. Carriage manufacturers, boat-engine makers, a wood supply, and a skilled labor force were located here. In Detroit, also, the market was divided between the wealthy East and the developing West. Finally, in Detroit were the entrepreneurs who succeeded in defeating competitors in New York, Philadelphia, Chicago, and elsewhere who also produced early cars. The decision of some Detroit builders to standardize and mass-produce vehicles was perhaps crucial. In any event, once it was powerfully established, Detroit's advantages of agglomeration and experience overwhelmed any transport or labor advantage of other cities. Detroit today remains very well-located with respect to inputs, although not quite so well with regard to final markets. Population shifts and the increasing costs of final distribution have led to a partial dispersal of body making and final-assembly operations to serve distinct regional markets.

Related industries are not far removed from Detroit. Parts suppliers in the United States are scattered throughout Michigan, Indiana, and Ohio. Glass production is concentrated in the nearby Toledo, Ohio, area, rubber tires in the Akron, Ohio, area. The rubber industry, which requires large coal inputs, located near to the eastern Ohio coal fields and also according to the preference of the early inventors; it is in addition reasonably close to Detroit.

Machinery. Machinery industries, both general and electrical, are very large and are basic to increasing the productivity of society. They consume much steel and other materials and add a high value during manufacture. A great variety of industries depend on their products, from primary producers such as smelters to the most consumer-oriented ones. Hence, it is difficult to speak of them as a group; their markets are diffuse and spread throughout the industrial core. Distribution costs on finished products are higher than on raw materials, but there are many customers, and a plant seeks to locate at their center. Electrical machinery is more dominant on the Atlantic seaboard, nonelectrical machinery, oriented to the automotive industries, in the central parts of the industrial belt, and agricultural and processing machinery at the western end. Almost all northeastern metropolises are strongly represented in machinery production, and the industry dominates many smaller and intermediate-sized cities as well.

Subdistrict specialties arose out of early inventions and spin-offs, and include the machine-tool industry centered around Cincinnati, the turbines and generators made near Milwaukee and Chicago, the textile machinery made in New England, paper machinery in Wisconsin and New York, mining equipment in Minneapolis, and printing machinery in New York.

Freedom of Location True freedom in choosing location is in fact nonexistent, although there are a few small specialty manufacturers in small, remote places who survive by the uniqueness of their brands and by employee loyalty. Large industries with powerful governmental influence, notably aircraft, ordnance, and missile and rocket development, may also be in peculiar locations,

partly out of security requirements and partly out of the half-conscious federal desire to spread wealth to some of the less-developed parts of the country or to aid politically powerful, but economically weak, peripheral areas.

The aircraft industry has always depended on rapid technological improvement, much at military instigation, for its growth. In its early days, locations were most common near spruce forests, such as in Michigan or the Pacific Northwest, and near large cities. Because of the good climate for experimentation and pleasure, the industry also grew rapidly in Los Angeles. Based on these early enterpreneurs and World War I contracts, some dominant locations were set: Los Angeles, Seattle, Hartford, St. Louis. Although transport costs are trivial (and hence the industry is called "footloose"), the need for large bodies of skilled labor enables established centers to remain dominant and metropolitan locations to be sites for future expansion. Only governmental pressure imposed in World War II created new centers at Wichita, Kansas; Marietta, Georgia; and Fort Worth, Texas.

Part Four

Spatial Interaction

6

Transportation and Trade

IMPORTANCE OF TRADE AND TRANSPORTATION

Movements—economic and social, of goods and of people, by means ranging from walking to telecommunication—make possible the specialization of location we have studied thus far. Even though a location may be defined mainly from its special character, that character may be most clearly understood not by the innate qualities of the location, but by its relations with other locations. Since almost nothing is consumed where it is produced, the pattern of interaction may be the key to the ability of a location to exist.

The goals of spatial organization should determine the optimum structure of movement. On the one hand, man desires to minimize distance and the cost of movement, but, on the other, he wishes to maximize the value of individual locations; the wealth generated by increasing the value of each location can justify fairly high levels of trade.

For instance, while a producer at a given location wishes to minimize the proportion of his revenues

that are needed for transport, society and the provider of the transport consider transport charges payments for services rendered, an alternate form of production, and thus values to be maximized. Also, since without transport the goods made at the location would be worthless, part of the value of the product must be attributed to the transport. It is thus incorrect to look on transport costs as a constraint to productivity; rather, the presence of transport services and the willingness of producers to use them make possible the high productivity resulting from specializing in a location. Society wishes to maximize the total value of production and transport services, and this goal at times requires more, and at times requires less, investment in transport.

Improvements in means of transport have made possible significant advancement of civilizations and have created major changes in patterns of human life—for instance, making control and exchange possible over wider areas and thus allowing more elaborate social structures to exist. The first Phoenician ship innovations made possible long-distance movement of goods and people and the maintenance of distant supply lines, and thus

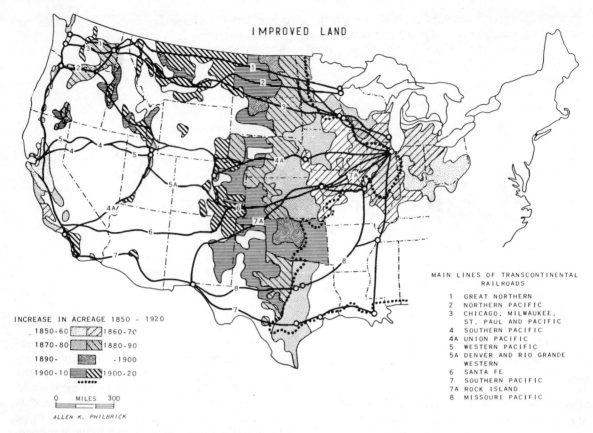

IMPROVED LAND

INCREASE IN ACREAGE 1850 - 1920

1850-60   1860-70
1870-80   1880-90
1890-   -1900
1900-10   1900-20

0   MILES   300

ALLEN K. PHILBRICK

MAIN LINES OF TRANSCONTINENTAL
RAILROADS

1   GREAT NORTHERN
2   NORTHERN PACIFIC
3   CHICAGO, MILWAUKEE,
     ST. PAUL AND PACIFIC
4   SOUTHERN PACIFIC
4A   UNION PACIFIC
5   WESTERN PACIFIC
5A   DENVER AND RIO GRANDE
     WESTERN
6   SANTA FE
7   SOUTHERN PACIFIC
7A   ROCK ISLAND
8   MISSOURI PACIFIC

Figure 6.01 Transport and land development. Opening of land for agricultural settlement accompanies the extension of the western railroads. (Reprinted by permission of John Wiley & Sons, Inc., from Allen K. Philbrick, *This Human World,* 1963.)

freedom to live away from a self-sufficient local area. Investment in road networks made possible the unity of the far-flung Roman Empire, and the deterioration of the roads in the Middle Ages reduced economic and social exchange. The railroad, by drastically reducing the cost and improving the speed of land transport, eased the development of interior resources and farming areas, especially in North America (Figure 6.01), Central Europe, and Russia. The car and truck, creating a demand for improved highways, made a wider and more diffuse area more accessible and reduced rural and urban cultural distinctions. The airplane and the radical improvements which have

been made in it—spurred by military necessity— have truly created "one world" in the geographic sense because no location—however primitive—is more than a few hours away from any other.

More important than these effects, perhaps, is the relation between better transport and improvements in productivity and living standards. By permitting specialization, improvement in transport leads to increased land and labor productivity and more efficient use of capital; costs of increased trade over greater distances have consistently been lower than the increases in productivity realized through specialization. As nations

TRANSPORTATION AND TRADE

or groups within a nation become willing to abandon self-sufficiency and more completely exchange their specialties, trade, wealth, and income rise rapidly.

Factors Influencing Trade

Trade is generated when transport cost and time become low enough that local specialization is possible. Most simply, the location of specialized production, the spatial separation that this specialization implies, the cost of overcoming this separation, and the demand for the goods so produced control the extent of trade. Production costs at locations dictate the amount of savings or additional wealth that scale and specialization will generate and thus determine how far apart related activities may be. Specialization and trade may increase so long as the production-cost savings exceed the increase in transport costs. For some activities, diseconomies occur at moderate scale, concentration is limited, and the optimum shipments are very short—even within the plant, for example—but for other activities, almost total concentration of production at a few locations is economic.

THE COST OF DISTANCE

The economic or social cost of the distance between locations which wish to interact is the fundamental determinant of spatial structure. Spatial structure as such could not exist without such costs, because any differentiation between areas would depend on inherent variations in the land and its owner.

Because distance as a direct barrier has been reduced, it has become popular to dismiss it. But with such progress, the indirect role played by distance has become greater. For example, the industries which have minute transport costs are tied to the large metropolises because the appropriate labor and management is immobile; distance separation obviously does matter. Vast public and private investments have been made to reduce the costs of distance, but even in areas that have the best transport, the volume of flows of goods and people drops rapidly with distance.

Measuring distance is, however, not easy. Its cost to movement and interaction may be expressed in at least these ways:

1. Geodesic distance—the physical mileage between two points.

2. The time needed to cover the distance via the given mode of transport.

3. Transport costs—the actual quoted rates or real incurred costs.

4. Psychological or social distance—interpreted by individuals.

5. Combinations of the above—for example, weighing both cost and time.

Although the impact of distance may be best expressed by a substitute such as time or transport costs, it is still the fact of spatial separation that underlies its effect.

Geodesic distance, the length measured as we walk or drive, is the most familiar measure of distance and plays a constant role in the average person's life—going to work, to the store, or to recreation. Yet, whether we consciously realize it or not, we may measure such distance by subtly transforming it to its costs in time; when we say we are willing to go only so many miles, what we may mean is that we are willing to be gone only so long. Existing central-place systems seem to show that changes in the speed of covering a distance is a factor that can alter the threshold of entry to the market and thus the success of places.

Movements of people, such as the journey to work, are more affected by time costs than are movements of goods, but the growth of air freight and innovations in freight handling installed by railroads illustrate that time is becoming at least

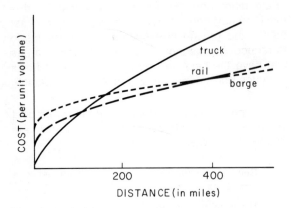

Figure 6.02 Carrier competition. Generally, there is a direct relationship between the capacity of a carrier and the distances at which it is most competitive.

tively, terminal and haulage costs could be expressed separately. However, many fixed costs are difficult to allocate to individual shipments, and the carrier frequently prefers to undercharge its very close and very far customers. Thus, the railroad, for instance, uses its middle-distance shipments—which are most competitive against other carriers—to subsidize competition at close range against truckers and at long distance against water and air movements (see Figure 6.02).

A characteristic of carriers in some countries, such as railroads in the United States, is quotations of rates by blocks of distance (so that they form a stair-step function—see Figure 5.09 again). This permits rates to be standardized so that only a finite number of rates exist.

The relation of transport rates to distance may vary from area to area because of differences in:

1.   Operating costs, due to such factors as topography, volume over routes, and characteristics of goods.

2.   Degree of monopoly control or effect of government regulation and rate-setting policies (Figure 6.03).

3.   The characteristics of carriers.

Topography has a strong influence on the cost of movement—initially, because of the high costs of construction and maintenance in mountainous and swampy areas, and, later, because over-the-road operating costs increase rapidly as gradients and curvatures increase. Rugged topography also incurs indirect costs because the speed of transport is slower. Natural barriers may impose costs (such as tolls on bridges) and thus, in effect, increase distance, although this is usually justified by comparing these costs to those of more roundabout routes.

Rate levels naturally vary by the kind of goods carried as well. Goods requiring refrigeration, special handling, or packaging incur greater costs

somewhat important to shippers, especially as the costs of holding inventories rise.

We may also modify "real distance" by our social and aesthetic perceptions; we may consider areas we don't like farther away, for instance, and perceived distance to shopping centers may be affected by our ability to pay and our image of the center's quality. Thus, the effective distance between areas of different economic or social status may be quite unlike the geographic distance.

For movements of most goods, the role of distance is best expressed by transport costs, since any business operation recognizes these costs explicitly. Transport costs represent either an increase in price to the buyer or a decrease in realized price to the seller, depending on who must absorb the costs.

The relation of transport costs to distance is fairly well known; the rate per mile decreases exponentially as distance increases, because terminal costs are included in the transport rate. Thus, total costs of transport increase more slowly as distance increases (refer to Figure 5.09). Alterna-

and bear higher rates. Shipments of less than standard-carrier size, especially those making up less than a railroad carload or full truckload, have many extra handling costs and are charged much higher rates. Carriers, with the agreement of the government, frequently exaggerate these differences by overcharging finished goods, even to the point of subsidizing some shipments of bulk raw materials.

Unit costs may be set lower where volume is great (see Figure 6.04). Economies of scale affect transport costs in two ways: individual shipments may be of large size or repeated shipments may reduce carrier overhead and result in lower rates; or a large volume carried over a particular route or to and from particular centers may raise the efficiency of shipments.

Also, where carrier competition to a particular place is keen, rates may be forced down and the difference made up by high prices on routes where the carrier has a monopoly. Governments generally attempt to prevent such high rates by determining prices that yield fair returns, but the rigidity of this method often produces inequities.

Error in the Interpretation of Distance

The cost of distance may be incorrectly or only hazily measured by individuals and firms. Even where there is an attempt to minimize distance and transport costs, errors in measurement are common and often result in suboptimal movements of goods. For example, a distributor may assume a freeway is the better route in a situation actually more suited to delivery via arterials. More commonly, shippers are uncertain about the exact amount of transport costs or have a tendency to see a range of distances or quoted rates as having essentially equivalent costs. Their failure to appreciate these fine distinctions in costs causes some unpredictable patterns of location and shipping.

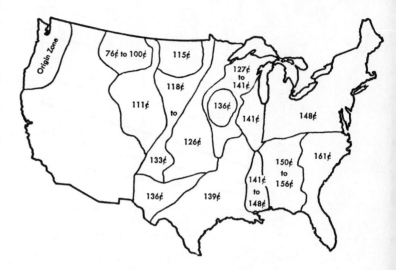

Figure 6.03 Transport rates for lumber (cost per 1,000 feet) from the Pacific Northwest. Rates increase with distance at a decreasing rate, but there are seeming anomalies due to government regulation (low rates in the Northeast) and competition (high rates in the Southeast). (Reprinted by permission of the Houghton Mifflin Company, from R.J. Sampson and M.T. Farris, *Domestic Transportation,* 1966.)

TRANSPORT SYSTEMS

Theoretical Transport Networks

Location of the Single Route Building a link between places is justified if, directly or indirectly, the cost of construction is repaid by the enhanced productivity of the places after trade is established between them. It may be optimal for the routes to depart from the straight line between the two points under certain conditions:

1. If the revenue and productivity gained by linking intervening places to the system offset the increased costs of transportation, congestion, and time loss (Figure 6.05).

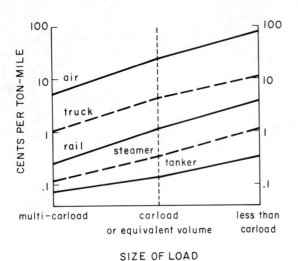

Figure 6.04 Over–the–road transport costs by carrier and volume. Not only do larger capacity carriers enjoy lower over–the–road costs, but for each carrier, costs are much lower if more units (trucks, railcars, ships) are assigned to a single shipment.

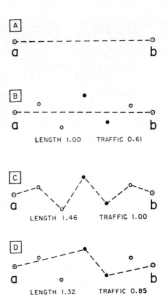

Figure 6.05 Deviation of transport routes for additional revenue. If only places a and b existed, a direct route would clearly be best. With other towns between (solid dots are larger places), the route may remain direct (with the shortest length and least traffic), deviate fully (the longest route with most traffic), or deviate to the largest places only. Deviation is justified if traffic (revenues) increases more than length (cost), as it does in D. (Reprinted courtesy of Edward Arnold [Publishers] Ltd., London, from Peter Haggett, *Locational Analysis in Human Geography,* 1965.)

2. If the costs of construction and maintenance over a longer route in easier topography are small enough to offset the increased distance of the route (Figure 6.06).

Transport costs may actually be lower on the longer route because the gradients will be less steep.

Theoretical Networks Location theory seeks to minimize distance traveled while allowing required interactions to be completed and maximizing the productivity of each location. Each movement is assumed to take place over the path of least cost available to it, subject to competition by other movements wishing to take the same route. It is also assumed that there is a rather complete transport network containing competing modes of travel, although movement associated with any particular activity, given the specialization of loca-

tions, should be concentrated on only a small portion of the system.

Agricultural location theory involves minimizing the costs of transporting produce to a central market. Transport costs in relation to market value probably do not change very much from regions near the center to those in the periphery; the attempt to keep this proportion stable results in competitive bidding for land and thus the agricultural gradient.

Agricultural gradient theory alone suggests a transport system that is completely center-oriented, radiating outward from the market. Decreasing fineness of the net will reflect the

Louisiana ROADWAYS

0   25   50

miles

Figure 6.06 Louisiana roads closely reflect local topography. The roads are rectangular in level areas, more complex in rolling areas, and absent from marshy areas along the coast and in the Mississippi delta, where construction is difficult. (Courtesy of the Louisiana Department of Highways.)

increasing size of farms and the greater distance between them. No crosslinks will be required, since all transport is to the market. The object is to construct the smallest network required to both provide complete access to all agricultural production and to minimize the mileage of the higher capacity segments, which are much costlier. Figure 6.07A represents a preliminary attempt to depict such an ideal branching system, but this scheme may be far from being the optimum one. Strictly minimizing distance requires a curved and continually branching system (Figure 6.07B), but society places a value on *straight,* direct routes and perceives the costs of indirectness as high enough to justify the slightly longer but more linear system shown in Figure 6.07A.

Central-place theory is based on minimizing the costs of distributing goods to consumers and of collecting goods from dispersed producers. Central-place theory requires a system oriented to many centers on several levels (Figure 6.08). Major roads and flows connect the largest places; lesser roads serve smaller places; and the pattern of transport mirrors the pattern of central places. In pure theory, settlement is homogeneous, and the central-place transport pattern is thus strictly regular, except that volume of transport and quality of the route reflect the level of the places connected. The central-place pattern according to the transportation principle (shown in Figures 4.05 and 4.06) is most efficient because the roads connecting two larger places pass through places of

A. A Branching Network(partial detail; continues outward)

B. A Continually Branching Network

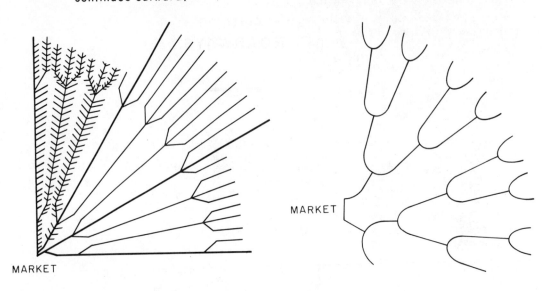

MARKET

MARKET

Figure 6.07 A and B represent two possible networks designed to move produce to a central market. B extends to points closest to individual farmers at the least distance to the market, but A may be more realistic because of preferences for straighter and more direct roads.

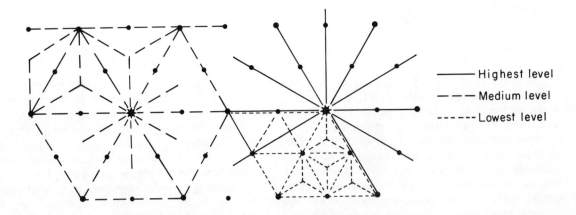

———— Highest level

– – – – Medium level

- - - - Lowest level

Figure 6.08 Flows in a central-place system mirror the geometric arrangement of places. The more important routes and flows converge on the largest (highest level) place (star) from equally large places outside the area (not shown). Medium volume flows and quality routes serve and connect the places of next lower order (large dots, left part of diagram), and local routes and small flows serve the smallest places. More important routes carry local traffic, too, of course.

TRANSPORTATION AND TRADE

the next lower order. Again, the mileage of the high-capacity, costlier segments is minimized; efficiency is increased by concentrating transport flows of large volume on major routes and restricting most small flows to local collection and delivery.

Agricultural gradients and central-place systems must be considered simultaneously to obtain even partial reality. What will the transport network for such a joint surface look like? Figure 6.09 is a first attempt at showing the ideal composite transport net. Essentially, the net is formed by linking laterally at intersections—defining these as central-place locations or smaller markets—the branches radiating from a large agricultural market and also by directing local and regional routes toward nearest central places.

Industrial location theory involves jointly minimizing the transport costs of assembling materials and of shipping products, although the importance of transport costs as a determinant of location varies widely. For some industries, such as sawmills or food processing, raw materials are collected from local areas over small-volume transport routes, and for others, such as urban newspapers, distribution is similarly local and small-scale. For the majority of industries, however, interindustry dependence means a pattern of fewer, larger flows, forming a shipping equilibrium that depends on the relative location of suppliers, producers, and markets.

Specific patterns of industrial location might not alter the basic structure shown in Figure 6.09, but they would tend to destroy its symmetry by creating regional variations in density, such as clusters of strongly linked plants that require particularly strong lateral connections not otherwise needed. Because industrial flows are generally large and less diffuse, transport may be more efficient and also cheaper per unit shipped than for movements of agricultural or central-place products.

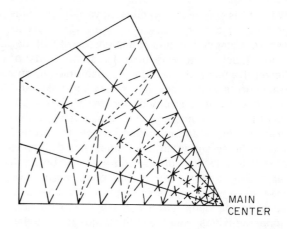

MAIN CENTER

Figure 6.09 Transport network on a joint agricultural gradient–central–place hierarchy surface. This figure shows a possible transport network to serve a landscape in which a central-place system is imposed on an agricultural (and population) density gradient. The wide solid lines are most important, wide broken lines next most important, thin solid lines next, and thin broken lines least important. See also Figure 9.01.

Evaluating the Transport Network

The amount of movement that may profitably flow on a given route depends greatly on the quality of the transport net. Components of the quality of a route include:

1. The relative characteristics of the transport modes available—carrier capacity, cost, frequency of service, and speed, for instance.

2. The vehicular capacity of the routes.

3. Connectivity—how directly places are connected.

4. Fineness—accessibility to local shippers.

5. Specific technical quality—surface, curvature, and gradient.

6. Stress—the likelihood that certain routes will be overused.

7. Density—route mileage per unit area.

Where it is physically practical, a variety of transport systems over a given route are desirable to assure competition and complementarity of demand (each system is best for some kinds of flows). Demand for transport is also uneven, and transport systems develop stress on links and nodes where topography or accidents of development limit route choice. Thus, roads converge on crucial bridges and mountain passes and around barrier lakes and mountain ranges. Congestion is most likely to develop in such areas or between large neighboring centers. This congestion, however, usually occurs at limited peak traffic periods, such as the daily journey to work, and for seasonal activities, such as beach-going. Queuing analysis can help in finding a capacity that will prevent all but small, acceptable congestion. A capacity adequate for the worst traffic would be extremely excessive most of the time and thus be an inefficient use of capital resources; the cost of providing the capacity for peak demand must be balanced against the costs of congestion, time loss, and deterioration of the system from overuse.

Directness measures the quality of the connections between places, and, again, the savings from avoiding probable congestion and time loss via indirect routings must be balanced against the costs of providing direct connections. A relatively high level of connectivity implies that the economy is advanced and can afford high-priority bypass links around intervening places.

The fineness of the net refers to its most local portion—its access to farms, homes, forests, and mines. Investment in such local access is costly because of the immense mileage involved, but inadequate access may cost even more by lowering productivity.

Since transport networks develop gradually over time out from areas of greatest development, they commonly exhibit certain problems arising over time. As technology improves, transport networks are subject to obsolescence—excessive curvature or inadequate capacity. Network analysis can reveal congested and circuitous links between places for which improvement is justified—such

as on a route between two cities that have strongly linked industries and poor transport between them.

Transport systems can also be analyzed to identify redundancy—overinvested links where revenues do not cover the costs of maintenance and handling traffic. For example, the least efficient 30 percent of America's railway mileage carries only two percent of the traffic. Such redundancy may result from a shift in transport mode to competitors or from technological responses to scale that make obsolete the too-fine network of an earlier era. In the United States, with its commitment to the private car and large public revenues for roads, there is some risk that roads would be over-extended if alternate investments were to yield greater returns.

The spatial allocation of transport routes has dramatic effects on development. Investment in major through-transport to the neglect of routes for local access risks unproductive agriculture and the depopulation and relative decline of most smaller places, while the reverse situation may foster inefficient regionalism accompanied by insufficient national specialization and trade (Figure 6.10).

Transport systems both compete with and complement one another. Each has an exclusive province where the others don't compete—ships cross the oceans and major lakes; the rails serve great mineral deposits; roads provide local access and major routes where the amount of traffic won't justify building a railroad; pipelines move bulk amounts of liquid and gas materials; air serves remote outposts unreachable by other means and allows people to rapidly communicate.

Water transport was the first fairly efficient form of transport. Today, water transport has great capacity, ranging from river barges with from 10 to 100 times the capacity of a rail carload to the giant bulk petroleum carriers that can carry 200,000 tons of crude oil. Where shiploads are made up of bulk products, and special loading and unloading techniques are available, the efficiency of water transport is unchallenged; costs may often fall below one-tenth of a cent per ton-

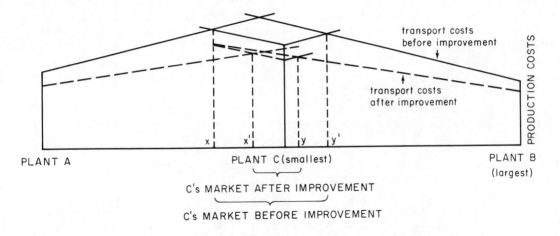

Figure 6.10 Impact of improvement in transport. Suppose that plants A, B, and C are located along a transport route. The size of the market of each is determined by the point where delivered costs from any two plants are equal. Before improvement, delivered costs are equal at points X and Y. After the route is improved, costs are equal at X′ and Y′, and A and B are able to expand their markets at the expense of C because of their larger size and lower costs.

mile. However, the costs of handling for general cargoes of mixed goods are rather high, even though the actual costs of transport are low. Water transport is also very slow and hampered by storms, ice, and—most important—the very limited location or origins and destinations on water.

Many canals, and even roads for a while, were rendered obsolete by the development of the rail-road. Rail transport has intermediate capacity (20 to 100 tons), terminal costs, and over-the-road costs. For multi-carload shipments of goods over medium distances, especially if the shipments are between plants or warehouses and no change in mode of transport is required, efficiency is high. The greater the number of train cars between a single origin and destination, the cheaper the rate and the quicker the trip; a train made up of cars with many destinations must be divided at major junctions (classification yards) and reconstituted.

Figure 6.11 shows the railroad network in the United States. The great concentration of mileage in the Northeast and Midwest reflects both the richness of agricultural and mineral resources and the historical economic dominance of the regions.

Trucks typically have a lower capacity than do railroad cars, ranging from 1 to 20 tons, and they cannot be linked into trains. Thus, handling costs for large volumes are high, but for truckload volumes are lower than competing carriers costs. Because of truck design and operating characteristics, trucks also have a competitive advantage for lighter, bulkier goods. Their greatest advantage, however, is that they make door-to-door delivery possible with no change in transport mode; the railroad network is skeletal and does not serve many good production sites, while motor vehicles can travel on the much finer road network. Thus, great savings in cost and time are often possible.

On the other hand, however, in spite of many subsidies, the over-the-road costs of trucks are high. Piggyback movements of trucks—where fully loaded truck-trailers are carried on railroad flat-cars for long hauls—represent efficient coopera-

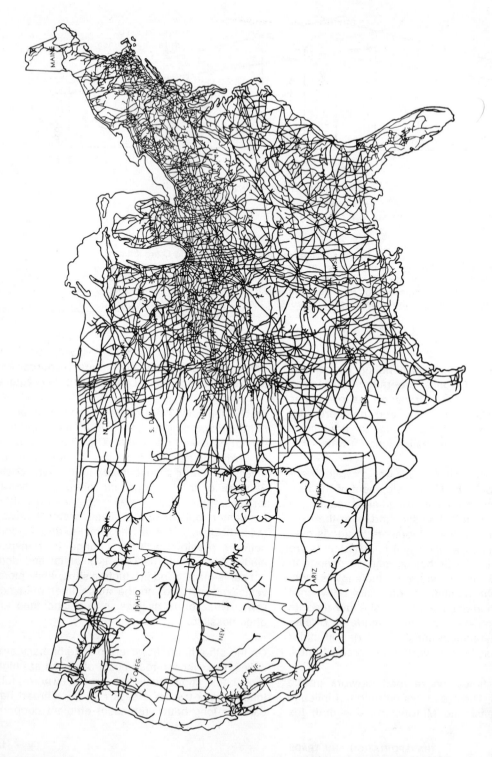

Figure 6.11 Pattern of railways in the United States, 1965. Note the concentration of routes in the rich agricultural Midwest and industrial Northeast, the gaps in hilly areas, and the sparseness in the low density West. (Reprinted by permission of the Association of American Railroads.)

tion between the two systems, minimizing the costs of both haulage and shifting transport modes and using the advantages of both systems.

Pipelines cost almost as little as water transport and have a high capacity besides. One technical advantage is their ability to traverse far steeper gradients than can other media; other advantages include low labor requirements, use of the pipe itself as storage, low haulage costs, and no necessity for a shift in transport mode. However, present pipelines are extremely slow—only three to five miles per hour—and time is becoming more valuable to firms and individuals.

Aircraft have the greatest freedom of movement and far superior speed, but they are limited by the costly equipment needed, restricted airfield location, small capacity, and, thus, high transport rates.

Electric-power transmission is a major source of energy transfer, competing directly with rail and water transport of fuels. Substituting electric power for coal and oil permits some industries to locate away from railways, and long-distance transmission means that remote hydroelectric resources can be developed and perhaps that some low-grade coal can be used without actually moving the coal. Transmission costs are high and usually exceed the cost of shipping and using fuels for power after about 300 miles.

Figure 1.08 indicated the inverse relationship of rates of speed and time needed for transport, and Figure 6.02 showed the direct, if variable, relation of rates to distance. Water transport is preferred for low-value bulk commodities with no time pressure; these commodities move by rail in areas where water routes are not available. Rails have a theoretical advantage for carrying manufactured goods shipped in lots of at least one carload with moderate time leeway. Road transport via trucks is best for products sent local to medium distances or over long, low-volume routes, for collection of farm products and final distribution to retailers, and for local interindustry transfers. Air transport has an advantage only in time.

Government preferences play a role in the choice of carrier. In the United States railroads are presently at a disadvantage; they have little political "pull" compared with the automobile–petroleum industries and the car-driving public. Government support for individual car owners also indirectly provides a sizable subsidy to the trucking industry by supplying exceptional roads, enabling truckers to capture much of the long-haul bulk commodity business perhaps technically better handled by rail. In other countries with state-owned railways, the opposite bias is often apparent.

Development of Transport Systems

Historically, transport network growth has both reflected and induced settlement, industrialization, and urbanization (Figure 6.12). In long-settled countries dominated by self-sufficient local economies, transport tends to be a complex, poor, but fine network, consisting of partially joined local roads and possibly a few military highways linking the capital to the provinces. With industrialization, penetration lines, usually using rail transport, are built from the earliest point of growth (usually the capital or major port) to the peripheral areas that supply agricultural products and other resources. Processing industries may in turn diffuse outward, and local feeders or access roads may develop for agricultural production. Lines of penetration extend farther, often connecting the major national centers, and industrialization spreads in a leap to these centers. The pattern then proceeds from multiple origins. Even before adequate transport covers the entire territory of the nation, intensive development near the origin demands replacement of the original penetration lines by higher quality, faster links.

A transport network has the ostensible short-run purpose of facilitating movement, but its fundamental long-run effect is to modify location itself; while many transport links are built in response to existing demand, fairly arbitrary decisions on penetration routes frequently may determine the location of future settlements.

ACHIEVING A BALANCE BETWEEN LOCAL SPECIALIZATION AND REGIONAL SELF-SUFFICIENCY

Selectively abandoning local self-sufficiency in favor of greater specialization while continuing to increase trade has traditionally been the direction of greatest efficiency, productivity, and wealth. Certainly, one may observe that lack of transport in many regions prevents the efficient use of resources (i.e., the realization of a comparative advantage in a specialty). Trade does cost money, as does transport improvement, but the overriding benefits of specializing in areas follow from variations in inherent natural productivity (such as differences between agricultural and forest land) and in man-made productivity (such as superior and inferior positions on the transport net), and from the realization of economies of scale and agglomeration. A dramatic long-run effect of specialization has been the geographic concentration of economic activity in a few favored sites and areas, notably large urban centers.

Are there limits to specialization? Is there any economic or geographic rationale for greater autarky—self-sufficiency of regions? The well-known risks of specialization are military and environmental; dependence on distant sources for strategic materials might be serious if enemies could sever those links, and concentrating the growth of an agricultural product in one location may cause serious shortages if weather conditions are too variable. Spatial concentration, along with industrial concentration, also increases the risk of control by a monopoly. The location may be efficient, but if monopoly pricing exists, it becomes more difficult to be certain.

One crucial test of specialization, however, is whether it tends to maximize short-run efficiency while not recognizing long-run suboptimality. For instance, it is extremely difficult and far too risky for a small firm to establish in advance whether a location that provides greater self-sufficiency will be more profitable in the long run. In 1800, as an example, it was more efficient in the short run for

the United States to buy manufactured goods from England than to produce them locally, but in the long run protection of infant industries at home was justified. In the USSR, also, construction of new "bases of industry" in Siberia involved costly subsidies at first, but the new industries have since become immensely profitable.

MODELS OF TRADE

The principal models of trade movements include the following:

1. International-trade or comparative advantage models.
2. Spatial equilibrium or transportation models.
3. Descriptive input-output matrices.
4. Interaction constructs.

The last model will be discussed in the following chapter (p. 135–152). The comparative advantage model is the most comprehensive in that location of production and trade are determined simultaneously, but this has been achieved so far only by using untenable assumptions. Input-output analysis is the most realistic description. The transportation equilibrium models are the most satisfactory both theoretically and practically and also possess great flexibility, but they, too, do not satisfactorily fuse location and trade theory.

The Comparative Advantage Model

This was originally an international trade model and includes several countries and several commodities. It is nonspatial. It assumes that the available supplies of productive agents—essentially labor—are known for each country and that the productivity of labor with respect to all goods is known—that is, the labor required per unit of output for each product is known. The proportion that each good provides of the total value of production is also known for each country. The problem, then, is to find the output of each good in each country, in that way determining the trade among countries and the net prices of goods that will use labor most fully and achieve the greatest production value. The model quantifies the concept of comparative advantage, and its solutions give both the optimum location and the optimum production volume of many goods in many countries, as well as the ideal levels of trade.

However, the model is limited in many ways. It assumes that labor can be completely substituted among goods; no limits on production except those set by regional labor supplies are admitted. The assumption that prices and consumption patterns are everywhere the same is unrealistic; in particular, transport costs are not included. It also does not admit returns to scale. The model uses the differential quality of regions, but not their spatial separation, and thus while the total amount of trade of each nation is determined, it may not be possible to determine the geographic pattern of trade.

In summary, the model's ability to yield the location, volume of production, and trade of many commodities seems impressive, but it is severely limited because only one factor of production, labor, is manipulated.

Transportation and Spatial Equilibrium Models

The comparative advantage model allocated production among nations on the basis of variations in labor supply. Transportation-type models instead allocate trade on the basis of the relative location of supply, demand, and interregional transport costs.

The theory of trade underlying the transportation model is simple and logical, if the location of production and demand are known. Under the simplest conditions, for example, military or perhaps intrafirm trade, where known quantities of goods must be shipped from certain areas and known

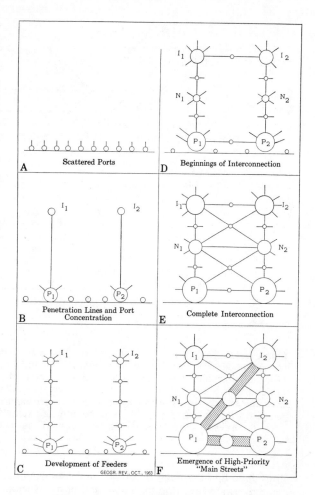

Figure 6.12 This figure illustrates one typical sequence of development, from initial small ports, to limited penetration of lines to inland centers (I), resulting in consolidation of port activity (P), growth of local access feeders, lateral connections, additional nodes (N), and, finally, the highest quality direct routes between the most related places. (Reprinted by permission of the American Geographical Society, from Edward J. Taaffe, Richard L. Morrill, and Peter R. Gould, "Transport Expansion in Underdeveloped Countries: A Comparative Analysis," *The Geographical Review* Vol. 53, 1963.)

quantities of goods must be received at other areas, the problem reduces to a basic geographic principle: to minimize the cost of transportation;

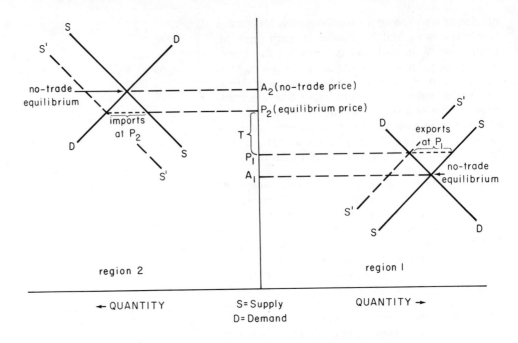

Figure 6.13 This diagram illustrates the volume of trade and regional price levels in two regions under specified conditions of supply, demand, and transport cost. In region 1, supply is too great. Demand will use up the supplies only at the low price A_1. In region 2, supplies are short; they can be sold at the high price A_2. The difference between A_1 and A_2 is greater than the transport cost T, so it pays region 1 to export goods to region 2. Equilibrium is reached when prices P_1 and P_2, given the adjusted supplies S', differ by exactly the transport cost, T. The difference between the two supply lines measures the quantity traded.

that is, to find the most efficient, least-costly shipments. However, finding such solutions is not easy; the relative location of surplus and deficit areas may sometimes require rather costly paths.

More generally, given levels of production (supply) and regional demand for a good in a set of areas, we can find the equilibrium prices (as set by supply–demand relations) that would exist if no trade were permitted (Figure 6.13). This state of affairs might seem absurd, but it makes a real point: trade will take place (in the two-region example shown in Figure 6.13) if the difference between the equilibrium prices in the two regions in the absence of trade exceeds the cost of transporting the product between the regions—the interregional transport cost. As trade flows between the regions prices fall in the importing

region as supply increases and rise in the exporting region as supply decreases. Because of the lower price, the importing region can consume much more of the good. At the same time, exporting producers in the surplus region earn much more because of the higher prices. Consumption is thus evened out between the regions. More trade is justified until precisely that point is reached where the prices in the two regions differ by the interregional transport cost. This equilibrium is stable; if even one more unit were shipped, the cost of transport would exceed the differential in prices, and the shipper would lose money.

Trade can take place then, if opportunities—price differences greater than transport costs—are present; furthermore, if trade takes place between two regions, the prices of goods when trade equi-

TRANSPORTATION AND TRADE

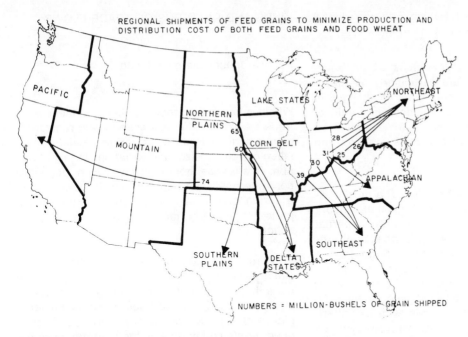

REGIONAL SHIPMENTS OF FEED GRAINS TO MINIMIZE PRODUCTION AND
DISTRIBUTION COST OF BOTH FEED GRAINS AND FOOD WHEAT

NUMBERS = MILLION-BUSHELS OF GRAIN SHIPPED

Figure 6.14 The optimal pattern of shipments of feed grains, using a spatial equilibrium model. Actual shipments are not known. (Reprinted from Earl Heady and Alvin Egbert, "Spatial Allocation of Crop Output," *Journal of Regional Science* Vol. IV, 1962.)

librium is reached will differ by the transport cost between the places. But the particular paths that are used—that is, the opportunities that are actually taken advantage of out of the many possible —will be those that can bring about a trade equilibrium at minimum total transport costs.

Although many specific and more or less complicated forms of the model have been developed, most are dependent or derive from the simple transportation model. Given a set of regions, their deficits or surpluses with respect to some good, and the pattern of interregional transport costs, the objective is to find the set of routes that will not only minimize total transport costs, but also remove all surpluses and satisfy all deficits. The spatial equilibrium model is a rather freer version of the transportation model; specific surpluses and deficits are not given, only regional production and demand. Not only are transport costs minimized and the direction of trade found in this model, but also the level of trade and final consumption.

The Value of Trade   The spatial equilibrium approach to trade not only provides a simple and reasonable theory to account for the volume and direction of trade, but also measures the value of trade to society. The value of final consumption (goods sold) increases, even after discounting the transport cost of the trade itself, because the use of supply is more efficient; consumers in deficit areas get more, supply in surplus areas is not wasted. A reduction in transport rates on a set of routes will similarly increase trade volume— perhaps at no increase in total transport costs.

Evaluation of the Efficiency of Trading Patterns
Since these equilibrium models are normative— they predict what would occur if distances were minimized and value of consumption maximized— it is theoretically possible to estimate the extent

to which the observed trading patterns depart from the best possible ones (see Figure 6.14).

Evaluation of Changing Conditions Equilibrium models such as these are particularly useful for short-run prediction of the impact of changes in transport rates, regional production, and regional demand (from population shifts, for example) on patterns of trade, regional consumption, and prices.

Limitations of Transport Models The most serious criticism of equilibrium models is that a theory of trade as such is necessarily only a partial theory. These models assume the location of production and from it predict trade patterns. But making decisions about location and trade simultaneously is the central problem of spatial organization and not easily resolved (see Chapter 9). A solution based solely on trade, with its pattern of prices and flows of goods, can, however, be helpful in shifting the location of production for greater efficiency.

A greater difficulty in these models is the restraints on substitution and variability of products. For example, where a transport model might indicate long-distance movement and a high price for a product, the importer might instead substitute another product for the high-priced one.

Input-Output Estimates of Trade

A table of interindustry flows shows trade relations only. It does not indicate distance, direction, or cost of transport, except that some transport services may be included as industries. An interregional table may specify flows between areas and industries. No theory of trade is explicit in such a table, but a theory of trade adjustment may be implicit when the matrix is used to evaluate expected changes in demand or output. However, it is probable that interregional trade links are less stable than aggregate interindustry relations.

KINDS AND PATTERNS OF TRADE FLOWS

Political Influences over Trade

Within a national economy political influences on trade are largely due to transport-rate regulation, government preference for certain carriers, regulation of vehicle size, and variations in local taxation. Trade has nearly always been politically controlled between nations, and, in newly industrializing economies, duties on imports and exports are often an important tool of government action.

In Europe, for several centuries, the road to national wealth and power was often seen to be more through trade than through internal development. In pursuit of more trade, the principal techniques of political control over trade were developed: tariffs and quotas. In the long run these are restraints on trade; they either raise the price of products and the cost of transport or they exclude and limit certain trading paths (Figure 6.15). Tariffs on incoming goods have three purposes:

1. To raise government revenue.

2. To reduce total imports, thereby improving the balance of trade and fostering the nation's internal development.

3. To protect internal production from outside competition.

Naturally, tariffs are conspicuously absent from demanded products not producible within the country. Duties on exports are used in developing countries as major sources of government or private revenue and may be imposed to discourage loss of particular resources. However, the use of export duties for income is limited by the risk of pricing goods above competing exporters of the same good.

Generally, as the internal economy develops, tariffs are used less often for revenue and to achieve a trade balance, but selected tariffs remain to protect infant and/or powerful or nationally desired industries—for instance, essential products that might be cut off in time of crisis.

War or serious political conflict can lead to embargoes against trading with certain countries; the United States, for example, has an embargo against trade with China and Cuba. Embargoes are a tool of economic warfare, used to hurt the economy of presumed enemies.

Controlled Liberalization of Trade: Common Markets

As nations gain confidence in the competitive strength of their industries or even wish to goad them into greater productivity, they may enter into tariff-reduction agreements, such as GATT—the General Agreement on Trade and Tariffs. Smaller groups of nations, especially the small but highly developed nations of Europe, recognized that the large internal markets and resources and absence of trade barriers within the United States and the USSR permitted greater specialization, agglomeration, and scale. To gain the same advantages, the EEC (European Economic Community), composed of France, West Germany, Italy, Belgium, the Netherlands, and Luxembourg, has almost completely abolished internal barriers to flows of goods, capital, and labor. The resulting marked increases in trade, income, and economic efficiency are well known. The EFTA (European Free Trade Association), including the United Kingdom, Portugal, Switzerland, Norway, Sweden, Denmark, and Austria, has eliminated industrial tariffs but has not at present dealt with agriculture.

Free Trade and Protection

It might seem irrational and self-defeating for nations to have any tariffs and for other areas of the world not to immediately form common markets, since tariffs increase transport costs, reduce trade, and restrict profitable specialization. However, if a country enters a period of excess imports and imbalance of payments, it may have to impose tariffs to restrict imports in order to maintain its national economy. More generally, the disparate levels of economic development presently existing among nations may require some protective tariffs to pro-

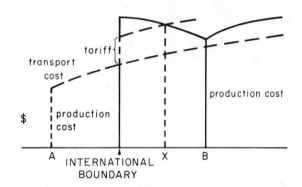

Figure 6.15 Tariffs can restrain trade and keep inefficient plants in production. A has much lower production costs (vertical dashed lines) and could sell its products more cheaply than B in B's country. By imposing a tariff, the nation to the right prevents A from competing any farther than point x into its territory.

tect the weaker countries. A common market consisting of very rich and very poor countries would tend to perpetuate the imbalance; unless the more developed nations chose to invest in the less-developed ones and support their industries during a formative period, the more developed countries would almost always maintain an overwhelming advantage in productivity.

In advanced economies the vast majority of production enters into trade. Because legal boundaries influence collection of data on trade, one is most aware of international and interstate movements. But the volume of local trade is actually greater; there is a rather regular decay in the value and volume of trade as distance increases (Figure 6.16).

These local movements of goods represent such a high proportion of total movement volume and cost because many material suppliers (such as farmers) and most consumer households are spatially diffuse. Intermediate-distance regional and interregional flows directly reflect the specialized structure of an economy. They are large-volume, more skeletal flows, located on only a few routes. International movements of goods re-

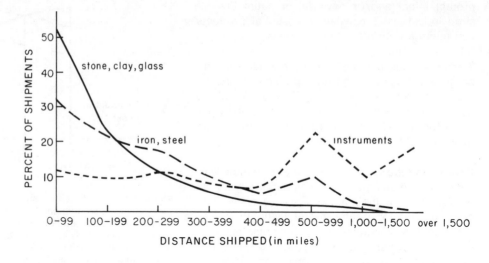

Figure 6.16 Distances traveled by selected commodities, United States, 1963. Although trade volume generally declines with greater distance, the less value per pound, the shorter distance a product is typically shipped.

flect mainly the specialization among national economies. International trade remains, however, biased toward raw materials and food; these are about twice as important as they are in most domestic trade.

Flows of Primary Products

Movements of primary products to processing centers is spatially a process of concentrating these products, typically from many scattered units of rural production, into a few urban centers (see Figure 6.17). In the United States, raw materials are collected locally in most areas, but the large interregional flows tend to be movements from peripheral regions to metropolitan centers.

International flows of primary products require a special discussion, since they have a great influence on economic development. Most simply, a "colonial"-type trading pattern has developed, in which primary products from less-developed countries are sold to processors in more developed countries. Duties on these exports constitute a large share of the national income of the less-developed countries, emphasizing the dual character of many such economies—a commercial export industry grafted upon a generally more subsistent agriculture. While these exports provide capital for development, dependence of this kind courts serious risks: great fluctuations in demand and price prevent stable development and repayment of loans; political considerations may destroy former markets, such as Cuba's loss of the United States; and if the income goes into the hands of a small aristocracy, there may be little incentive for internal development. The weakness of many competing small countries against large, industrial, consuming countries is also apparent in the very low prices paid for their primary products in comparison to the high prices the small countries must pay for capital or consumption goods. This trade is not irrational; it does respond to valid demand and trade opportunities, but it is not strictly fair because of the disparities of power and development.

TRANSPORTATION AND TRADE

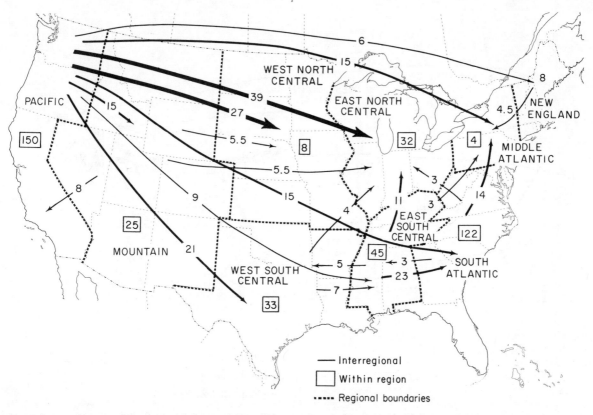

Figure 6.17 Lumber shipments, 1963. Lumber flows centrally toward the northeastern urban-industrial core. In this case, one region, the Pacific Northwest, is an unusually dominant source. (From the U.S. Census of Transportation.)

The major commodities involved in these international flows are petroleum products, agricultural goods (tropical fruits, sugar, rubber, fibers, wheat, meat, livestock, coffee, tea), and minerals (metal ores). These trade patterns exhibit surprising stability, reflecting long-established mother-country–colony ties translated into continuing preferential agreements that, to some extent, may not be most efficient for either party.

Primary products also flow in great volume between more developed countries, reflecting surpluses of local resources and production specialties. A few advanced nations that enjoy high resource-to-population ratios, notably the United States, Canada, Australia, New Zealand, and perhaps Sweden, are in the enviable position of possessing both demanded resources and developed manufactures. The resulting trade surpluses help make these five the richest nations in per capita income.

Flows of Manufactured Goods

The spatial converse to the collection of raw materials is the distribution of manufactured goods to consumers. The distribution proceeds down the central-place hierarchy—from manufacturers, to

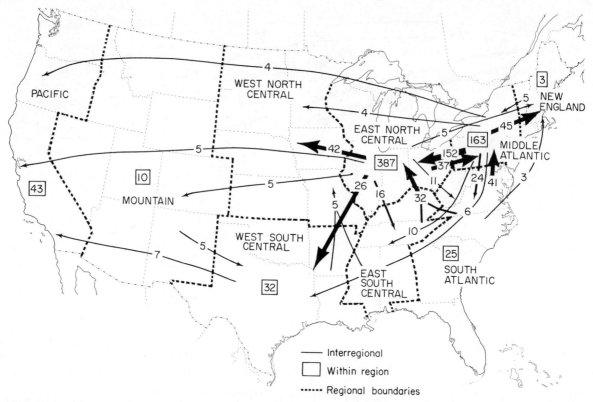

Figure 6.18 Steel shipments, 1963. Most flows are shorter and move within or out of the industrial core—East North Central and Middle Atlantic regions. (From the U.S. Census of Transportation.)

wholesalers, to retailers, to the consumer—and regionally, from the industrial core to the peripheral territory. This exchange system operates at great volume imbalance; the bulk of the collected raw materials exceeds many times over the bulk of the manufactured goods, and inefficiency in the use of carriers is the unavoidable result.

Flows of manufactured goods (Figure 6.18) can be contrasted with those of primary goods (Figure 6.17). Although the greatest value of the flows occurs within the industrial core itself, there is a sizable outflow to the periphery. On an international scale, manufactured goods from highly industrialized nations tend to be exchanged for the primary products of less-developed areas. In addition to the simple colonial-type exchange discussed above, there is an intermediate kind, typified earlier by Japan and now by India and other developing nations, in which the less-developed nations may themselves import some raw materials and then export cheap labor-intensive manufactures.

Exchange of Manufactured Goods

Within and among advanced nations, most of the volume of trade is in manufactured goods. In con-

TRANSPORTATION AND TRADE

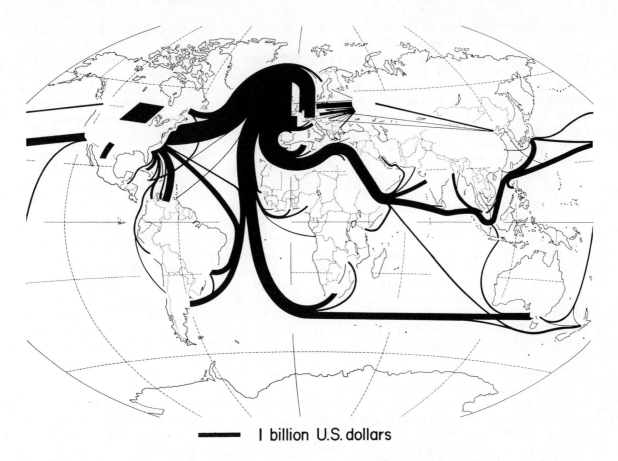

I billion U.S. dollars

Figure 6.19 Pattern of world trade (1958). Flows of goods to and from Europe are dominant. The pattern remains the same today. (Reprinted by courtesy of H. Bosch, ed., *United Nations Yearbook of International Trade,* 1958.)

trast to early theories of trade, which emphasized the colonial exchange system as the route to wealth, actual experience has shown that greater profitability results from specialized exchange among competing industrial powers. This effect is, of course, merely an extension of the benefits of specialization and scale that can be developed within an economy; to some extent, such trade represents exchange of products for which countries or regions of a country have a clear comparative advantage. For example, paper and basic steel are exchanged between Sweden (specializing in paper) and Germany (specializing in steel);

food products and heavy industry goods between Denmark and Germany; and, within the United States, petroleum products are exchanged for machinery and vehicles between the Southwest and Midwest, and other exchanges occur between manufacturers who prefer metropolitan and those who prefer small-city locations.

However, this regional product specialization cannot account for all trade. Even for what is apparently the same product, seemingly inefficient movement of similar goods in opposite directions (cross-hauling) is profitable, usually because the product is not really the same. American and European cars vary greatly in size, price, and appeal to consumers, for instance, and most kinds of machinery vary in their specific capabilities. Brand preferences and maintenance programs, such as with aircraft, may also be influential. Variations in productivity and price resulting from differences in mechanization, labor costs, and market size may also serve as a short-run creator of trade.

Overall Patterns of World Trade

The pattern of world trade has a striking spatial form. There is an inner web of strong and close ties, generally oriented toward western Europe, with smaller webs around lesser nodes (such as Japan) and only weak links at the periphery—the same kind of pattern observed within a nation and for the internal structure of a city.

Western Europe remains central to and dominant over world trade (Figure 6.19). Not only are many of the largest flows internal to western Europe, mainly consisting of manufactured goods, but most of the remaining large flows move to and from Europe, consisting mainly of primary materials shipped to Europe. A few rival trade centers have developed that can challenge this dominance, notably the United States with respect to Canada, Latin America, and Japan; Japan with respect to its neighbors; and the USSR with respect to nations within its sphere. To be sure, the small size of European nations makes their role in international trade seem even greater than that of, say, the United States and the USSR, but the conclusion holds even if western Europe is treated as one nation. This pattern of world trade shows much inertia, but it is not necessarily inefficient; it is a reflection of the developmental history of the colonial period and illustrates that economic change can lag far behind political.

Patterns of Internal U.S. Trade

The internal American pattern of trade movements is similar in structure to the world pattern in that an intense core of trade, some competing centers, and sparse center-oriented flows from the periphery can be observed. However, the American economy is smaller in area, the quality of the transport is fairly high over much of the territory, and development disparities are thus much less severe. Hence, the American economy is more tightly interconnected by trade.

The northeastern urban–industrial core is dominated by intense internal movements of manufactures, although local movements of primary products (coal and food) are great, too. From the periphery foods and other bulk products and some specialty manufactures flow toward the center, while the reverse flow consists largely of machinery and other finished products and consumer goods. Again, competing centers have begun to emerge, notably California and, to a lesser extent, the Gulf Southwest.

7

Interaction:
Movements of People and Ideas

As with the trade of goods, movements of people and communications between them are part of all theories of location, since some kind of distance minimization is normally a major component of such theories. Since locations are separated and specialized, there is a strong demand for interaction with other persons and for goods and services that are not available at one's own location. People are willing to devote much time and income to such movements—at all levels of spatial organization.

In a spatially restricted society, interaction is highly localized, and demand can be met within the range of a few villages. Yet, in the absence of telephones and reliable roads, achieving interaction may involve as much effort as for members of a highly interdependent economy traveling much greater distances; in advanced economies the quality of the transport system and the cheapness of travel permit more movement over a greater distance for the same effort, thus allowing extensive specialization and greater separation of activities and people.

KINDS OF MOVEMENTS

Many trips for personal interaction and communication are temporary:

1. Personal interactions between businesses.

2. Interactions between consumers and local businesses—that is, trips for goods and services.

3. The journey to work.

4. Interactions between persons for social purposes, much of which can be accomplished by mail or telephone (as can many interbusiness interactions).

5. Interactions between consumers and distant businesses—such as tourist trips for recreation and "exploration."

Some moves requires a temporary change in residence (transient moves):

6. Military reassignment.

7. Movement of migrant labor.

8. Attendance at colleges.

Some moves are permanent:

9. Migration for economic improvement.

10. Migration for social and psychological reasons.

11. Migration because of political necessity or force.

12. Migration for retirement.

Temporary movements of people are necessary for the efficient day-to-day functioning of society. If they cannot be made, the volume of production and consumption will fall. If they are excessive, the structure of locations is probably inefficient. But temporary movements do not alter the pattern of location; rather, temporary movements and location mirror each other.

Permanent movements of people, however, are adjustments in location. They may either reflect or initiate shifts in the location of activities. For instance, investment in new activities or, conversely, a decline in present activities may induce inflows and outflows of people, while in pioneering agricultural settlement, migration stimulates change in location of activities and an increase in the value of production in the area.

Location Theory and Associated Movements

Agricultural location theory involves mainly minimizing movements of goods. In extending the theory to urban areas, personal movements become of great importance (see Chapter 8). The density gradient part of the theory involves, in cities, minimizing the cost of necessary center-oriented journeys to work and to shops; the sector aspect of the theory of urban structure (see Chapter 8, pp. 155–174) involves minimizing intergroup friction and enhancing intragroup social and business interactions. In urban areas we find zones of decreasing density because people—not goods—differ in their willingness and ability to move.

Central-place theory concerns minimizing transport costs for the interactions of scattered household consumers and farmers with centralized businesses, and also interactions between agglomerated businesses themselves.

Industrial location also includes mainly movements of goods, but minimizing the cost of movements of people is vital for certain branches of industry, such as publishing, apparel, and research and development, and important enough to many other branches to help cause much industrial agglomeration. The differential quality of land and resources is significant to two kinds of movements of people:

1. Areas that are perceived as having a high recreation value cause long-distance tourist movements, and

2. People may migrate permanently to amenity areas (usually those with mild winters) for retirement.

Static location theory, however, does not in general predict migrations. Dynamic modifications in the theory that allow for population growth, increasing demand for land and resources, income growth, shifts in demand, changes in economic structure, and technological change in transport and production all explicitly predict population redistribution through labor migration.

TEMPORARY MOVEMENTS

Interbusiness Movements Businesses of all types are major consumers of each other's services and goods. Those that require the greatest volume of contacts and can least tolerate time lost traveling to each other will tend to agglomerate in centers or parts of centers. Such contacts include those between publishers and advertisers, apparel makers and designers, courts and lawyers, banks and retailers, and retail and office locations and restaurants.

Shopping and Service Trips Some shopping and service trips, such as those for gasoline and for quickly needed bread or cigarettes, are usually single-purpose and inflexible in time; such trips are short and fairly efficient, usually to the closest supplier. Travel to elementary schools is similar. However, trips for many purposes require comparison shopping, such as those for clothing, furniture, and weekly groceries, and, in order to save time and travel, the shopper may wish to combine several purposes in one trip. For these sorts of purposes, larger nucleations of different activities are preferred. Large centers are better known and offer a greater variety of goods; these and special-purpose centers, such as clusters of furniture stores, automobile dealers, nurseries, and hospitals, will attract customers from greater distances. Overlap of paths is great (see Figure 4.11); customers may not go to the closest location for a given good or service.

Much overlap of trips, however, can be explained by the real—or perceived—differences between centers regarding brand availability, quality, and selection; many persons, for example, skip the closest hospital in order to visit one associated with their religion.

The Journey to Work   The trip to and from work dominates the local travel patterns in advanced societies (Figure 7.01). Because their jobs are so important, people are willing to travel farther to work than to shopping centers. The larger and more specialized the employment center, the more widespread its laborshed—the area from which its workers commute.

Trips for Social Purposes   Two kinds of movements are involved here. Trips to visit family and friends are between residences and tend to occur within an area of fairly homogeneous socioeconomic status and age, although a family's travel pattern may include visits with friends who have moved to the suburbs or, conversely, with those who have remained in the city (see the movement patterns shown in Figure 1.04).

Trips for recreational purposes are oriented partly toward nucleated recreational centers, such as a downtown entertainment center, and partly toward space-consuming activities located in the periphery—golf, racing, and rides in the country.

Tourist Travel   Most recreational trips are temporary and limited to the distance an individual can reach and return from in a day. The limitation of one day for travel, in order to be ready for work and to avoid paying for lodging, is a powerful one and places great pressure on local recreational resources. Freedom from work on holidays—increasingly common in the affluent society—permits longer recreational trips, typically of one to three weeks.

An important portion of tourists travel from small places to large cities, especially the greatest metropolises. A more obvious portion travel to areas having some special scenic or recreational quality—distant mountains, beaches, and lakes. The attraction of such areas is partly a function of the degree of difference from home; for example, in winter, tourists travel from the northern cities to Florida or southern California or Hawaii, or to the western deserts and mountains. Public awareness of such places is important; national parks and greatly publicized private resorts get disproportionate amounts of people.

Important geographic effects of such travel include the transfer of income (such income may constitute much of the income of scenic but otherwise economically limited areas) and the spread of information about other places and opportunities, leading, perhaps, to permanent movements and creation of a more unified culture.

Temporary Movements and Choice of Transport Mode ____

In advanced societies, the automobile is dominant at the local level, but poorer and older people, especially in Europe, must use buses and streetcars. Besides being the most popular form of transportation, the private car can be cheaper than public transport so long as there is more than one person in the car, parking costs are

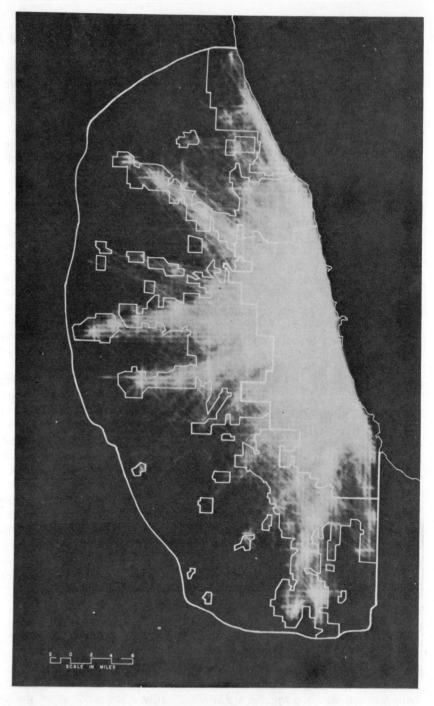

Figure 7.01 Journey-to-work flows, Chicago, 1956. Fuzzy white lines represent work trips, usually toward the center from the periphery. The irregular solid white lines are the boundaries of built-up areas, the outer line is the boundary of the Chicago region. (Reprinted by permission of the Chicago Area Transportation Study from their *Final Report,* Volume 1.)

negligible, and the trip accomplishes several purposes. Although a trip by a lone driver is apt to be more expensive than a bus trip, the driver may feel that the greater flexibility, avoidance of waiting, and typically greater speed gained by using the car offset the extra cost. Only where parking costs and driving congestion are high do public transit trips actually have a clear advantage.

Theoretically, trains are more efficient than buses (which are in turn more efficient than cars) because costs are spread among many more passengers. The seeming inconsistency, then, of larger carriers having higher rates than smaller ones is explained by their high fixed costs for personnel and equipment, the little flexibility they have, and the severe problem of providing for peak loads and then dealing with slack capacity the rest of the time. However, where cars must compete on a profit-making basis with the other forms of transportation—taxis, in other words—they are indeed the costliest.

For long-distance travel, the choice is between personal car, bus, railroad, and air. Long-distance auto travel is preferred for business purposes when a variety of smaller places must be visited (by a traveling salesman, for instance) and for family recreational travel because it is both the cheapest and most flexible kind of transport. Air travel is still used chiefly for between-city business trips, since the higher costs are usually covered by expense accounts. However, as incomes rise and air costs fall relative to other transport, a higher proportion of social and recreational trips will be by air. Air travel is efficient also for one person traveling alone and whenever time is sufficiently valuable.

Substitutes for Temporary Movements:
Communications

The major geographic role of communications— in the sense of nonpersonal meetings—has always been to maintain organizations larger in space than those that individuals can maintain physically, such as nations and widespread companies. Complex decisions can be made and goods and money can be transferred by mail. The telegraph and, later, the telephone accelerated communication in a revolutionary way and permitted a much faster and more efficient response to distant problems. The mass media—newspapers and magazines, and particularly radio and television—have national and international connections and are efficiently molding a national culture by disseminating the same information and ideas over a large and diverse territory. Generally, all these means of communication effectively save time and transport costs by acting as substitutes for movements of persons, communicating their decisions, demands, and feelings.

While communication is hardly free, it is so much cheaper than personal contact that distance is in effect overcome significantly, at least for many business and governmental transactions. The money cost of mail may remain constant within an economy, but the amount of mail declines fairly sharply with distance, partly because the probability of knowing someone declines with distance and partly because mail is relatively slow, especially between smaller places.

Telephone communication is more expensive and charges, if not the real costs, do increase with distance—in the United States, rather sharply within a state, and gradually across states. Hence, the frequency of telephone calls decays perhaps more steeply with distance than does mail. Again, however, the decrease in the likelihood of knowing someone at a long distance is a more important reason for the attenuation than the rates charged.

TRANSIENT MOVEMENTS

Military requirements involve the redistribution of large numbers of people. In the United States, over three million men plus their many dependents are moved away from their original homes and many may prefer not to return home. Within the United States there is a strong military relocation to the West and South, where most of the bases are located. Very probably the information effect —the knowledge gained while visiting an area— helps explain the postwar and continuous growth of California.

Students away at college represent another large transient group within the United States; perhaps two million are away from home. Most students go to schools within their home state, although there is a large movement to the older, more prestigious institutions in the Northeast—a population movement opposite to the military transfers to the South and West. As in military movements, shifts to schools often lead to permanent moves, especially since the young and college-educated are at any rate a most mobile group. However, college graduates do not so much remain in educational centers as become concentrated in the larger cities.

Some occupations involve much transiency—for example, airline flight personnel and long-distance rail and truck crews are subject to much movement. Another transient is the traveling salesman; his need to meet the maximum number of customers in the least amount of time and shortest distance has led to special models for finding the most efficient paths for such trips.

Migrant, transient labor is common, especially in agriculture, since many crops have heavy demands for seasonal labor; many migrants move from crop to crop as the demand dictates (Figure 7.02). Most migrant farm workers are unskilled and uneducated and have not been able to find permanent jobs. In the United States the number of migrants has been maintained by discrimination, prevention of union organization, and both legal and illegal importation of temporary contract labor. Migrants represent a serious social problem not only because of their extremely low wages and severe poverty, but also because their transience hinders adequate education, health care, and political representation. Such semi-continuous migration is thus very costly and damaging to society, if not to the farmer; where migrant labor is not available, farmers have learned how to employ workers permanently or have become more fully mechanized. Efforts at organization of migrant workers, various aid programs, and increased farm mechanization may reduce the problem's severity.

PERMANENT MOVEMENTS: POPULATION MIGRATION

The migration of people may be viewed as an efficient response to their desires and opportunities. Population transfers also depend on improvements in transportation and perhaps communication (so that people may be aware of the opportunities at other locations).

Although world history is characterized by constant movements of people, it is apparent that people are less mobile than goods. There is much greater inertia; people are willing to accept a lower income than is necessary for long periods or even indefinitely because of fear, lack of knowledge, and the greater importance of other values.

Importance of Migration

Despite these restraints, migration has been of immense significance.

1. It accompanies and makes possible the spread of settlement and the colonization of new areas.

2. Rural-to-urban flows makes possible rapid industrialization and urbanization.

3. Transfers of slaves and contract labor for agriculture and mining have brought about new mixtures of people, thus having great social and economic impact.

4. Migration provides the manpower needed to develop new resources.

MOVEMENTS OF PEOPLE AND IDEAS

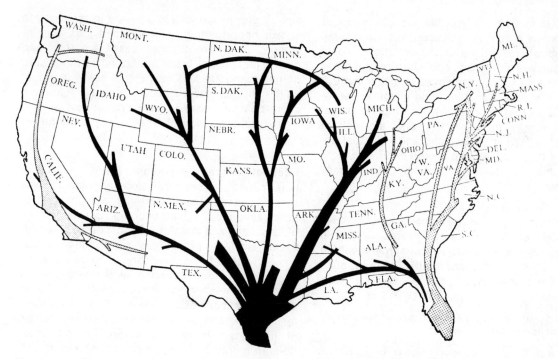

Figure 7.02 Major migrant worker movement in the United States. Texas, California-Arizona, and Florida are the origin of and winter-work areas for migrants. In spring and summer, migrants move northward, following planting and harvesting demands. (From the U.S. Department of Labor.)

5. Migration constitutes a mechanism for alleviating, or at least responding to, inequities in national and regional development.

6. Migration is the principal mechanism for spreading technology, language, customs, and most other social behavior.

Migration, then, is one of the primary mechanisms used to achieve equilibrium in society. Since land is immobile, people must move to the new areas that society evaluates as having greater productivity and more opportunity. To the extent that people respond to the possibility of having higher income or social status, migration can aid in the process of regional convergence—lessening the inequalities in income among regions. However, migration will not necessarily lead to such convergence if, for example, the out-migration from the poorer area consists mainly of the most tal-

ented groups. Migration may also aggravate the difference in the total level of activity by reducing population in the regions of out-migration.

World Population Movements

In the pursuit of better opportunities, man has continually migrated (Figure 7.03)—at times impelled by overpopulation at home, at other times attracted by the hope of large rewards, and at still other times forced to move by invasion or defeat. Migrations have been both centrifugal and centripetal—men have at times aggressively pushed into new, unsettled areas and at other times flowed into already crowded and successful areas.

Population movements typically occur in response to two kinds of motivation—economic and social. In a subsistence village economy, social movements, such as intervillage and intertribal searches for wives and visits to relatives, are dominant. A food crisis may generate long-distance movements of a group for reasons of economic necessity, frequently involving war and the risk of annihilation. When commercial and industrial activities are introduced, a powerful economic motivation—the opportunity for a money income—may take hold.

In developing and advanced economies, the largest volume of movements beyond the local level are made because of expected improvements in income, security, and opportunity. Spatially, such moves are of three types:

1. Those made to develop agricultural resources—that is, frontier settlement.

2. Those made to develop mineral or forest resources, also apt to be at the frontier.

3. Those made to take advantage of urban opportunities.

Migration for Economic Reasons

Rural to Urban Migration   Economic growth has occurred predominantly in towns and cities and has led to the major population movement of the last three centuries and the present era. In most of the world, rural populations are excessive, and poverty is severe. The possibility of finding a job in the city, no matter how lowly and no matter what the filth and misery in the city, has led to the vast rural-to-urban flow of people that has probably transferred at least 200 million persons to urban areas in this century alone (see Figures 7.04 and 7.05). This process of concentration generally represents an efficient response to existing needs and opportunities and has made possible vast increases in total wealth.

Not all population movements are in response to known opportunities or guaranteed jobs. For instance, one can observe cases where urban growth far exceeds urban opportunities. Since care of the urban jobless is much more costly than that of the rural jobless—who are typically ignored—overurbanization has become a direct cost, hindering development in many less-developed countries.

Intermetropolitan Migration   During urbanization, migration from rural areas and small towns to cities is dominant, but after a high level of urbanization is reached, migration between urban places becomes greater. Large flows occur between similarly prosperous metropolitan areas, some of these flows consisting of students, some of military personnel, some of the young or of the retired heading for amenity areas with better climates or more exciting cities. Some are movements of personnel transferred within companies at the managerial level; some are due to fluctuations in employment in particular industries; and some may be due to the feeling that "the grass is greener over there" or to the desire to get away from home. In any event, the movers believe they will increase their opportunities or satisfaction by shifting, and since most of these movements are to areas that are fairly close, the cost of movement is low.

Nonurban Opportunities   Not all economic opportunities are urban; millions have migrated from crowded, poverty-stricken rural regions to regions having more agricultural opportunities. The most dramatic of these shifts was the agricultural settlement of Canada and the United States from peoples of Europe during the eighteenth and nineteenth centuries, when some 50 million persons—who otherwise might never have left their native villages—traveled 5,000 miles to a new and uncertain life in the Americas. Given that the farmer is normally conservative, this movement attests to the extreme gap between local opportunities and what America was at least perceived as possessing. Perhaps the possibility of owning a large tract of land was a powerful attraction.

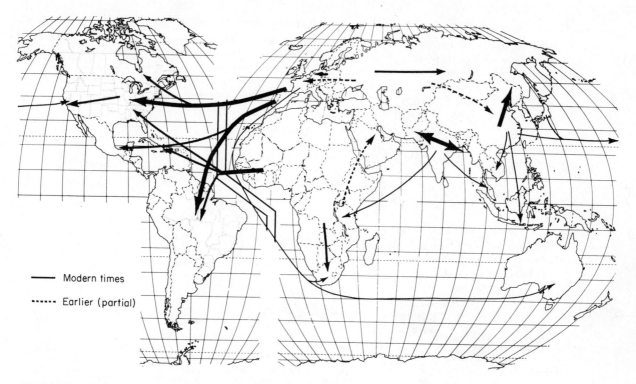

Figure 7.03 World population movements. In recent centuries, colonial and slave movements (from Europe and Africa to the Americas) have been dominant, but, recently, political moves have been sizable (from India and Germany). Flows are consolidated for simplicity; part of Europe's migration, for instance, is shown migrating to all of South America.

— Modern times

----- Earlier (partial)

Migration for Social or Political Reasons

Major population movements have also resulted from political and social persecution. In this century, European and other wars have led to vast redistributions of peoples, such as the expulsion of Germans from eastern Europe, the transfer of Moslems and Hindus within the subcontinent of India, and the settlement of Israel by Jewish migrants from Europe, Africa, and Asia.

Within the United States there has been a vast movement of blacks from the more discriminatory South to the less discriminatory North and West—for both economic and social reasons. Since the First World War, when industrial opportunities in the North were first opened to blacks, several mil-

lion have left the South. Most moved directly from their extreme poverty as sharecroppers to the large, industrial cities; as unskilled workers, they thus were employed at very low levels. Even the slum dweller segregated in a ghetto, however, preferred it to the rural poverty and more pervasive discrimination of the South—partly because he hoped for better education and employment opportunities for his children.

The original importation of slaves, of course, mainly to the Caribbean, Brazil, and the United States, was one of the most colossal forced migrations in human history. Probably some 20 million persons were brought to the New World from 1550 to 1850, and a substantial portion of these evidently died in transit.

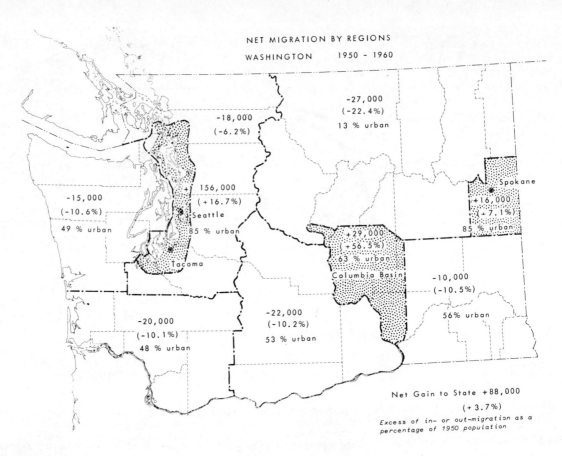

NET MIGRATION BY REGIONS

WASHINGTON   1950 - 1960

-27,000
(-22.4%)
13 % urban

-18,000
(-6.2%)

-15,000
(-10.6%)
49 % urban

+ 156,000
(+16.7%)
Seattle
85 % urban

Tacoma

Spokane
+16,000
(+7.1%)
85 % urban

+29,000
(+56.5%)
63 % urban
Columbia Basin

-10,000
(-10.5%)
56% urban

-20,000
(-10.1%)
48 % urban

-22,000
(-10.2%)
53 % urban

Net Gain to State +88,000
(+3.7%)

Excess of in- or out-migration as a
percentage of 1950 population

Figure 7.04 Rural-urban migration. An example of shifts from rural areas to more urban ones. (From R.L. Morrill, "Regional Growth and Net Migration," *University of Washington Business Review* Vol. 21, 1962.)

Movements for retirement represent an increasing proportion of migrations. The retired family, having more income and greater freedom than in the past, tends to seek urban or suburban locations in zones having a warmer climate—Florida, Arizona, and California in the United States, for instance.

The Mechanism of Migration

Migration of people is like trade in the sense that if the potential increase in income—the value dif-

ferential (when the motivation is economic)— is perceived as greater than the economic and social cost of moving, the migration is possible (Figure 7.06). Or, to put this concept in familiar geographic terms, the interaction between places will depend on their degree of complementarity (value differential) and transferability (cost versus ability to move). In general, the flow of migrants between two places can be considered a function of the perceived quality of the source and the destination and of the relative location of the places.

When there are few rural opportunities, there is a greater chance that persons will migrate to cities.

MOVEMENTS OF PEOPLE AND IDEAS

The perceived attractiveness of a city, in turn, depends chiefly on its volume of economic activities, its rate of growth, its income relative to other areas and cities, and the public's image of these factors. The probability that these opportunities will be acted upon depends on how well-known the opportunities are, the direct cost of movement, the presence of closer opportunities, and—often—the social cost of a shift in cultural environment. Areas where income is low and unemployment is high or where the prospects of employment for young people are poor will have many persons willing to move.

The public's view of the opportunities in places is not strictly accurate and is probably biased toward amenity areas. Also, the cost of distance *per se* may not be as strong a deterrent to movement as the fact that people's knowledge of opportunities available declines with distance from the opportunities. For many, too, nearby opportunities, while not as potentially valuable, may be preferred if they permit the family to maintain its social environment.

The Role of Information   Even taking into account these "push-and-pull" factors—disadvantages that push migrants out, advantages that pull them in—and the intervening opportunities and costs, migration is strongly concentrated on certain favored routes. Such concentration occurs because information available to an individual or region about presumably equivalent places varies greatly; the migration process has an important feedback mechanism, which works as follows: people who have moved write back about opportunities to family and friends still living in their former home. Thus migrants from particular communities and even particular counties tend to follow certain paths (see Figure 7.07). This same mechanism is perhaps even more important in determining the destination of immigrants from overseas.

Although between any pair of places many more migrants travel to the larger or richer place, a reverse flow also exists. This may be economically

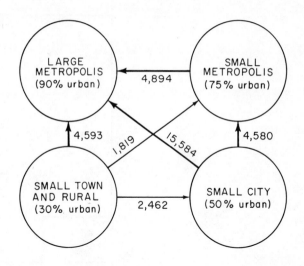

Figure 7.05   Net migration flows from less urban to more urban areas. Counties that are less urbanized have net migration losses—more people migrate from than to them. Thus, there is a net shift in population toward more urban and metropolitan areas. The large metropolis includes Seattle; the small metropolis, Spokane and Tacoma. (Washington state, 1955–1960).

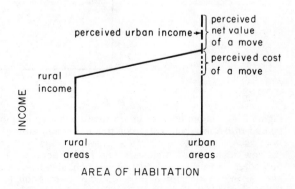

Figure 7.06   When persons in rural areas perceive that the cost of a move will be less than the gain from the move, they tend to migrate toward urban areas.

rational for some population subgroups, and for individuals who cannot adjust to urban life, the social gains obtained by returning home compensate for the economic loss.

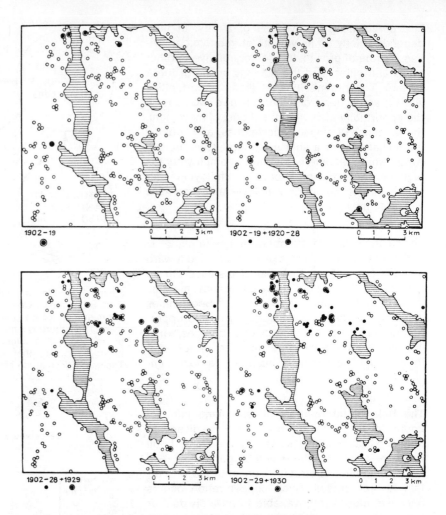

Figure 7.07 Importance of information for the spread of innovation. These figures trace the spread of cattle tuberculosis controls in a small area of Sweden. Open circles are potential farm accepters, dots in circles are new adopters, and solid dots are old adopters. Note that the new adopters are in clusters near former adopters, illustrating the importance of information obtained from nearby friends and acquaintances. Migration is also greatly influenced by such an information spread. (Reprinted by permission. From T. Hägerstrand, "On Monte Carlo Simulation of Diffusion," in W. Garrison and D. Marble, eds., *Quantitative Geography,* Studies in Geography, No. 17, 1967, Northwestern University Press.)

Effect of Migration on Population

Migration plays a basic role in redistributing population from weak and declining areas to strong and growing areas. Net migration has tended to flow:

1. "up the urban ladder"—from rural areas and small places to large cities.

2. from more stagnant to more growing regions.

3. from areas of greater to those of lesser discrimination.

4. from areas having fewer to areas having more amenities, such as from inner cities to suburbs and from harsher climates to more pleasant ones.

Population growth reflects these flows, of course, but natural increase and loss—the other component of population change—can modify the effects of migration (Figure 7.08).

In the fastest growing areas of the United States, the amenity regions of Florida, Arizona, Nevada, and parts of California, population increase is due especially to migration. For suburban areas and some rapidly expanding industrial and service cities, both components of growth are large and about equally important. Places growing just a little faster than the national average are apt to have only a very small net in-migration.

There are very large areas (see Figure 7.08) that have small to average population gains only because a large natural increase offsets net out-migration. In these areas the economy is expanding too slowly to utilize even the region's own natural gain. Several of the large, older metropolises belong in this category; their fairly large absolute population gains mask their slow rate of growth. Larger areas consisting of mixed agriculture and small towns and cities often follow this pattern also. Here, the large out-migration from the rural areas is masked by their equally large natural increase or by slight gains from migration to the small cities. However, in the rural areas of the South and Midwest and in isolated hilly areas everywhere, the out-migration is so great—including perhaps one-third of the population in one decade—that natural increase cannot make up the difference. In both this case of absolute population loss and in the preceding case of small population gains due to natural increase, much of the out-migration is of the younger, most productive age groups, and prospects of economic growth are thus even further reduced.

EFFECTS OF HUMAN MOVEMENTS ON TRANSPORT SYSTEMS

While the motivation for much construction of transport routes may be to facilitate movement of goods, the demand for movement of persons can be quite important. Without doubt, many roads have been built and maintained to permit easier control, both cultural and military, over a territory; in the United States the popularity of the car among people adds greatly to the demand for more and better roads, and the density and quality of the road network is thus far higher than is necessary for movements of goods.

Some transport systems have specifically developed in response to the need to move people. During the railroad era, the demand for passenger service was great. Within and between cities, elaborate streetcar systems laced major arterials, and commuter railroads permitted suburbs and satellite cities to develop in rays about cities. As the private car met more of the demand and permitted residences to be more widespread, however, the rail and streetcar system, which required high-density traffic, became unprofitable.

The demand for fast movement has helped bring about the rapid growth of air travel and the establishment of new routes; many people are willing to pay more for the time savings and greater convenience. Since air routes may be rather direct and, unlike land routes, can ignore intervening places, the route structure may fairly closely reflect the demand for connections between any two places.

MODELS OF PERSON MOVEMENT

Trips of people, migration, mail, and telephone calls are all interactions between locations of people and locations of businesses, recreation, and other people. The economic cost of such movements is not always the dominant influence. Also, the number of movements of people is many times greater than the number of goods shipments. Thus, whereas goods will tend to be shipped over a restricted number of cheaper paths in order to minimize costs, individuals can merely reduce the frequency of contacts on more expensive paths and still tend to minimize the cost of the interactions believed necessary (see Figure 7.09). For

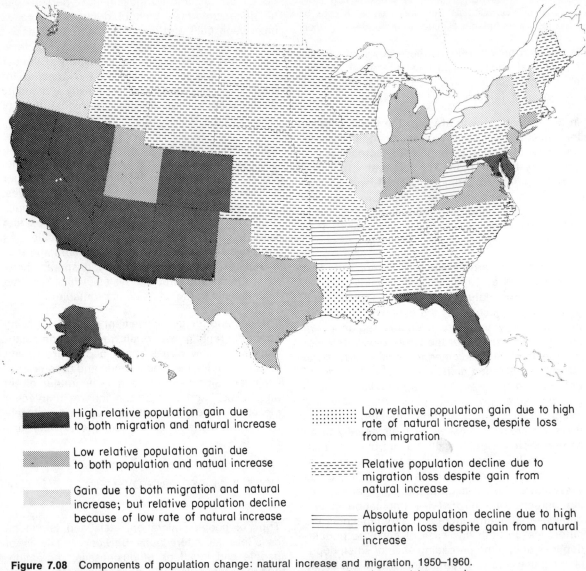

Figure 7.08 Components of population change: natural increase and migration, 1950–1960. States of the nation may be classified on the basis of migration of and natural increase in population. "High relative gain" is population growth at more than twice the rate of the entire nation. "Low relative gain" is growth at more than the rate of the nation; "relative decline" is growth at a lower rate than the national average.

Legend:

- High relative population gain due to both migration and natural increase
- Low relative population gain due to both population and natual increase
- Gain due to both migration and natural increase; but relative population decline because of low rate of natural increase
- Low relative population gain due to high rate of natural increase, despite loss from migration
- Relative population decline due to migration loss despite gain from natural increase
- Absolute population decline due to high migration loss despite gain from natural increase

instance, a shopper can buy his groceries in the closest store only, but the satisfaction he gains from visiting several stores may more than offset the increased distance or time necessary. For an-

other example, the prospective migrants from some city could all travel to the nearest place having opportunities, but, in fact, individual migrants will interpret differently the opportunities existing

MOVEMENTS OF PEOPLE AND IDEAS

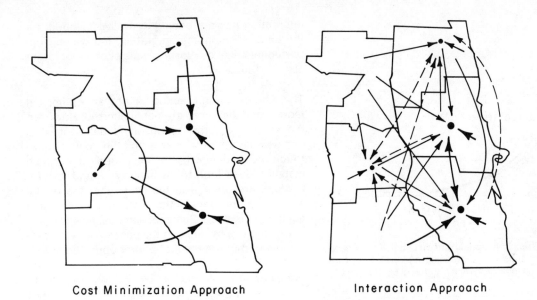

Cost Minimization Approach   **Interaction Approach**

Figure 7.09 Interaction and cost minimization: two approaches to movements of people. Example: movements to hospitals in one part of Chicago. The cost, or distance, minimization approach, useful for goods, is not appropriate for person movements because far too few flows are permitted. The interaction approach is far more realistic. Dots represent hospitals (larger dots are larger hospitals), and lines are flows of people.

in and the cost of reaching a number of places; some will thus be willing to travel farther than others. For these reasons, the models used to find optimal transport patterns, based on minimizing costs, are not adequate for most movements of people.

Most models of person movement, therefore, have been of a descriptive character rather than attempts to optimize movement, recognizing people's more diffuse movement patterns. In fact, most are modifications of the "law of migration" proposed by Revenstein in 1888. Later called the gravity model, this inverse relation between frequency and distance has been found in almost countless studies to describe fairly well a wide variety of flows: migrations, vacation trips, shopping trips, mail flows, telephone calls, journeys to work (see Figure 7.10 as an example).

The Gravity Model and Related Models of Interaction

This theory contains two principal elements. First, the maximum or ideal number of contacts from or to a group of people is proportional to the number of people in the group; and the number of contacts between any pair of groups is proportional to the product of the sizes of the groups. For example, at the extreme, every person in one town could interact with every person in another town. Second, the proportion of the maximum possible contacts actually realized is diminished by some function of the distance, or an appropriate substitute for the distance, between the locations. The decay in the number of contacts is definitely not linear as distance increases, but rather exponential or hyperbolic (Figure 7.10). Such a form for the decline of contacts with distance may theoreti-

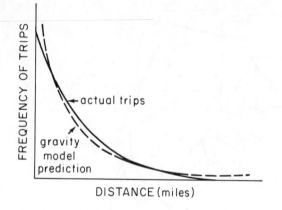

Figure 7-10 Trips to hospitals and distance. The decline in frequency of trips with increasing distance from Chicago general hospitals is well predicted by the gravity model.

cally exist because people perceive distance and the cost of overcoming that distance exponentially; greater distances may be seen as farther or shorter, and the cost of overcoming them greater or less than they actually are. Even when the cost of overcoming the distance is significant, the probability that a person knows about an opportunity also decays exponentially with distance. Such a decay in knowledge about opportunities implies that an individual has an information field (pattern of contact) within which the direction and the length of trips are not wholly random, but biased toward favored routes and destinations.

Many people perceive the separation of places not as distance but as intervening opportunities. It is logical to argue that, where the direct cost of distance is not very great, the presence of closer opportunities will reduce the perceived advantage of more distant ones somewhat proportionally to the size of the closer opportunities; the more nearby opportunities there are, the less advantageous the farther ones will appear. Intervening opportunities are obviously a restraint to interaction at greater distances, but what constitutes intervening opportunities for the various kinds of

interaction has not been very well developed; for the case of economic migration, intervening opportunities may be closer places of equal or larger size and income.

This theory of interaction is not an optimizing model, and distances are not minimized. However, the model conforms to observed behavior; it is behaviorally rational. Also since the cost of separation does diminish the likelihood of contact, distance does tend to be minimized, and its predictions are optimal in the sense that the model maximizes the satisfaction of a population at a minimum distance. Such satisfaction, however, requires the use by some of the people, or by all individuals part of the time, of poorer opportunities.

Demands for interaction are closely related to individual preferences for space. Each person evaluates the surrounding world according to its usefulness in satisfying his needs and desires, and makes a list of his preferences for destinations from those places that he may visit or contact. For example, a family is faced with a variety of recreation sites around a city. Their satisfaction is not maximized by always going to the closest site, but, instead, satisfaction from a variety of trips to several places will more than offset the added cost of transport. For the individual family, this model can give the probabilities of their going to the various parks; for the mass of people in the city, the model can give the proportions of trips made to each park.

The effect of differential feedback—information about places, usually supplied by friends and relatives—can be included as another element in the model; feedback increases the frequency of travel on some already-used paths and decreases it on others. Barriers to interaction, both physical and cultural, can rather easily be treated in this model.

Interaction models do a fair job of predicting the total movement to centers and the distribution of lengths of trips, but since many trips are multipurpose, and multicentered (to more than one center), such models fail to generate typical shopping patterns. An interaction model can be used to assess the probability of a trip to various centers, but a separate analysis is needed to give the probability of extending the trip to more purposes and to more centers.

THE SPREAD OF IDEAS AND INNOVATIONS: SPATIAL DIFFUSION

A third class of movements, after those of goods and people, is movements of ideas, concepts, methods, and rumors. These movements are frequently accomplished through persons traveling for social, business, educational, or military purposes; the movements may also be by newspaper, magazine, book, radio, or television. If the movement of an innovation results in change in the landscape and is accompanied by movements of people as well, settlement itself spreads. However, most ideas can move and even alter the landscape without the movement of people.

Spread of innovation—technical change in processing or ways of doing things—has been the most studied and is likely to have the greatest effect on the landscape. Since in most countries agriculture is carried out in many small units, how much any improvement spreads—whether of tools, seed and animal quality, methods of cultivation, or marketing possibilities—is of great significance for farm income and national output. Knowledge of industrial innovations spreads more quickly, since the number of production units is relatively small, but the ability to act is restricted by the cost of new capital goods, licenses, and royalties. Hence, the spatial effects of innovation will be outweighed by economic and technical factors.

Innovations that are used primarily for agriculture or are basic to economic development and settlement, such as the growth of a rail network, are diffused fairly continuously over space (Figure 7.11). Innovations that may be adopted by the entire population, however, are diffused through society's centers of control, the cities. Thus, clubs

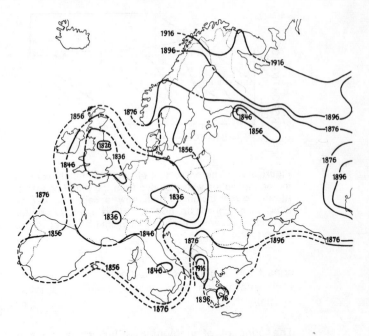

Figure 7.11 Areas within which railways had been built by specified dates, Europe. Note the general spread from the England–Belgium core and lesser spread from other metropolitan capitals—Rome, St. Petersburg, and Prague. (Reprinted by permission of the Department of Geography, University of Lund, Sweden, from S. Godlund, "Ein Innovations Verlauf in Europa," *Lund Studies in Geography* No. 6, Series B.)

and organizations, clothing styles, television, and fads seem to spread down the hierarchy of places, from the largest metropolises to their satellite centers and then gradually to surrounding small towns and rural areas.

There are three major factors controlling the spread of ideas and innovations. First, people, even in the same area, vary in their psychological and economic ability to accept change; often, but not always, the more educated and more prosperous will accept change before the less educated or less prosperous. Once having accepted change, people vary in their willingness to tell others about it. Second, the most effective means of information spread are interpersonal and, third, all per-

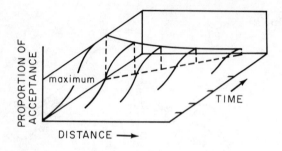

Figure 7.12 The proportion of people typically accepting an innovation with distance from the origin and time. At any given distance, note how acceptance begins slowly, then speeds up, and later slows again. At greater distances, acceptance begins later and never becomes as complete.

sons have a network of contacts, which we call their information field, that is highly restricted spatially.

The concept of innovation diffusion as a wave arising from an origin and moving outward is a rather good analogy, where the changing form of the wave describes the pattern of acceptance at any distance and time from the origin of the innovation (Figure 7.12). The crest of the wave—the zone of most active acceptance—moves outward from the origin, and the overall probability that people will either accept the innovation or tell

others about it falls slowly as distance from the origin increases and time passes. Hence, the final level of acceptance often declines slowly with distance also. Over time, the acceptance of the change at any point in space will follow an s-type curve (since the *rate* of acceptance will be very low when the innovation is still far off, will be highest as the innovation reaches an area, and will then fall off because most people who will accept the change have already done so).

The actual movement of the innovation wave is accomplished as the pioneers who first accept the change tell others in their field of personal and business relationships. Thus, nearby acquaintances are the ones most likely to be told about and to adopt the change (see Figure 7.07). In turn, these accepters tell other people about the change, perhaps people beyond the range of the pioneer's contacts. The rate of spread will depend on the persistence in telling about and the resistance to change and on the spatial extent of an individual's field of acquaintance.

As societies become more affluent, they demand higher levels of services. Thus, a greater proportion of movements are of people rather than of goods, and the quality of the transport system comes to depend more on people's preferences for routes.

MOVEMENTS OF PEOPLE AND IDEAS

Part Five

Spatial
Organization

8

The Urban System
and Urban Structure

THE SYSTEM OF TOWNS

In advanced economies, not only do cities dominate the life of the citizen, but also contain the vast majority of the population, even though cities occupy only the smallest segment of the nation's space. Cities are complexes of those activities—control, exchange, culture, processing—for which efficiency is obtained by intense spatial proximity. Geographically, in the large view, cities are but tiny scattered points in a vast area of land and water, the principle evidence of man's impact upon nature. In the small view, these concentrations of people are covering increasingly large areas with high-intensity use, a vast investment in the direct alteration of nature.

In the more advanced areas, cities have become the supporters and organizers of the economy. Not only are up to 80 percent of a nation's population city dwellers, but rural dwellers depend on the city far more than cities depend on the farmer. Cities ultimately depend on farm and mineral resources, to be sure, but the majority of the population living in the cities produces goods and services for other city dwellers.

Cities are vehicles of social, economic, and cultural control and of administrative rule; they are centers of demand for the exchange of goods, centers for the accumulation and use of value and wealth, centers for the creation and support of cultural, educational, and artistic institutions. As the centers of control and culture, cities are also the foci for passing on the traditions of society.

Yet, cities contain within themselves also the means for change in society—sources of unrest, social ferment, and even violence. In the small area of a city are contained a variety of people, occupations, and industries acting to enrich the experience and increase the expectations of all city dwellers—a source of both unrest and creativity. As centers for communication and for the transient and traveling populations, cities are subject to invasions of new ideas and knowledge of alternate ways of life. Cities are centers of fashion and innovation, and their large size permits them the luxury of tolerating the aberrant—the idealist, the reformer, and the critic—which rural society cannot endure.

Spatial Patterns of Urban Settlement:
Theory of Urban Location

The advantages of agglomeration and scale provide the basic rationale for concentrating population in urban settlements. Whether cities are designed to control a population or to exchange and process goods, costs are reduced and the value of the activities is enhanced by concentrating them at one point. However, because of the fact of space, its differential quality, and because even central-place and processing activities use space, activities and population must be somewhat disaggregated and dispersed. A complex pattern of towns and cities emerges, since it is impossible to concentrate all activities in one giant city.

We define as *rural* activities and settlements (homesteads or hamlets) directly engaged in exploiting land and forest resources. As soon as nonagricultural activities (including mining, services, and processing more advanced than family handicraft) become established, a different organization of space is present that we may call urban, even if the settlement is but a hamlet.

One set of town-building activities, central-place activities, provides service, exchange, and collection service to more dispersed customers. The volume of demand for, customer willingness to travel to, and best combinations of activities vary, and a hierarchy of different city sizes in a network of central places will thus emerge as the most efficient and profitable way to serve a population. As already discussed, such a network would ideally have a hexagonal structure, distorted, however, in four ways.

1. Variations in productivity affect the frequency and spacing of settlements.

2. Variations in topography shift settlements toward points of natural communication, such as ports and fords.

3. Some variations in settlement density are due to developmental history.

4. The presence of processing activities distorts the pattern.

The alternate set of town-building activities, processing activities, transforms raw materials, into demanded products. Clusters of closely spaced urban settlements tend to develop where the resources are concentrated in a few areas.

The freedom of many processing activities from direct need for agricultural or mineral resources and their response to the advantages of large-scale production lead to a preference for location in large urban settlements—that is, cities—whether the cities are of central-place or processing origin. When manufacturing becomes concentrated in such larger places, central-place activities will follow, so that in a highly industrialized economy a far higher proportion of central-place activities may exist to serve the metropolitan population itself than to serve the rural and small town population.

Variations among Cities and Towns

Cities show great variation in size and importance, function, form, and relative location. The most obvious variable is size; in theory, larger size may result from the provision of central-place services of higher order or from the differential response of processing activities to returns to scale (some plants operate well with 10 employees; others may need 1,000).

Central-place and processing activities reinforce each other. A larger, higher order place is itself a large market and a distribution center. It thus is attractive to a wide variety of manufacturers, who in turn support a larger population, which increases the demand for and thus the level of services. The metropolis becomes more and more self-sufficient as the size of the internal market justifies satisfying internally more and more demands. Consequently, many economies exhibit a top-heavy structure of city sizes—a "disproportionate" (from a central-place viewpoint) share of the population and the activities resides in the larger metropolises. An increasing variety of activities become profitable with greater size, exports and imports decrease, and more economies of scale are realized. However, as the metropolis continues growing, costs are increased and the economies of scale are eventually reversed (Figure 8.01). Thus the size of metropolises is somewhat limited, perhaps reflecting at least these two spatial restraints: the excessive cost and time needed for finding sufficient food, other raw materials, and markets; and the internal diseconomies, such as congestion and blight, resulting from inability to organize space. Therefore, a set of regional metropolises is necessary and able to compete as well.

Primacy   The size of a territory, especially that territory within which an economy developed, influences the distribution of large cities. The smaller the territory, the greater the proportion of economic activity that can optimally be located at one center. Hence the phenomenon of primacy, where a high proportion of the total urban population of a country is located in one place. Primacy is essentially a product of territorial size and may be economically efficient. Economies contained in a large territory such as the USSR, U.S., and Canada, or those that have merged several small separate ones, such as Germany, Italy, and Spain, lack such national primacy but may exhibit regional primacy.

Size and Relative Location   Within an economy, smaller places tend to be more prominent in areas of extensive agriculture, such as the Great Plains of the United States, in areas of extensive forests, and in areas of rugged topography, such as Appalachia and the Ozarks, where most settlements are hamlets. Conversely, larger places are concentrated in the areas of oldest development, such as the northeastern United States, and in positions of high natural accessibility and ease of communication.

Optimum Size of Cities   Seeking one optimum size for a city conflicts with both the real demand for different levels of central-place services and real variations in the scale economies for different forms of processing. One may observe, however, that very small places cannot sustain even mini-

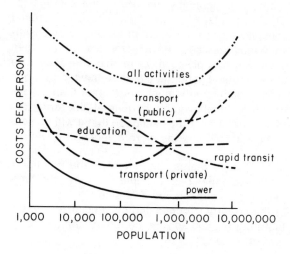

Figure 8.01   Returns to scale with urban size. Moderate-sized cities seem more efficient than either very large metropolises or small cities and towns.

mal services, that people seem unable to live together harmoniously in the large numbers and high spatial intensity of the very largest cities, and that at some point economic and social costs begin to exceed further gains from agglomeration.

Not until a city size of 250,000 to 350,000 is achieved is a threshold level reached that can provide some self-sufficiency in central-place services and high-quality cultural and educational amenities, and also attract modern industry. The most efficient population range seems to extend from this level to a population of perhaps one to two million, which can support a very wide range of services and activities, is rather self-sufficient, and can support an efficient internal transport system without the severe social and congestion costs of the giant metropolis (see Figure 8.01).

Classification of Cities   Functional variation among cities in their activities has led to many systems for classifying cities. Generally determined by its employment structure or sometimes by the value of its activities, the class of a city depends on the specialized activity of the place—the activity that makes up a disproportionate share of its economy, relative to the average for all similar places. Many measures of functional specialization have been proposed, and essentially they are useful devices for describing urban emphasis and giving a distinctive character to a place. Diversification is the state in which no one activity occurs very much more often than it does on the national average. In general, the larger the place, the greater the likelihood that it will be self-sufficient and thus the more diversified it will be.

In the United States, the pattern of the functional classes of cities has a simple structure: the largest regional capitals are diversified, the core area of the country is dominated by specialized manufacturing places, and the periphery contains centers of trade.

While large cities tend to be diversified, those in the northeastern United States specialize somewhat more in manufacturing, while the "gateway" cities of the Plains and the regional capitals of the South and West specialize more in wholesale and retail trade, transportation, and services. At the small city level, some peripheral industrial towns based on agricultural, mineral, and forest resources appear. There are also other classes: scattered towns specializing in administration or education, usually containing state capitals or colleges; mining towns, especially in the West, Appalachia, and the Gulf South; and a few transportation cities in crucial transit sites.

Role of the Particular City (Economic Base)
More important than its functional class is the role of a city in the regional and national economy. This is revealed largely by the pattern and the strength of its external relations to the surrounding hinterland and nation (Figure 8.02). The central place usually provides services for a spatially contiguous, limited area; some processing centers, however, serve an entire national economy and even beyond its borders. In an economic and spatial sense, it is these exports to surrounding areas that make possible the existence of the "unnatural elements"—the cities. The exports provide the income by which a city may purchase the special goods, the raw materials, and the food that the city does not itself produce.

The population directly engaged in export activities demands other internal products and services and thus indirectly makes possible another class of activities, so-called nonbasic activities, which may soon exceed the export or basic group in quantity and value. It is important to understand that this group of internal activities is not parasitic; these activities create value just as do the export activities and are necessary for a high standard of living. Just as to exist the city ultimately depends on the productivity of the country, so do its nonexport activities depend on its exports. However, the larger the place, the greater the proportion of relations carried on internally and the easier it is to sustain a disruption in traditional exports.

The export, or basic, share of the economy may come from any economic sector. From small towns, central-place activities are "exported" to the local countryside. The larger the place and the higher its level, the greater the spatial extent of these exports (Figure 8.02) and the greater the share of wholesale trade in the city's economy. Excluding the local region, manufactured goods are apt to dominate a city's exports and determine its national importance, if any.

Urbanization

Cities have been in existence throughout recorded history, often functioning as points of religious, political, and economic control for the territories on which they depended for sustenance. However, not until the industrial revolution vastly raised the productivity of processing and agriculture, so that farmers could produce significant surpluses, did urbanization—the transition to a life dominated by cities—really begin.

The ancient and medieval cities were mostly small; only a few were able to control supply lines for food and material sufficiently long and large enough to support large numbers of people. When these lines were cut, the cities immediately declined. The modern rise of cities began with the development of international commerce and new

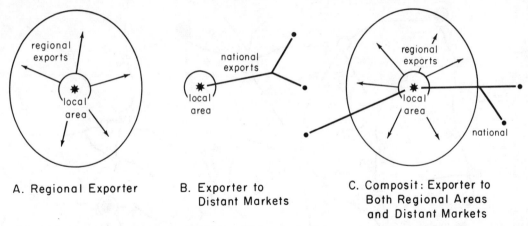

A. Regional Exporter   B. Exporter to   C. Composit: Exporter to
                           Distant Markets   Both Regional Areas
                                                  and Distant Markets

Figure 8.02 Economic base: spatial types. A. Cities emphasizing central-place activities export services chiefly to local (up to 10 miles) and regional (10 to 100 miles) markets. B. Cities emphasizing mining or industrial activities export mainly to national markets. C. Most large cities do both.

ways to transport goods long distances. Some of the existing capital, however, also found its way into internal manufacturing and local communication networks, and the market town and the mill town began to arise. Since both central-place and processing activities helped build these new towns, and since urbanization was not simultaneous everywhere within even one economy, instead spreading out gradually from points of early financial and economic power, it is clear that a theory explaining the location of cities must combine central-place concepts, industrial location and resource-use ideas, and, in addition, recognize historical processes of diffusion.

In moderately rich agricultural areas with few alternate opportunities, such as parts of Europe and America, we can discover a fairly pure geometric central-place net. Similarly, in areas having very rich mineral resources, notably coal, we can observe typical industrial clusters of mining centers and heavy industrial towns and cities (Figure 8.03).

In regions where processing and central-place activities are of about equal importance, historical study often reveals a complicated interplay between different location forces. One may trace

historically the gradual elaboration of an urban net on a rural population (see Figure 1.06, for example). New central places serving agricultural populations often developed at midpoints between two earlier existing places—often in a rather regularly spaced pattern. At the same time, industrial towns based on specific resources or the entrepreneurial ability of single men were clustered in districts that were often poor for agriculture and also along railroads, which connected distant important places. Gradually, these industrial towns took on service functions, distorting the central-place pattern and redistributing population along major transport corridors.

In the United States, because of the homestead pattern and the importance of local control over schools, rural farm settlement was accompanied by a pattern of small, closely spaced hamlets. Villages and towns containing a wider variety of service functions were often rather arbitrarily located and encouraged by the railroad builders and state decisions locating county boundaries and county seats. Yet, in retrospect, the arrangement has proven surprisingly rational and efficient. Only the most recent period of cheap and fast auto travel has shaken this central-place

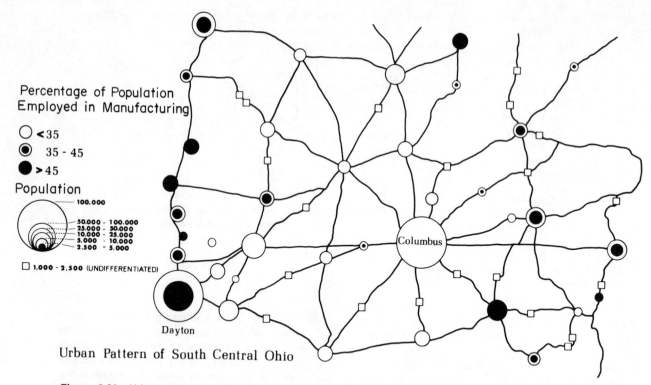

**Percentage of Population
Employed in Manufacturing**

○ < 35
◉ 35 - 45
● > 45

Population

100,000
50,000 - 100,000
25,000 - 50,000
10,000 - 25,000
5,000 - 10,000
2,500 - 5,000

□ 1,000 - 2,500 (UNDIFFERENTIATED)

Columbus

Dayton

Urban Pattern of South Central Ohio

Figure 8.03 Urban pattern, south central Ohio. This local urban pattern illustrates both a central-place pattern (especially the area around Columbus) and an industrial one (the linear set north from Dayton).

structure and perhaps rendered obsolete the smallest set of places.

In earlier periods, U.S. industrial settlement was small and often depended on easily accessible water power. Thus, from New England to the southern Piedmont a fairly fine network of small industrial towns can still be found, especially at falls on streams and smaller rivers. Some of these towns, too, have been rendered obsolete; they have not been able to adjust to shifts in power sources and consumer demands.

Larger U.S. cities often were partially creatures of the railroad. In the interior of the country, sites where early railroads crossed natural barriers, such as the Ohio, Mississippi, and Missouri Rivers and the Rocky Mountains, often became major cities—Cincinnati, St. Louis, Kansas City, Omaha,

and Denver, for instance. Places chosen for railroad junctions or end points often prospered also, including such towns as Los Angeles, Portland, Seattle, Indianapolis, Minneapolis, and Atlanta. Even the old pre-railroad port cities were very much affected; those with early and good connections to a large interior area prospered—New York, Philadelphia, and Baltimore—while others, such as Charleston and New Orleans, suffered. Other industrial cities were based on concentrations of resources; break-of-bulk ports grew up and spawned linear clusters of manufacturing towns, from which factories gradually diffused outward.

In short, present urban patterns are products of relatively efficient locational behavior, subject of course to adjustments as the economy changes. At any one moment the pattern has inefficiencies; some places are declining after losing their origi-

THE URBAN SYSTEM AND URBAN STRUCTURE

nal base of people or resources, others from a location that has become inefficient under a changed technology. Still other places gain from such things as shifts in population, use of new resources, responses to new scale economies, and greater importance of amenities.

Present trends in urbanization reflect opportunities for developing new central places and manufacturing locations and attempts by existing locations to adjust to change. Very small places are generally declining, even disappearing, because we can travel two or three times as far as we would 50 years ago with the same—or less—effort, and also because individuals prefer larger centers for their amenities, and industries prefer larger places in order to use their labor supply, business services, and markets (Figure 8.04). Conversely, large places are growing disproportionately fast as services multiply, industries become even more market-oriented, and inter- and intra-metropolitan transport improves. Yet, even in the most advanced countries, the element of diffusion is still present; regions of a nation are at different stages of urbanization. In the northeastern United States, the first section of the country to be industrialized, a mature pattern consisting of large metropolises and an extensive wealthy exurban fringe has emerged. In the South, however, the emergence of central places and the creation of new industrial clusters is just beginning. In the rich agricultural interior, the decline of small centers and consolidation of population into larger cities is evident at present.

Metropolitanization   Some scholars suggest that current trends in city growth are leading, ultimately, to an extreme metropolitanization—a pattern in which most (80 to 90 percent) of the population will reside in a set of regional metropolises, each containing from 1 to 25 million people, and in which the larger portion of territory (95 percent) will be occupied by the minimum rural and small town population needed to carry on extensive agricultural, forest, and mining activities.

Recent data do not support this theory, however. Cities of all sizes beyond 10,000 people are grow-

ing about equally fast, although the smaller metropolises containing 250,000 to 1,000,000 people are perhaps growing more rapidly. This trend will cause the metropolises to include an increasing proportion of the total population, but the nearby satellite cities that are not part of the great metropolises are growing faster, indicating that some investors and at least part of the public are responding negatively to extreme city size. Indeed, a fair proportion of the population seems willing to get along on a much lower income in order to remain in the country.

However, metropolitanization in the economic and cultural sense, where most of the rural, small town, and small city population is dominated by a few large metropolises, seems to be growing. In particular, the increased speed of land travel and the use of air travel in business encourage consolidating higher management, exchange, and financial functions in the largest places with the best connections. These few cities—perhaps only 35 in all the United States—govern the economy and culture of wide territories. This kind of system of metropolitan regions is not at all new, though; the major change in the last half century has been this concentration of power in fewer places, primarily reducing the role of regional centers having from 25,000 to 250,000 people.

Some nations have attempted to control the pattern of urbanization. British attempts date back to the end of the nineteenth century. Since World War II, particularly, government and industry have together built new towns—towns in nonmetropolitan areas—that otherwise would not have been built. The Soviet Union, too, has long had similar policies, and the national government's control over investment has permitted it to establish and encourage a widespread pattern of intermediate-level urban places and smaller metropolises.

Urban Life

Urban life seems in the present age to have overwhelming advantages and attractions. Economic

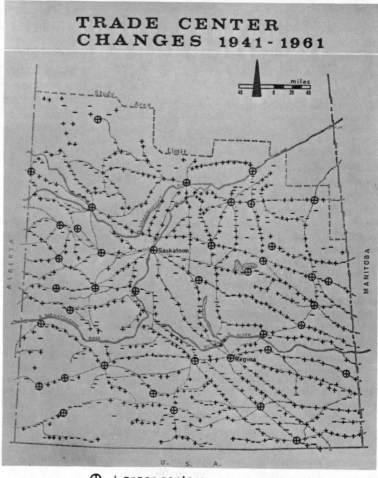

Figure 8.04 Trade center changes, 1941–1961. On balance, smaller and less accessible centers not near transport junctions are declining. Most larger places are gaining. (Reprinted by permission of the Regional Science Association, from G. Hodge, "Prediction of Trade Center Viability in the Great Plains," *Papers and Proceedings of the Regional Science Association* Vol. XV, 1962).

diversity is greater in urban areas; economic opportunities are concentrated there, perhaps to a more than efficient degree. Educational and cultural superiority follow this concentration of talent and wealth. The efficiencies of agglomeration and greater scale reduce costs and raise living standards. Culturally, mixing ideas and people enriches individual experience, reduces prejudice, and encourages innovation and tolerance to progress. The anonymity of the individual is an attraction to

THE URBAN SYSTEM AND URBAN STRUCTURE

many persons. In the city are excitement, opportunity, and comfort.

The disadvantages of urban life are well-known, but for the majority of people do not outweigh the attractions. Many persons, especially those brought up in the country, feel estranged from nature and often live in the rural fringe to get the best of both worlds. Others are accustomed to a cozy community and strong family ties and cannot adjust to the psychological isolation of the city. The different peoples and cultures are impossible for some to accept, and the sheer concentration of so many people in so little space and the social control needed to regulate them conflict with our traditional belief in individualism. The congestion, speed, noise, and intensity of life create insecurity and increased illness. The concentration of such a large number of people often makes differences too obvious, heightens conflict, and leads to social breakdown, increased crime, and delinquency. Society has not yet learned how people can live individually in a communal space.

THE INTERNAL STRUCTURE OF URBAN CENTERS

Although the city on the map of a nation is only a point, that point is a significant space—so intensively used that it contains more people and wealth than do the vast rural lands. Moreover, the spatial organization of the city seems to follow the same principles as those governing rural land use, so that in a sense the city is a microcosm of the larger rural region.

Theory of Urban Structure

Urban land uses are by definition those which respond to the needs or benefits of agglomeration and which themselves need very little space (in comparison to such rural uses as agriculture or forestry). It is not obvious, however, where an urban land use ends and a rural one begins. We may tentatively class as part of the urban area of a city those activities and areas from which there is much commuting to the city and in which the natural landscape is clearly altered. But any such arbitrary distinction cannot ignore that there is really a continuum of intensity of activities and land use (Figure 8.05), from nonuse in remote rural areas to the most intensively used downtown corner. The urban region contains just the more intensive, less space-consuming end of the continuum, those activities that are most able to compete for a central point. Since this is the case, the theory of internal urban location will be in part, at least, an extension of agricultural location theory.

The same elements applied to agricultural regions apply in the urban context. The familiar concentric ring concept describes the density gradient of the city, from the point of highest accessibility and value downtown to the least accessible and least valuable areas on the urban fringe. The sector concept stresses the variety of demands for locations that are equally accessible and valuable, just as an agricultural zone of a given intensity may be divided into several parts, as a result of climate, soil, or cultural differences. In addition, central-place theory applies to the urban scene and predicts the hierarchy of shopping centers, from the central business district (CBD) to the isolated store.

Gradient Theory Urban land uses, like rural ones, vary in intensity and type. Among urban activities, for example, many shops require little space while such uses as parking, cemeteries, and single-family homes require relatively much. Since activities are urban because they need to be as near each other as possible, they compete for the limited space around the point of greatest accessibility (Figure 8.06). As in agriculture, the "best" locations have the highest price and thus units tend to be small and intensity very great. Shops and services with a high turnover whose success depends on accessibility to the maximum number of people can afford the highest rents. A home, however, needs to be accessible to only a few people, and residents are willing to accept larger

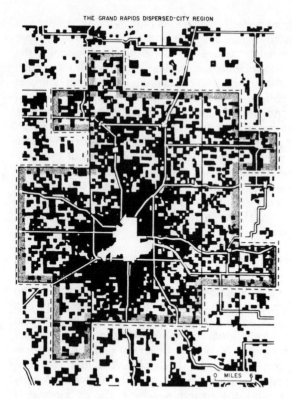

THE GRAND RAPIDS DISPERSED-CITY REGION

0 MILES 6

Figure 8.05 The urban-rural continuum. Areas of predominately nonfarm occupance (black areas), including residences of commuters to the city, extend far beyond the city itself. This extension is often termed "the dispersed city." (Reprinted by permission of The Association of American Geographers, from H. Stafford, "The Dispersed City," *The Professional Geographer* Vol. XIV, 1962.)

units of land that are less accessible. As in farming, the same total land value per enterprise unit—shop, home, and so forth—can be found from the center to the edge of the urban area; the area of each unit, though, increases as the land becomes less valuable and less accessible.

The simplest model of urban structure, suggests, for example, a zonation of land from:

1. The retail core, to

2. A wholesale–industrial ring, to

3. An apartment zone, and

4. Single-family homes.

However, each activity occurs at a variety of intensities, and a more realistic gradient would be:

1.	Central business district commerce.
2(a).	Wholesale and central manufacturing.
2(b).	High-rise apartments.
3(a).	General multifamily homes.
3(b).	Outlying business districts.
4(a).,4(b).,4(c).	Single-family homes, increasing lot size.
5(a).	Peripheral manufacturing and wholesale trade.
5(b).	Exurban residential.

Many studies corroborate in a general way the existence of the land gradient, but since the gradient theory takes into account only some of the factors affecting location, the observed pattern departs from the predicted one.

As with agricultural activities, physical variations play a role in the location of urban activities. Level land is more suited to manufacturing, and rising and rolling topography to residences (especially land with a view). Arterial roads, when necessary, follow valleys and easy ridges and thus influence commercial location. River and lakefront lands often are desired for industrial, public, and residential use—leading to conflict. Microclimatic features such as a prevailing wind may affect location; to avoid smoke, high-value residential buildings are placed to windward, industry to leeward. Physical variations, then, will tend to impose differentials in the use of the land within an intensity zone and, as in agricultural gradients, will distort portions of the zone. A wedge of slopeland with a view, for instance, may have higher land values than its surroundings, and an area of rough topography or swampland may have less value.

Sector Theory Even without physical variation, however, we should not expect rings of homogeneous activities around the CBD. A variety of

THE URBAN SYSTEM AND URBAN STRUCTURE

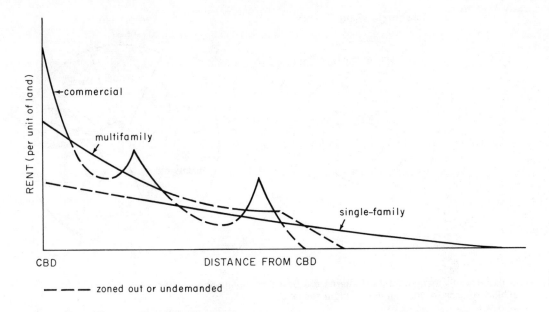

Figure 8.06 Ideal urban rent gradient. Competition for land results in an ordering of land use from commercial, to multi-family, to single-family residential. In some cases, the highest value use is not permitted, and there is often demand for single-family homes even where that use pays less rent than other uses. Commercial activity peaks at different locations, since business districts seek local markets to dominate.

somewhat mutually exclusive activities may actually be of similar intensity and thus compete for land at the same distance—for example, manufacturing facilities and apartment houses, different racial groups, or different income groups might compete. This competition leads to a sectorization by class and land use. In its pure form, this sectorization will lead to wedges—sectors—of different uses, with internal variations of intensity within them (see Figure 8.07). Thus, within the upper-class sector, for instance, the gradient will go from wealthy shops, to expensive high-rise apartments, to older upper-class apartments, through newer upper-class residential suburbs and industries that utilize professional skills, such as research laboratories. In the lower-class sector, the progression will move from mixtures of inexpensive shops, wholesaling firms, and manufacturing facilities, to older homes that have been subdivided to provide rooms and apartments (including the ghetto), to smaller homes, and finally to suburbs containing low-cost housing and heavy industry. Although racial ghettoes typically occupy a high-intensity zone within the lower-class sector, the ghetto itself may become a wedge after sufficient variation in income develops (Figure 8.08).

Another wedge—or more than one wedge—located along the major access railroads may be devoted almost entirely to industry. This separation of manufacturing activities from residential and commercial uses results from both personal preference and zoning laws; historically, however, the need to be near one's place of work led to a mixture of manufacturing plants and lower-class residences, which is still prevalent.

If it were not for racial, religious, and income differences, much of the sectorization would disappear. However, social differences are persistent

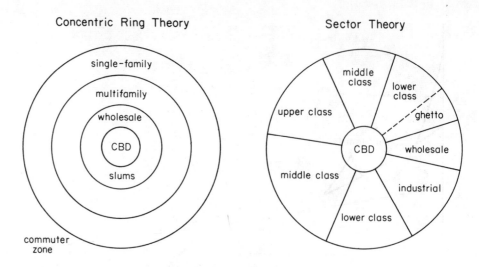

Figure 8.07 Two theories of urban structure. Patterns are based on competition for access and the incompatibility of uses. A combination is more realistic.

and strong, and this joint gradient–sector model offers the best approach to a theory of urban structure. There are other reasons for considering sector theory. Sector theory most easily allows for growth; increased demand for some activity simply causes an extension of the wedge. Much intraurban migration, such as movements to the suburbs, also evidently occurs within a sector. Finally, even in the absence of social differences, a powerful force for wedge-shaped development is the radical, center-oriented structure of the transport network to the city center.

Central-Place Structure of the City   One element is still missing from our urban structure—the hierarchical structure of central-place activities that should be imposed on the overall gradient–sector system. The location of shopping centers follows central-place structure and at the same time both reflects and modifies the intensity gradient; for example, the distance between equally sized shopping centers increases as one moves outward from the city center because at lower suburban densities larger areas are needed for a center to reach its threshold of support.

Since the city is a bounded space, limited in extent, the central business district tends to become the dominant center. A fair time passes before competitive centers begin to emerge. Theoretically, when the total market served by the original center becomes large enough to support seven of the smallest shopping districts, six competitors will simultaneously emerge (see Figure 8.09). The central business district will support the highest level activities by using the total urban market. Thus, the central-place administrative principle is theoretically most efficient in an urban setting. Since overall density decreases outward from the center of the city, the position of the central business district is further enhanced because it is closest to the urban region of highest density. The outlying shopping centers will thus have to draw their trade from larger but lower density areas farther from the center.

The system of arterials connects major shopping centers first to the central business district and then to each other. The arterials, and especially the centers themselves, locally raise the intensity of land use and the value of the land, in propor-

THE URBAN SYSTEM AND URBAN STRUCTURE

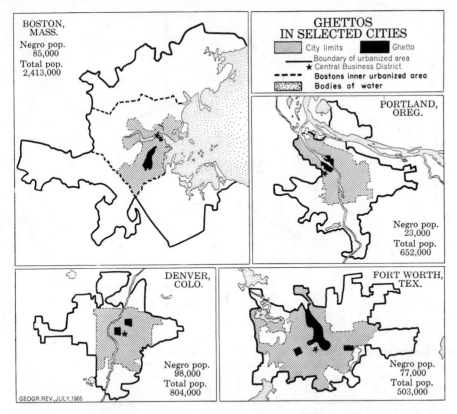

Figure 8.08 Representative Negro ghettos in U.S. cities. Most ghettos occupy older housing near the center. The Fort Worth ghetto, however, has become a wedge. (Reprinted by permission of the American Geographical Society, from R. Morrill, "The Negro Ghetto: Problems and Alternatives," *The Geographical Review* Vol. 55, 1965.)

tion to their size. Thus, the intensity gradient is changed by business districts and arterials, so that lesser peaks and ridges of intensity dot the urban landscape (see Figure 8.10). The central-place structure in turn is affected by sectorization, and the structure is weaker in industrial and low-income areas, where purchasing power is less.

In fact, however, the theoretically optimal structure of central places—in this case shopping centers—within an intensity gradient has not yet been fully worked out (discussed more fully in Chapter 9; see Figure 9.01). Clearly, pure hexagonal trade areas will not be found, although the general principle that the smallest centers are located approxi-

mately midway between two or three larger ones can be supported. In summary, a static theory of urban structure includes an intensity gradient modified by a central-place structure of business districts and divided by sectors having different uses and different social groups.

Urban Land Use

Commercial Uses Commercial activities require easy access and high visibility. The center of the transport net and other major intersections create the central business district and the major shop-

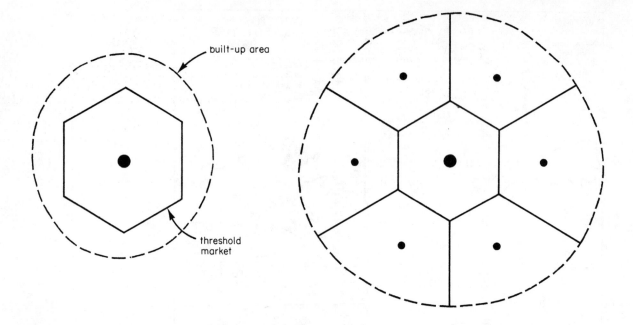

Figure 8.09 Growth of the shopping center hierarchy. When the built-up area of the city grows to many times the threshold necessary to support one center, outlying centers (small dots) will arise. The original center (large dot) continues to dominate the entire market for higher level goods and services.

ping centers, and the routes serving them are sought by arterial-oriented businesses.

The complexity of the commercial structure is a function of city size. A village has only one business center and some arterial business out from it. The town will add some isolated stores, and the small city (population 10,000 to 25,000) will be able to support one or more centers for convenience goods. In the metropolis, at least these levels of commercial structure are commonly recognized:

1. The central business district.

2. Major outlying shopping centers (at least two or three, and perhaps as many as six), with branch department stores.

3. District shopping centers, with a variety of specialty stores, banks, movie theatres, and so forth.

4. Neighborhood shopping centers, emphasizing groceries, drugs, cleaners, and the like.

5. Local stores, mainly for gas and groceries.

In addition, interconnecting arterials may contain two or three levels of businesses, depending on the volume of traffic and the density and income level of the adjoining areas. Arterials thus provide both convenience goods for local residents and goods and services geared to the traveler.

In most cities, business districts developed at a time when streetcars prevailed, and they located at intersections or arterials served by streetcars. Since land use and traffic flows were intensive, the shift to the private car led to severe traffic congestion and parking shortages. Developers of planned shopping centers in the last 25 years adapted to the car by building a new kind of structure: an intensive core of stores with a pedestrian mall, surrounded by parking space. Given the automobile, this is far more efficient than lining stores along roads; the planned centers have less congestion, and more can be accomplished in a given time without walking as far.

The development of outlying shopping centers as a city grows is a natural central-place process; at the same time, the nature of the central business district changes as its relative share of all business declines. Auto travel has led to the decline and demise of many local stores, mainly in the inner city, because shoppers can travel to larger, newer, suburban centers with greater variety (Figure 8.11). Some small, isolated stores manage to survive by offering special hours, products, or services.

Even more than with country stores, the trade areas of business centers overlap (Figure 8.12). Since centers are typically only a mile or so apart and are subtly differentiated—such as by different grocery, drug, or bank chains and, at higher levels, by different department chains—and since people cannot distinguish between small differences in distance, centers that have a spatial monopoly over an area are rare. Another reason for this overlap of trade areas is the high degree of internal urban mobility, and many people maintain previously established shopping habits, particularly with regard to doctors, dentists, and banks.

Even the central business district, small as it is, is strongly differentiated internally. There is an inner zone of intensive pedestrian movement for the activities requiring a high volume of customers and a peripheral ring of stores requiring moderate customer volume, divided into "interest" areas—finance, general office, hotel–entertainment, wholesale, lower-class retail, and high-class shops. This specialization within the central district also implicitly recognizes the division of the population into economic and social subgroups.

Residential Use Residential land use varies in density, quality, racial occupancy, and age. In the United States, as the city grew, single-family

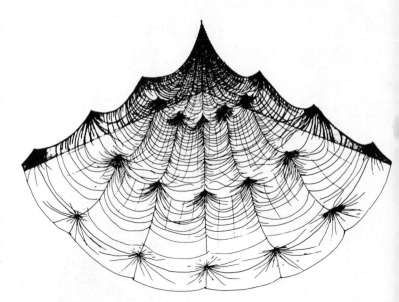

Figure 8.10 The urban density surface. Land value and intensity peak at points of greater accessibility on major arterials. (Reprinted by permission of the University of Chicago Department of Geography, from J. Simmons, *The Changing Pattern of Retail Locations,* Research Paper No. 92, 1964.)

homes extended its circumference. In the higher class sectors, the inner, older homes were typically replaced with upper-class, high-rise apartments. In the poorer sections, the older homes were divided into small apartments and frequently deteriorated into tenements. Although land value and taxes were high and per family rents low, net revenue per property could be quite large, given a high density of population and low maintenance costs. Minority groups, often regardless of income, and poorer groups dependent on public transport or walking to get to work are forced to reside in such areas. However, after the inner city severely deteriorated physically and especially after rather cheap private car travel was possible, thus reducing the central area's advantage of accessibility, land values, too, declined in the central districts.

The original gradient of land value and intensity has weakened as access to the center becomes of less importance and the car is perceived as much more convenient than bus travel. Indeed, as with

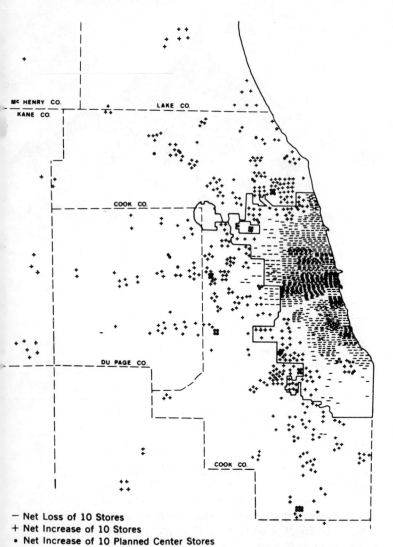

- Net Loss of 10 Stores
+ Net Increase of 10 Stores
• Net Increase of 10 Planned Center Stores

Figure 8.11 Changes in Chicago retail establishments. Retail stores follow the population to the suburbs. (Reprinted by permission of the University of Chicago Department of Geography, from B. J. L. Berry, *Commercial Structure and Commercial Blight,* Research Paper No. 85, 1963.)

agriculture, as transport cheapens, the quality of the land becomes a stronger determinant of the value of the land. In addition, the optimal location for apartments was previously as close as pos-

sible to the city center; their location today is determined by the location of demand for that type of housing, even in suburban areas.

Subpopulations vary in their preferences for housing and amenities and in their ability to pay. Some, most often people without children or cars, prefer closer-in locations, exchanging higher rent for reduced transport time and cost and proximity to the downtown amenities. Others, especially those with young children, prefer more space and are willing to pay more for transport in exchange for suburban space and cheaper land. They may also be seeking homogenous neighbors—in other words, they are fleeing minority groups—or may simply desire newer or more modern housing. Indeed, the suburbanite seems willing to spend more for housing and transport combined.

The highest income groups have the widest choice of location and type of residence, since their ability to pay enables them to achieve the environment they desire. Middle-income groups may not be able to pay for a rebuilt central-city environment and are thus likely to move to outer, moderate-quality city districts and suburbs. The poor occupy the oldest, smallest homes and are often closest to industrial areas. Suburban homes are not always available to the poor, and those that are available are apt to be intermixed with suburban industry.

Other Urban Land Uses   Industrial land occurs in wedges or clusters within the metropolis or city. It includes an older, inner industrial zone near the central business district that uses little space, and, adapting to car-driving workers, newer space-extensive industries in intermediate and fringe locations and along railroads and major highway links.

The observed decentralization of industry in most cities is due to a lack of space and to excessive land costs for the space that is available. Only manufacturing that requires face-to-face contact with other industries and services, can utilize the labor of nearby poorer groups, and does not require much space will seek and pay for central

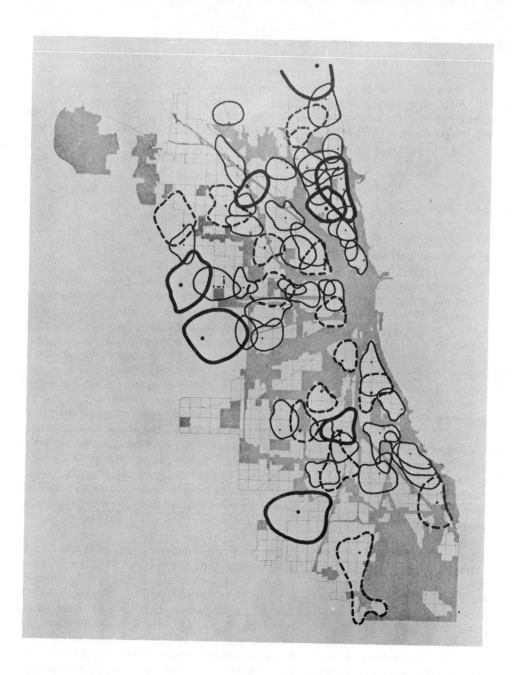

Figure 8.12 Trade areas for convenience goods: Chicago. Overlapping customer trade areas around major Chicago shopping centers. Width of lines indicates size of shopping centers (dots). Dark gray areas are industrial and commercial. (Reprinted by permission of the University of Chicago Department of Geography, from J. Simmons, *The Changing Pattern of Retail Locations,* Research Paper No. 92, 1964.)

locations. Examples of such industries are printing and publishing, apparel, and pottery. On the other hand, many industries prefer more spacious peripheral sites, such as refineries, metal processors, and fabricators. Also, specialized small manufacturers whose employees are skilled and for whom local accessibility is not important prefer peripheral locations in or near middle-income suburbs.

Internal Social Variation

The concept of incompatibility between social groups and the resulting segregation in the sector model are necessary to understand internal social variation. Separation of income groups is achieved mainly by separating housing of varying values; similarly valued homes tend to cluster because of location relative to industry and topographical quality and because developers construct such clusters. Separation of groups by their national origin, color, and religion follows from both the internal preferences within the group and external discrimination against the groups.

In cities all over the world, minority groups of a distinct religion, color, or national origin have long been set apart from the rest of the populace—perhaps willingly for self-protection—and the separation has often been legally enforced by the majority. The European Jewish ghettos are the most obvious examples. Also, as each different group has immigrated to large American cities, it has been forced to occupy the poorest area, or ghetto, when it arrives. Despite their poverty, these ghettos do offer a community of people like oneself to aid in the transition to a new society.

The most recent migrants to the city are blacks and Puerto Ricans. Blacks differ from earlier groups, however, in that color is a greater barrier to dispersal among the rest of the population than religion or language ever was. Negro ghettos are maintained by both preference and discrimination; the black minority is not able to disperse because of individual prejudice and real estate, financial,

and even legal barriers. Thus black communities have been able to accommodate internal growth only by a slow block-by-block extension. Growth into lower-middle income areas has typically been easiest, since neighboring low-income groups are often the most resistant to black residents, for both psychological and economic reasons, and since the middle-class population can afford to move to the suburbs. In other words, growth most often occurs outward in a wedge rather than through similar housing (see Figure 8.08).

Urban Transport

The existing transport routes usually determined the pattern of growth of a city and the location of the central business district and major industrial tracts as well. As the size of the city increased, stress was placed on these routes and demand arose for better quality transport, especially to the central business district. The routes were then modernized by using streetcars, and the center was enhanced and use intensified along the affected routes; arms of development began to extend outward along these routes in stellate (star-like) fashion (see the pre-auto development pattern, Figure 9.07, p. 187). With further growth and a shift to automobile transport, obsolescence and congestion of existing routes again occurred; as the central business district suffered, competing centers arose.

Efforts to improve access to the CBD have led to such transport improvements as rapid transit and freeways. As far more intensive than a freeway system, rapid transit tends to concentrate activities in the downtown area and at outer nodes (stations). It is a viable and efficient system so long as most commuters do not have or use cars. However, even in areas having rapid transit and the highest intensity of land use, people demand cars, and severe congestion results (as in New York, Boston, and London.) Central densities may then decline as more people demand space for their cars, and the transit system will become less and less profitable.

THE URBAN SYSTEM AND URBAN STRUCTURE

A freeway system will tend to decentralize people and activities and again will cause some unavoidable congestion in the large metropolis. For the smaller metropolis, though, where highways can accommodate the volume of cars generated at the center, a freeway system may be optimal. Improvements in the speed of either system will encourage expansion of the city outward along the transport routes, since commuters may then enjoy newer housing and larger open spaces at no increase in travel time.

Growth of the Town or City

Most cities in advanced societies have experienced more or less continuous growth over varying periods of time. Expanding the edge of the city and changing the use of areas within it are two of the most exciting and dynamic spatial processes.

The growth of population and the increase in activities generate increasing demand for space not only at the edge of the city, but also at good locations within the city. Thus, the city grows in both extent and intensity. The density of the inner areas increases because of competition for the limited, more accessible space. However, the advent of the automobile caused many cities to spread out more rapidly than they intensified, and overall densities fell.

For short periods and in smaller places, all growth may at times be accommodated by extension of the city alone or, if land is severely restricted (either legally or topographically), by intensification alone; in any longer time period, though, both processes will occur. Central land intensities must rise as the competition for good sites enhances land values and increases rents; and the outer limits of the city must extend because part of the demand is for new single-family houses, and because areas that could intensify often lag in their response.

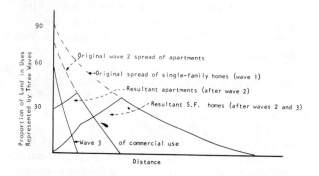

Figure 8.13 Waves of urban expansion. As a place grows, single-family homes spread outward from a small commercial core, and the inner, older homes become replaced by the growing commercial core and a surrounding zone of apartments—the older of which may later be displaced by expanding commerce.

As intensity increases, older homes and apartments surrounding the CBD will gradually be taken for commercial use. Apartments will extend, especially along arterials, into former single-family areas. In more desired areas, such as sectors of middle or high income, new apartments tend to replace older homes. In less desired areas, homes are often subdivided into small apartments. Together this overintensive use and lack of landlord and tenant maintenance help create slum tenements. As well, the concentration of low-income residents in one area also hurts preexisting businesses and leads to commercial blight and deteriorating services for the poor. Rehabilitation and code enforcement are attempted, but with little success. Urban renewal at least shifts the burden of building maintenance to the public sector, even if it does not prevent other manifestations of the slum.

Obviously, public officials favor building highrise and townhouse projects designed to attract high-income groups back to the city, but success here is limited by the preference of the rich for suburbs and space. At the same time, other residents of older areas move to new housing at the edge of the city. In some cases, the move is impelled by a radical change in the social or economic status of their neighborhood, such as when people flee before an advancing ghetto, but more often it reflects their demand for newer and more modern housing.

In the American city at least, which has little central planning, the expansion of the edge and the process of successive uses within the city may be described as a diffusion process. The outer edge is a fairly wide zone of transition from areas that are solidly city to more widely separated homes and subdivisions. Since far more land is available for subdivisions than is demanded, their specific locations are in a sense random. Given a free, speculative land market, the probability that a parcel of land beyond the solid city area will be developed is a complicated function of housing preferences; distance from the edge, from employment opportunities, and from services; the size of the parcel; topography; and the speculative behavior of the owner. Both premature development and late development are common, and at any one time much land within the suburban fringe is in "speculative nonuse"; it has been sold by the farmer who originally owned it, but not yet subdivided.

The process of succession, too, is complicated. More areas are ripe for renewal, more homes available for replacement by apartments, and more sites available for commercial upgrading than are demanded. Thus, as with subdivisions, their locations are in a sense random.

A microlevel theory of urban growth suggests that the demand for space by new activities may be separated into a series of waves (see Figure 8.13):

1. A wave front of single-family homes, from the place and time of earliest settlement to the present outermost suburban edge, and including necessary supporting facilities: parks, schools, and convenience-goods stores.

2. A central commercial expansion, which is as much upward (more intensive use and higher buildings) as outward.

3. A rather slow replacement wave of apartments, which comes a little later.

4. A wave of poor immigrants, intensifying the use of existing older housing.

5. A renewal wave of high-rise apartments for the wealthy and public housing for the poor.

At any point in time, there is a density gradient (leaving out the subpeaks caused by business districts), and over time this gradient shifts both upward and outward.

THE URBAN SYSTEM AND URBAN STRUCTURE

9

Spatial Structure of the Landscape

SUMMARY: THE THEORY OF SPATIAL STRUCTURE

We now summarize what has been suggested so far to account for the spatial patterns of economic activities. A location is given meaning or identity by specializing, which implies that it forms a set of spatial relations with other locations. We examined locations and the interactions between them in order to discover their structure in space, if indeed there is any. On the one hand, structure or organization implies that a territory may be divided into regions, and, on the other, that the regions are arranged in a hierarchical structure. This systematic structure is produced by the rational attempts of a population to achieve some goals of spatial efficiency. These goals are:

1. To use each separate parcel of land and, simultaneously, the sum of all parcels of land to the greatest profitability and utility, and

2. To achieve the highest level of interaction at the least possible cost between locations needing such interactions.

Obviously, other goals and desires also affect the appearance of the landscape, but we will discuss here only what can be understood about the landscape from just these two spatial goals.

The spatial goals give rise to certain spatial structures through a small set of interrelated spatial decisions, or substitutions, that can be made.

1. A substitution can be made between land costs and transport costs when seeking accessibility to some point. Expensive sites close to the site can be chosen and then used intensively, or farther sites may be chosen and used less intensively—with the same total costs.

2(a). A substitution may be made between production costs at sites and transport costs when seeking the optimal market size and scale of operations. The cost benefits of larger production volume must be balanced against increased transport costs for procurement of raw materials and distribution of finished goods. Most activities have a limited optimal scale of production, but this varies greatly by industry.

2(b). A substitution between production-cost savings from agglomeration and transport costs can be made. The savings gained by proximity to related industries must be balanced against the risk of having no even partially monopolized supplies or markets.

2(c). A substitution is possible between self-sufficiency (higher production costs) and trade (higher transport costs). Importing higher quality resources or goods from outside the region, involving greater transport costs and the risk of political and military interference, must be balanced against using lower quality local resources or producing goods locally at a higher cost.

When we attempt to describe the order, or spatial pattern, of locations and their interrelations, we observe at least five kinds of behavior, together defining the real landscape. The existence of space together with the goals of spatial efficiency induces two kinds of regularity:

1. Spatial gradients of land use.

2. A spatial hierarchy of regions.

The differential quality of space results in:

3. More irregular but predictable patterns of location and interaction.

Elements that distort theoretical patterns include

4. Spatial error resulting from nonoptimal behavior.

5. The process of spatial diffusion; the unfolding of the spatial structure over time as conditions change.

Spatial Gradients

In theory, spatial gradients are the inevitable result of the competition between activities for the limited space near a point of maximum accessibility. The resulting patterns of land use and travel should maximize the value of the land and minimize the transport costs, while at the same time satisfying the demands of society.

A point exists in any area that is central to all other points and thus minimizes the total distance to points in the surrounding area. This is the market. As the distance of any activity from the market increases, a producer will incur greater and greater transport costs and thus lower and lower net revenue per unit area until eventually he cannot survive; net revenues will equal transport costs.

Given activities that are of varying productivity and transportability, a spatial ordering of activities results. Activities with very high transport costs have limited ranges where they may survive and must be produced very intensively near the market. Thus, activities that incur lower transport costs are displaced to more distant locations, substituting greater acreage for greater intensity. In theory, at any one point in time an optimal gradient order will exist. This equilibrium is brought about by the competitive bidding of potential producers for the more accessible land, thus raising its value (the cost of purchase, or rent). Such a gradient is continuous from the farthest edge of the market to the most intensive urban location. However, we cannot expect to observe such a pure gradient pattern, since the gradient *per se* is but a partial picture of the theoretical landscape. The important point to remember is that gradient behavior exists, and gradient tendencies may be observed.

Spatial Hierarchy of Market Areas

Whereas the spatial gradient results from competition for the space around the most central point, the spatial hierarchy includes a whole system of such points, each attracting producers and serving consumers within its market region, but seeking to be separate from other, similar centers. This behavior creates an efficient division of space into regional markets.

A very large number of different economic and social activities, including control, exchange, and other service functions, require little space in which to operate and depend for support on the final consumer, who is generally scattered spatially. These kinds of different activities are mutually attracted to each other, a concept evident in the very notion of a market. Different activities that have similar thresholds (sales needed to sustain the activity) and ranges (distance customers are willing to travel) find it profitable to locate together in a cluster, since customers typically wish to minimize the effort needed to consume goods and services that they seek with similar frequency. Hence, by enabling customers to satisfy many purposes in the same trip, agglomeration of these activities achieves large economies.

Sellers of the same good or service, however, are mutually repellent. Each seeks a spatial monopoly —an area in which only one seller of the good has customers. This competition thus induces sellers to locate just far enough away from each other so that each can enjoy a profitable spatial monopoly, but close enough together so that not enough purchasing power remains in the space between the sellers to allow another seller to spring up between them. Ideally, this process results in a triangular arrangement of sellers, each one equidistant from the others, and these triangular patterns will together form a hexagonal network.

As soon as we find activities that require larger markets than in the basic system above, a hierarchical structure emerges. One rather optimal arrangement when such an activity emerges is for every other central place to add the new activity. Similarly, for activities requiring even larger markets, every other one of these second-level centers would acquire the activity. Thus, we would create an even higher level. In this way, a territory is divided into a hexagonal structure of markets and spatial monopolies having as many hierarchical levels as the economy will support.

Under a given technology, an arrangement of centers will theoretically exist for the entire economy such that the population can satisfy all its demands on all levels at the least possible total distance, while at the same time all sellers are profitable. In summary, the central-place hierarchy is the result of balancing a number of goals: locating as many activities in as few places as possible and realizing the greatest economies of agglomeration, while at the same time keeping the number of trips and the total distance traveled to a minimum.

Gradient Hierarchies   If space were everywhere identical and no activities existed except ones like those already introduced, the landscape would have a joint hierarchical and gradient character (see Figure 9.01). The gradient results when activities compete for space on the basis of their productivity, and it induces some dispersal of population and activities. However, if the territory of the economy around the main market is large enough to permit the emergence of smaller competing markets and central places, a central-place structure begins to be formed. The larger the space the economy contains, the more elaborated becomes its hierarchical structure and the less important any single center; modifying the overall gradient around the main market are local gradients around regional markets (see Figure 8.10). In the U.S., for example, we observe a dispersion of central places over the territory, an overall gradient of intensity of population and activities outward from the Northeast, and lesser gradients outward from the other regional centers.

The internal structure of a city also illustrates this structure (Figure 8.10 again). When small, the city center contains all the distribution facilities, and there is a gradient of land use outward from the center. As the area of the city increases, the threshold for establishment of competing centers is reached, the original gradient becomes punctuated by areas of greater intensity around district shopping centers, and, when the city becomes very large, a complex central-place hierarchy develops, consisting of hundreds of nodes at many levels with their gradients overlapping.

Spatial Quality

Space, however, is not homogeneous, but differs markedly in its productivity, attractiveness, and—especially—endowment of resources. Variations in

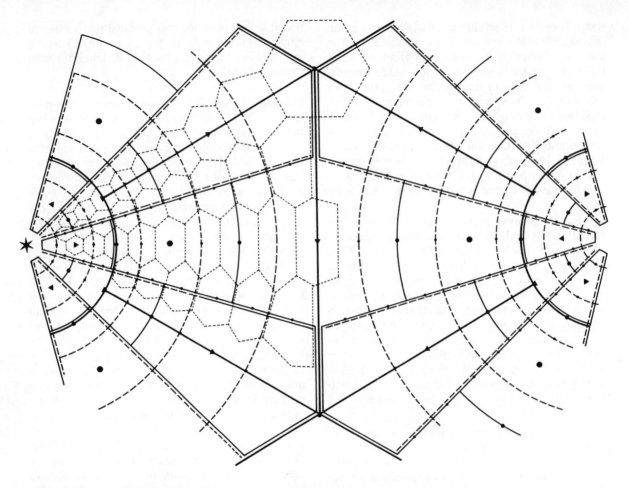

Figure 9.01 Gradient–hierarchy landscape. This is one attempt to combine rent-gradient and central-place theories. Central places (dots) and their trade area boundaries (lines) are developed to serve the area between two large centers, which are agricultural markets. The hexagonal shape of the smallest market areas is maintained (for clarity, not all are shown), but the market areas become larger and centers farther apart with distance from the major centers. Compare with Figure 4.05 showing the usual central-place patterns.

spatial quality alter the patterns presented so far, usually by creating variations in the intensity of land use and concentration of activities. The gradient–hierarchy landscape will thus change.

Variation in quality works in several ways. If land productivity varies over very wide areas (such as with a seasonal monopoly), it will alter the agricultural gradient and likewise increase or reduce the spacing of central places. More localized differences in land productivity create rather predictable local irregularities, such as upgrading or downgrading the use of the land, or favoring larger or smaller farms than would be expected. Where transport is relatively cheap and differences in land productivity great, the agricultural land use gradient may be greatly modified.

SPATIAL STRUCTURE OF THE LANDSCAPE

The Industrial Landscape The most common case of response to variation in spatial quality, however, is industrial location, which involves obtaining needed raw materials from a limited number of specific locations distributing finished products to other industries with very specific locations, rather than to more widespread final consumer markets. Whereas the gradient–hierarchy landscape consists of central markets serving widely diffused farmers, the industrial landscape shows greater concentration of activities at large markets and material sources. Rather than seeking locations away from each other in order to obtain spatial monopolies, many industries cluster at locations that have proven profitable, hoping to share all or much of a national market.

For industries in which transport costs on finished products are most important and markets are diffuse, location is similar to that for a central-place activity. Other industries in which the transport costs of raw materials are the dominant expense seek a spatial monopoly, or a local supply area. On a macro-scale, such places will often seem to have located in a cluster, but on a micro-scale, it will be apparent that each plant has sought a separation from the others that will assure it a local supply area.

Industries for which transport costs on both materials and finished goods are significant may locate at either resource or market or at major junctions between. The less important the transfer costs and the more important other cost differences between sites (such as the quality and cost of labor), the more the industrial pattern will become one of clusters of producers at several locations where costs are least.

The net effect of these patterns of industrial location is, first, to create clusters of similar urban settlements near major concentrations of resources. Second, industries that share national or large regional markets and for which transport costs are not great tend to locate near the largest single markets—the bigger metropolises—to obtain labor quality and supply, and prestige, or to minimize risk. The effect on the landscape is to concentrate population and production in fewer, larger places (Figure 9.02)—disproportionately few in comparison to the pure gradient–hierarchy landscape serving an agricultural population.

Distorting Factors

At least two distorting factors are present to complicate the picture still further: spatial error and spatial diffusion. By spatial error, we mean that the optimum locational decision is not always made. Most decisions are made without all the facts available, and they thus contain much error. Even with good information, error can be introduced when the data is interpreted. In addition, many persons, governments, and businesses often make decisions which are satisfying rather than optimal; they follow a conservative, safe course that is profitable, even if another, riskier course would be more profitable.

This error is most apparent in locational mistakes, paid for in extreme cases by economic failure, but more generally by inadequate profits and income and operation at less than capacity. The effect on the theoretically ideal landscape is to blur its precision; to confuse its boundaries between agricultural and urban uses and between market areas, resulting in both zones of interpenetration, such as between crops, and zones of indifference, such as customer choice of a shopping center; and to loosen the rigidity of the hexagonal structure randomly.

However, even if the optimum decisions are made at one point in time, these may be rendered imperfect quickly by the second distorting element: change over time in location factors and the locaters. If, as has been typically the case historically, population, activities, and knowledge spread from a small number of points having greater power, access to markets and capital, and ability to achieve the optimal goals, then a static theory can be considered only a partial one. Not only does economic development spread outward

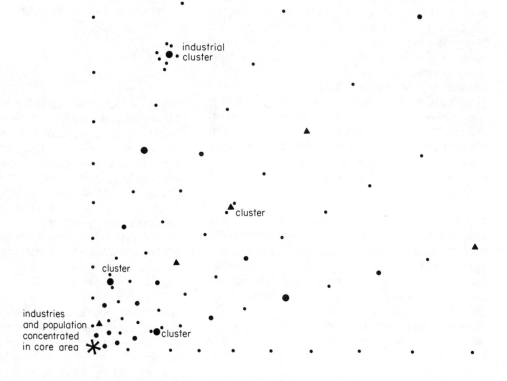

Figure 9.02 Addition of industrial clusters to the gradient–hierarchy surface. When such variation in spatial quality as resource location is considered, the gradient–hierarchy landscape is distorted. Clusters of industrial towns appear. Because of their industrial importance, some larger places are closer together than in Figure 9.01. (Only urban places are shown here.)

from a few origins, but social, political, and economic conditions change over time: technology, transport quality, productivity, kind and volume of demands, manufacturing processes, and population all change. The effect of these changes on the landscape is to make existing locations obsolete and to force enterprises and individuals to adjust their behavior.

The effects on the landscape of dynamic spatial growth and diffusion are complicated. One impact

is the creation of another kind of gradient. Most obviously here, population and transport density decline outward from the hearth areas of a population to the margin of settlement (Figure 9.03) (for example, westward in the United States from the Atlantic seaboard). Also, industrialization and urbanization typically diffuse slowly from early centers of economic power (from Boston–New York–Philadelphia in the United States). As a result, both absolute and per capita income usually follow the same gradient (see Figures 9.03 and 6.12).

SPATIAL STRUCTURE OF THE LANDSCAPE

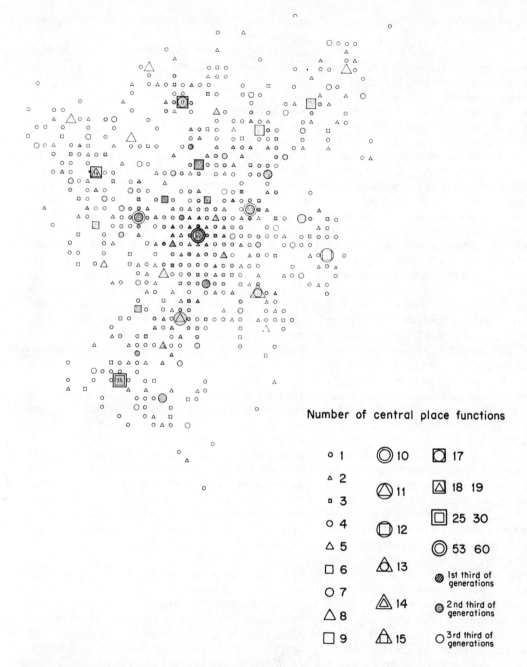

Number of central place functions

∘ 1	◎ 10	▣ 17
▵ 2	◭ 11	◪ 18 19
▫ 3	⬓ 12	▢ 25 30
∘ 4		◎ 53 60
▵ 5	⬓ 12	
▫ 6	◭ 13	⬙ 1st third of generations
○ 7	◭ 14	⬤ 2nd third of generations
△ 8	◬ 15	○ 3rd third of generations
□ 9		

Figure 9.03 Growth of central-place systems over time. This figure shows an experimental and hypothetical pattern of central places, as might have developed over perhaps 100 years. Note that the density decreases outward from the center (the distance between the places increases), but that denser clusters of central places occur at various points.

SPATIAL STRUCTURE OF THE LANDSCAPE

Movement Patterns

While this summary discussion has focused on the location of activities and people, it should be made clear that the whole structure is maintained by interactions between locations—trade, movements of people, and communication. The differentiation of the landscape has increased, of course, as transport and communications have improved and become cheaper; thus greater advantage can be taken of superior locations and site quality. Organization of locations means specialization of functions, which requires movements to make the specialization profitable. Without movement between places, no organization of locations could exist; there would be only a surface containing individual man–land relationships.

All the locational models and theories discussed could, in fact, be called movement or interaction theories, since the goal of minimizing distance was inherent in each model. The gradients of agricultural and urban land use result from minimizing the costs of supplying agricultural products to markets and the costs of reaching work and shopping within the city. The extent of both the market and the city is governed by transport costs as well as land rent (price).

Central-place theory, too, depends on minimizing transport costs when satisfying different sets of central service needs. Again, the extent of one central-place system is controlled by the relation of transport costs to possible revenues. However, partly because people are willing to travel much farther for some purposes than for others, minimizing transport costs applies to a variety of levels. Figure 9.04 depicts movement patterns to agricultural markets on two levels and to central places on three levels for a small area.

Much industrial location involves specific, irregular movements from raw material sources and to markets. Theoretically, industrial location rests heavily on minimizing transport costs, but these costs are to a complex of markets and from a complex of sources, rather than to just one market. Thus, the resulting location and movement patterns are less regular—they are no longer center-oriented and diffused, but instead, few, larger, and overlapping.

Spatial Organization

In the light of the five kinds of spatial behavior we have just discussed, the landscape can be seen to show systematic variation in intensity and extent of land use and interaction. The spatial structure of a society is perhaps best described by the patterns of intensity of land use and by the complex pattern of interaction that each location has with the world around it. Try to imagine all five patterns of spatial behavior placed together on one map. It is obviously difficult to analyze such a complex pattern; one component cannot be readily isolated from the others. We attempted here just to summarize the major elements that, in commercial societies at least, seem to interact to produce typical landscapes.

Theory and Reality   There are many ways to test portions of theory. Many of these methods were discussed earlier, and warnings were given not to expect simple patterns, such as hexagonal trade areas, in a real landscape. Finding evidence of efficient behavior in the location of activities requires more sophisticated tests; in the central-place example, for instance, adjustments must be made for topography, population density, age of settlement, other activities, and some acceptable range of error.

The evidence given by the more careful tests shows thus far that optimal or nearly optimal spatial behavior and much spatial order can be seen in location and interaction patterns. However, the effects of rapid changes in technology, population, and other forces are perhaps greater than anticipated, and we have not yet well enough incorporated into our theory the dimension of historical change. On the other hand, the presumed role of irrationality has become smaller and smaller as we have improved our concept of opti-

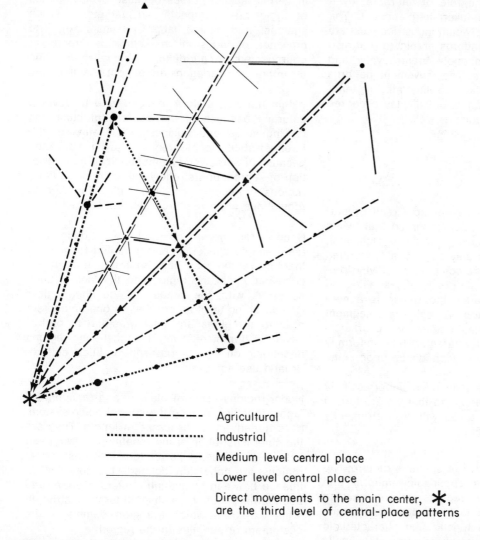

Figure 9.04 Partial movement pattern for a gradient–hierarchy–cluster surface. Movements serving the spatial pattern are shown in Figure 9.02.

mizing behavior, as we have looked at larger sets of relationships, and as we better understand the multiple meanings of distance and other spatial characteristics.

Distribution maps provide the most simple evidence of spatial structure. Distributions of land use, farm size, and per-acre value of farm output corroborate the existence of an agricultural gradient, as well as showing the effect of land quality and entrepreneurial differences. Maps of the areas of retail and wholesale trade in urban centers and analyses of how places are spaced support central-place theory, so long as variations in population density and the role of alternate town-building activities are taken into account. The location patterns of individual industries illustrate the kinds of optimal patterns predicted, but also show the effects of monopoly, brand loyalty, and other distorting factors. The movement patterns of goods and people likewise illustrate this tendency to minimize distance, but display a degree of indifference to distance as well.

REGIONAL STRUCTURE

In this chapter we first presented a realistic pattern of locations and interactions so that, when the region was discussed, it would be clear that, in theory, the region is only a practical, simplified way to look at the more complex underlying pattern of behavior. For purposes of planning and administration, of course, the region is a necessary and practical tool. A region is a segment of space that is bounded together and character-ized by some common characteristic—uniformity of land use or common dependence upon some center, for instance. However, such "pure" common characteristics extend over embarrassingly small amounts of territory, so that we are forced to accept as regions areas with less stringently defined common qualities.

With respect to theories of spatial structure, two kinds of regions are applicable—uniform and nodal regions. Uniform regions are areas having some given use or character or possessing some other common characteristic (the characteristic varies within the region only to some statistically acceptable limit). Whether having in common a single factor or multiple factors, uniform regions may be diverse in other respects.

Uniform regions are the result of spatial agglom-eration and the incompatibility of some land uses and social groups. Uniform regions having the same agricultural land use, for example, tend to occur within a certain range in the intensity gradient out from a central market. Specific por-tions of the zone at that distance tend to specialize in certain specific crops because of advantages of agglomeration (specialized markets, research stations, and skilled labor, for instance). The presence of industrial markets is a strong en-couragement to agricultural specialization, and environmental variations are of course significant.

Within the city, uniform regions tend to develop naturally because of the benefits of clustering for industries and businesses, because of dif-ferential ability to pay rent (or buy homes), and because of perceived incompatibility. The motiva-tion of segregation strongly helps create uniform regions of income, religion, and color. Zoning regulations often reinforce the natural trends.

Uniform regions are now able to be defined by fairly simple clustering and grouping techniques that insure the maximum contrast between the cohesion within the region and the lack of such cohesion with the areas outside the region. Obviously, no territory consists of one unique set of uniform regions; any small area may be part of several different relatively homogeneous regions depending on the criteria used—politics, culture, or land use, for example.

Nodal regions—central places—and their hinter-lands, together forming the central-place system, have already been discussed at length. They are the chief illustration of the repetitive, hierarchical nature of space. Like uniform regions, nodal regions, are not rigidly defined—the zones of in-fluence between competing centers overlap, and boundaries should be defined in terms of strength —the extent to which a region dominates the customers or supplies in the region.

Any small area is part of a whole set of nodal regions, from the smallest hamlet to the national economy (Figure 9.05). The smaller regions, in general, nest within the larger ones, although there are many cases in which a smaller area is divided in its allegiance to larger ones. The higher the hierarchical level of the region, the more self-contained its culture and its economy.

The structure of metropolitan regions has been the most studied. Metropolitan divisions are based

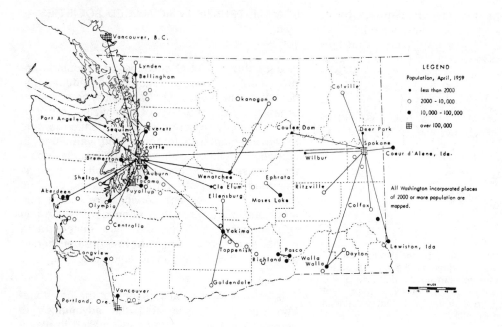

Figure 9.05 Nodal regions of Washington. One clue to the nesting of smaller nodal areas within larger ones is given by an analysis of telephone data. In this example, it was assumed that if one town places more calls to another than it receives, it depends on that town. Thus, Seattle receives from all places more calls than it sends, including the next most important place, Spokane, which in turn dominates its local region. (Reprinted by permission of the Regional Science Association, from J. Nystuen and M. Dacey, "A Graph Theory Interpretation of Nodal Regions," *Papers and Proceedings of the Regional Science Association* Vol. VII, 1961.)

mainly on wholesale and financial patterns (Figure 9.06). Although boundaries are typically drawn between these regions, it should be clear that the zones of influence have a wide overlap, especially where metropolitan centers are close together and their hinterlands are large.

Political regions are legally defined by specific boundaries, so that our lives must conform to these boundaries to a degree. Administrative efficiency in large areas requires a hierarchical, repetitive structure, such as in the central-place system (nodal economic regions). A question that is interesting theoretically and also important practically is to what extent these sets of regions —political and economic—coincide. Central places

often arise at midpoints between large centers. Boundaries between larger places pass through smaller ones, but it is administratively more efficient to include entire subunits within larger ones—for example, to include entire parishes within a diocese, entire schools within a school district. Thus, the economic and administrative principles conflict. If the economic forces are stronger, the later administrative structure will be less than optimal—including too few or too many subdivisions and off-center administrative centers. Administrators and planners generally favor making economic structure subordinate to administrative efficiency, which might be optimal from the viewpoint of the entire society (using social and political as well as economic criteria).

SPATIAL STRUCTURE OF THE LANDSCAPE

METROPOLITAN REGIONS-1948
(After Bogue, 1949)

0 500
Miles

Figure 9.06 Regional structure of the United States. Here, all counties were assigned to the closest major wholesaling center, thus minimizing the distance of the population to such centers. (Reprinted by permission of The Johns Hopkins Press, from Otis Dudley Duncan et al., *Metropolis and Region.*)

Still, political units and economic regions conflict more often than not; the hinterlands of such centers as New York, St. Louis, Kansas City, Omaha, Chicago, Cincinnati, and Portland cross state lines (see Figure 9.06).

The solution to this apparent conflict between administrative and economic organization is that economic subareas often nest entirely within higher ones, even though this does not strictly minimize distance. Branch Federal Reserve bank districts, for example, nest within major districts, and retailers in a smaller city midway between larger ones will obtain most wholesale goods from only one of them.

In summary, regions do exist, they do have meaning, and we can delineate them. However, they are not clear-cut areas in which activities are confined. Rather, regions are useful more as a system of classification; they are imperfect generalizations of the underlying spatial complex, which itself can be better described as the connections of countless individuals, farms, plants and businesses.

SPATIAL TRENDS IN ADVANCED SOCIETIES

In agriculture, central services, and industry, improvements in transportation have reduced the cost of distance and thus the dominance of spatial organization by the goal of minimizing transport costs. Thus, in agriculture more attention is paid to environmental differences and variations in response to inputs. Similarly, individuals locate their houses more because of amenities (such as view and amount of land), services, and prestige location. Industries and services are responding more and more often to economies of scale and agglomeration, and thus becoming concentrated in the fewer, larger places having greater market and labor stability and more amenities.

It is becoming popular to speak of the new location freedom, to say that the advantages of centrality and accessibility have ceased to play a decisive role, and to ask whether the city, the central business district, the hierarchy of cities and services, and — indeed — much of present theory is becoming obsolete. In fact, of course, distance is still important. Our new ability to go greater distances for the same cost has extended the range of our activities and lengthened our relationships. But that the goals of accessibility and minimizing distance are still powerful is shown by today's even greater concentration of activities in the few places that are most accessible. Similarly, the structure of distribution of goods and individual shopping is still hierarchical, although the number of levels have been reduced, and centers of a given level are farther apart.

A larger portion of manufacturing, as of agriculture, can today respond to local variations in quality and returns to scale in order to penetrate more distant markets and reduce the spatial monopoly of other producers. Yet, the growing demand for goods and services that can be delivered immediately in time — such as entertainment, recreation, and repair work — is stimulating a counter-trend toward greater regional self-sufficiency.

SPATIAL STRUCTURE OF THE LANDSCAPE

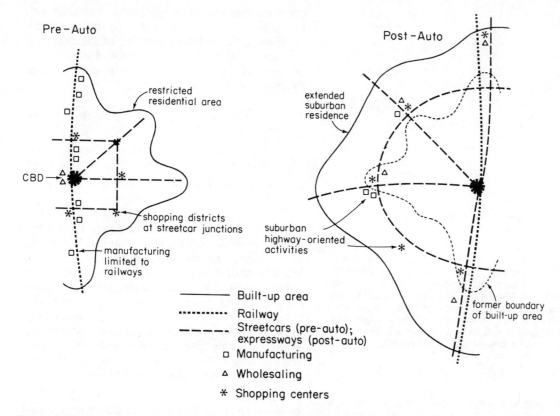

Figure 9.07 The urban pattern: pre-auto and post-auto. The automobile has made possible a more extended residential area and a dispersal of manufacturing and wholesaling activities to suburban locations.

Within the city, cheaper transport and the shift to the automobile have had an even more radical impact (Figure 9.07); the entire urban area may now be within the range that an individual is willing to travel in his car. However, the freedom given by the car tends to transform the greatest asset of the center — its accessibility — into a liability — congestion. As a result, some activities are dispersed to more distant points with only moderate accessibility but more space. In this case, a more complicated pattern of rent and land values emerges, showing far more emphasis on local differences in environment and amenities. But the problem of the congested center results from a technical inability to adjust to an altered transport mode; the change in transport does not bestow real "location freedom" but instead permits competing centers to arise because their freedom from congestion offsets their slightly lower accessibility.

Thus, even with change, spatial order does not disappear. Businesses remain aggregated to maximize information exchange and reduce total transport charges, but even more aggregations become appropriate as the city area increases and its density decreases; an individual store that chooses a separate, low-rent site, even though technically more accessible, risks lack of awareness by consumers and subsequent bankruptcy

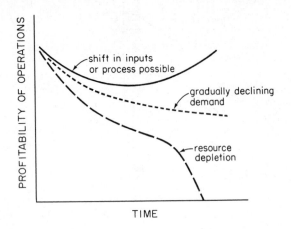

Figure 9.08 There are three possible outcomes for an investment at a location. If a necessary resource depletes and there is no substitute, profits will decline, and the location will fail. Often a location slowly loses profits as demand gradually declines (such as a small store when large stores take a greater share of the market). Successful adjustment without new investment may be possible if inputs or products can be changed.

because of its spatial isolation. The dispersal of shopping in metropolitan Los Angeles is not the result of "location freedom," but rather is precisely the result of the difficulty of moving to one center from such a vast, built-up area. Here, stores are not randomly dispersed, but cluster in regional shopping centers rationally located to the distribution of population. However, the absence of a dominant downtown center may result in having fewer of those goods and services that need the entire metropolitan market for their support, for even in Los Angeles most travel is local, and people are no more willing to travel to distant locations to a specialized shop than if it were downtown.

SPATIAL ORGANIZATION: EFFICIENCY

Although we do not know very well what constitutes social and economic efficiency, we can compare the predictions of spatial behavior with the real landscape in order to measure the "efficiency" of existing patterns of location and interaction. The fairly high degree to which businessmen depart in the short run from optimal or rational behavior suggests that:

1. Other social or psychological goals may be paramount.

2. People may be uninterested in optimal economic efficiency and be satisfied with lesser returns.

3. People make mistakes when they attempt to be rational.

Inasmuch as it is difficult and costly to find the optimum decision, which is at any rate not too stable over time and may involve real risks to attain, it should not be surprising that there is a great deal of profitable and satisfactory location and movement, but not much that is theoretically optimal. On the other hand, location or movement that is highly irrational will cause measurable economic costs and suffering, and such errors are not hard to find; however, most activities are rationally located and seem not too imperfect.

As we have frequently observed, technology and demand change more quickly than the useful life of an investment in a location. Thus, at any point in time some inefficiency due to obsolescence (Figure 9.08) is to be expected. Until profits disappear and even after losses set in, a location may not be abandoned.

Evidences of a fairly efficient spatial structure would seem to be these:

1. The enterprises are profitable and operate at the most economic scale.

2. Physical and human resources are fully utilized.

3. Unnecessary cross-movements do not occur.

4. Regional differences in income are not extreme.

In sum, these criteria imply that shifts in scale or location will neither raise profits nor decrease costs.

Information and Power: Barriers to Efficiency

Efficient spatial structure presumes that the price system is relatively free to operate and, in turn, that information is freely available and there is no monopoly power. If some groups have such superior, monopoly information, they may obtain short-run advantages that will destroy producers who are basically more efficient or better located. If a region possesses such advantages, it may prevent production that would have been more efficient in another region. The primary spatial effect of regional monopoly is to exaggerate differences in regional development and income. Indeed, we may view the slow diffusion of development partially as a function of the uneven distribution of power and information.

10

Problems of the Spatial Structure of the American and World Economies

This book has been concerned principally with presenting concepts and models of ideal spatial location, and with finding how observed patterns follow these principles. In this context, we made frequent mention of deviations from the ideal models. Variations in regional and world levels of development and income are the most obvious examples of such deviations, and at least a brief discussion of economic development is thus called for.

Both the American and the world economies exhibit much evidence of spatial (regional) inefficiency. To judge from the criteria given at the end of the previous chapter:

1. Many enterprises are far from being reasonably profitable.

2. Unnecessary cross-movements seem rather common.

3. Resources, both physical and human, are not fully utilized; rather, they are frequently misused.

4. Differences in regional income are far greater than is theoretically justified.

The main reasons for this inefficiency seem to be:

1. Variations in the power of groups and areas and in their access to information and capital.

2. National political divisions and variations in size, resources, and popular attitudes within such divisions.

3. The inability to make rational decisions.

4. Differences in technology and the development of history.

5. Superiority of ideological or prejudicial values over spatial optimizational goals and economic values.

6. Technological change, resource depletion, and other causes of obsolescence.

SPATIAL EFFICIENCY OF THE AMERICAN ECONOMY

At any one time, many enterprises within the economy can be observed to be either failing or unprofitable. Many factors account for this. For example, presently unprofitable factories may have been optimally located at one time, but resource and labor costs may have risen, the location of markets shifted, or the technology of production altered too rapidly. These outside conditions may have made adjustment impossible, whatever the behavior of the firm. Similarly, many stores that were well-located during the streetcar era cannot possibly adapt successfully to the present car-oriented transport network. Thus, some inefficiency as a product of change in time is unavoidable.

Many firms are unprofitable, however, because they are uneconomically small and their operator is unwilling to shift to a more profitable location or occupation. This problem is common in agriculture, trade, and services. Other farms and businesses are unsuccessful because of ignorance and bad locational decisions. In our society, where small businesses may enter relatively freely, a great many failures of this kind should be expected, despite the caution of banks in lending capital.

Some unnecessary cross-movements and some excessively long and costly movements should also be expected because of ignorance and the occasional superiority of noneconomic values. For example, individuals may ignore good, nearby shops and services because their image of them is bad, or ideology may dictate part of a nation's trade, probably raising costs as a result. Excessive movements may also result from monopolistic control. Monopoly ownership of closer resources may force competitors to use far distant sources; similarly, control by hospitals over the physicians allowed to affiliate with them forces many black and poor patients to travel farther for care than otherwise necessary (Figure 10.01). This kind of inefficiency may be rather costly to society.

Inefficient use of resources can take many forms. Land held in speculative nonuse around cities is common (Figure 10.02). Physical resources, such as water, may be irrationally allocated because political divisions and groups have different

amounts of power. Under-utilization of available human resources is common, too, because of such factors as prejudice against certain groups, Negroes and American Indians, for instance; discriminatory state laws and differences in the quality of education; and the relative immobility of labor.

Regional Inequality in Development and Income

The single best piece of evidence for spatial inefficiency at the local and national levels is excessive inequality in income levels. If the price system were truly free and groups and regions did not vary in power and information, then the limited inequalities that existed would not be inefficient, but rather necessary products of spatial separation; some areas are better located than others and pay less for transport. If, however, variation in income exceeds what might be expected for these reasons, then the spatial structure of the economy is inefficient.

In spite of almost continuous economic growth and the world's highest per capita income, America is beset by incongruent problems:

1. Continuing unemployment, beyond that technologically induced.

2. The persistent poverty of as much as a quarter of the population, shown by severe inequality in income.

Not only do sections of the country differ widely in prosperity (Figure 10.03) but portions of cities as well (Figure 10.04). It is generally recognized that these variations are greater than would be expected under truly optimum conditions in a unified economy.

Regional Convergence   One common explanation for this unemployment and income inequality is that there has been a lag in regional adjustment. According to this theory, as the economy has grown, some rather large areas have not been able to adjust to the changing conditions in transport, technology, and demand and as a consequence have much unemployment and lower per capita income. For example, some mining and lumber areas are declining because demand, labor requirements, and resource levels have fallen. Technological unemployment in such areas is common. Also, many agricultural areas contain inefficient, small farms that cannot generate sufficient income per family. So-called underemployment is the result.

In the process of adjusting, surplus labor from declining areas has migrated to more successful areas, usually larger cities—not rapidly enough for the declining areas to achieve internal economic equilibrium (including full employment) at a higher income level, but too rapidly, given the migrants' few skills and lack of education, for the metropolis to absorb. Thus, although rural out-migration from the poorer farm areas of the South has been rapid, the farms remain far too small, partly because of high rural birth rates. Presumably, equilibrium will be reached in the long run in these presently backward areas, and those farms remaining will be large, efficient units. Regional income should then tend to converge.

There are some doubts concerning this convergence process in America, however. Even if the economy is moving toward this equilibrium, in which most people will live in metropolises, there remains some question about whether the pattern is truly the most efficient one, economically and socially. There may be benefits lost by under-utilizing resources in the areas relegated to extensive activities, and there are also the enormous, unexamined economic and social costs of congestion in very large metropolises. The United States should perhaps examine the alternative, preferred by many other advanced nations, of developing more evenly across her territory.

However, there also exist underlying structural deficiencies in the economy which seem to make the above adjustment futile in itself. This author believes that the regional variation in development and income in America is excessive; and that the

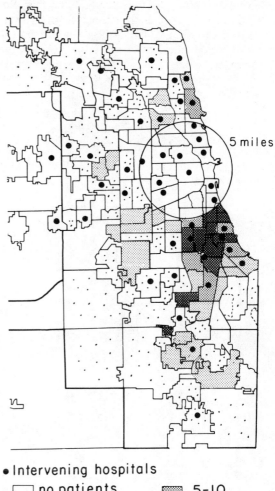

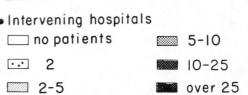

Figure 10.1 Unnecessary cross movements to Cook County Hospital from persons living over five miles away and located closer to other hospitals. Most poor patients have been forced to seek care at the Cook County Hospital. Thus, many patients from the poor south side of Chicago must travel beyond closer, intervening hospitals which they cannot afford — an example of spatial inefficiency as well as economic discrimination. Data are from 1968. Patients within five miles visiting the hospital are not shown.

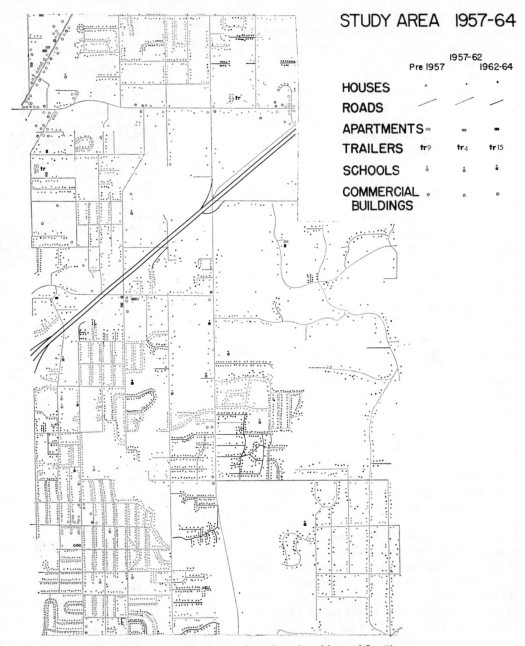

STUDY AREA 1957-64

	Pre 1957	1957-62	1962-64
HOUSES			
ROADS			
APARTMENTS			
TRAILERS	tr 9	tr 4	tr 15
SCHOOLS			
COMMERCIAL BUILDINGS			

Figure 10.02 Urban fringe settlement. In the sample section from the urban fringe of Seattle, the scattered, sprawling nature of subdivisions can be seen. Most of the vacant area is held for speculation; none is used for farming. Provision of services and schools to the dispersed suburban population is costly. (Reprinted by permission of the Regional Science Association from Richard Morrill, "Expansion of the Urban Fringe," *Papers and Proceedings of the Regional Science Association* Vol. XV, 1965.)

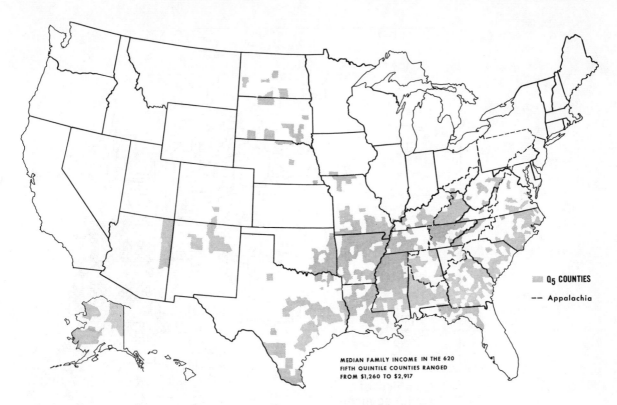

MEDIAN FAMILY INCOME IN THE 620
FIFTH QUINTILE COUNTIES RANGED
FROM $1,260 TO $2,917

Figure 10.03 Poorest areas of the United States. The fifth of counties (Q⁵ counties) with the lowest median family incomes are shown. Note the prevalence of poor counties in Appalachia and in rural portions of the South. (Source: U.S. Department of Commerce.)

depressed and poor regions of the country are not just products of temporary maladjustment.

1. The economy emphasizes short-run maximization of profits—quick return on investments.

2. The price system seems unable to allocate income correctly.

3. There is discrimination — often governmental — against minorities, women, the very old, and the very young.

These factors are reflected by the very large numbers of poor and unemployed in the most prosperous places, such as Chicago and Los Angeles, and even among long-time city residents. Even the most successful places are unable to achieve full employment and to eliminate poverty, despite the presence of the best transport and economic and cultural opportunities. If the economy sets too low a price for the services of certain workers and then further discriminates against many of them (because of race, for instance), then even in the most prosperous city poverty will never be removed by education or migration. Thus, merely relocating people from unsuccessful areas to the cities might well only aggravate their poverty.

Similarly, if the economy sets too low a price for forest and agricultural products, migration from these areas will not bring those people remaining to adequate income levels because individual

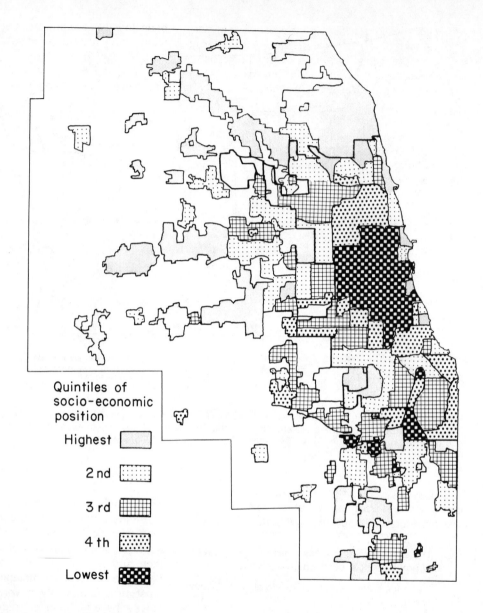

Figure 10.04 The socioeconomic position of Chicago-area communities. (Reprinted by permission of the University of Chicago Department of Geography, from J. Simmons, *The Changing Pattern of Retail Locations,* Research Paper No. 92, 1964.)

Quintiles of socio-economic position

Highest

2 nd

3 rd

4 th

Lowest

operators will not be able to either find a profitable production process or handle a large enough area to be profitable with the existing process. Prices might be high enough for adequate incomes if all farmers had high productivity on moderate acreage, but in some highly competitive sectors, distributors are strong enough to keep prices below even this level.

THE SPATIAL STRUCTURE OF ECONOMICS

Apparently, great variation in the power and bargaining position of different groups and the partly monopolistic control of prices by private industry and government prevents the price system from allocating income correctly. Weaker groups are paid too little, and thus differences in income exceed differences in actual productivity. One consequence is that the economy depends too much on saturating high-income consumers, while much of the population represents enormous latent demand. Excessive income inequality can thus be a deterrent to economic growth; the increase in production, employment, and mass consumption and the reduction in poverty following the 1964 American income tax cut is illustrative.

Discrimination against less powerful groups, blacks for example, also has great economic consequences. Negroes are systematically excluded from higher paying jobs, particularly at the local and small business level, and an unaccountable waste of resources and potential talent results. On the other hand, the uneven distribution of power gives other groups deferential treatment, such as depletion allowances and indirect subsidies—perhaps exemplified by highways aiding long-distance truckers.

Many discriminatory constraints in the economy are a consequence of state economic autonomy—minimum wage variations, right-to-work laws, and the like. While an attraction to industry in the state's early stages of industrial development, low minimum wages are also a deterrent to the state's internal economic growth, since most consumer goods are nationally priced. Right-to-work laws, too, weaken the normal process of increasing income levels through collective bargaining.

Regional Planning

Regional planning is action taken to improve the efficiency of the economy, particularly regarding problems of regional imbalance. Regional planning is, of course, very limited in a federal system under free enterprise; past regional planning has been mostly confined to interstate river development under federal jurisdiction.

At the broad policy level, the United States has two alternatives:

1. To encourage present trends of concentration in the large metropolises, leaving a veneer of efficient agricultural and recreational areas on the rest of the land.

2. To foster more even development over the entire country.

Present regional developmental programs—such as highway construction and educational improvement—actually may encourage the former alternative, since improved roads extend the domination of the larger, more successful centers, and the better trained and educated must necessarily find jobs in the cities. Improvement of access to local areas, such as in Appalachia, may encourage tourists and speed the marketing of farm produce, but it does not provide alternate employment opportunities for those in rural areas.

Without doubt, the most successful examples of regional development and income improvement in the United States have been due to either climate or governmental action. The sheer volume of the migration of already skilled and educated people in search of better climate to Florida, Arizona, and California caused a more general economic expansion, first in services, later in manufacturing. Even more important, the partly deliberate allocation of governmental expenditures for defense and space to selected areas, particularly California, Texas, Alabama, and Florida, induced a level of growth and prosperity in those states that otherwise could not have been achieved.

In the absence of such investment, economic expansion will almost always be located in the already successful areas, especially the northeastern core and a few regional metropolises, even if other locations might be more profitable in the long run. Thus, the gap between the more and less successful regions will become even greater, more migration will occur, and the prospects of the weaker areas will be reduced still further.

Although it is certainly possible for a region to grow without increasing its exports by increasing its productivity or expanding internal production of goods formerly imported, even this is less likely to occur in poorer regions than in the successful ones.

More even regional development would require more radical programs—for example, increased investment aid to new business in weaker areas, perhaps by exempting them from federal taxation for some period; greater incentives to encourage large companies to decentralize; and the creation of "new cities," not merely as suburbs to the already successful metropolises, but rather as centers in stagnant and depressed regions, to act as catalysts for regional development. These would need to be of small metropolitan size (250,000 people or so) in order to reach reasonable economic and cultural thresholds and still be located within commuting distance of most of the population; without the prospect of such moderately sized regional markets, few industries would find it advantageous to decentralize. Such massive governmental investment can theoretically be justified because, presumably:

1. Resources would be more fully utilized.

2. Income levels would rise—more than enough to return the cost of the investment—and consumption would be increased.

3. Congestion costs and diseconomies in the metropolises could be controlled (see Figure 10.05).

Spatial Inefficiency of the City

Since urban patterns have developed over time under constantly changing conditions and since urban decision making is so subject to error and the influence of unequal distribution of power, cities contain many obsolete and inefficient locations. Much of this inefficiency may be due to the inability of activities located on once optimal sites to adjust to changed conditions. Thus, while there may not be much demand for some older housing, there may also be not enough demand for the site to justify building new housing. As well, although businesses move constantly toward new locations of demand, they tend to show some inertia in their present location.

As observed before, political fractioning of the metropolis results in obvious costs and inefficiencies. Urban sprawl, too, is inefficient; sprawl requires costly school bus service, new roads, and utility extension in sparsely populated areas, and it often disrupts surrounding agricultural operations.

THE WORLD ECONOMY: INEQUALITY AND INEFFICIENCY

It is not, of course, strictly possible to evaluate the spatial efficiency of the world economy, because there is not just one world economy or society but national and even local economies having only tenuous connections to each other. These different economies greatly vary in their organizational complexity and spatial interdependence.

International trade does constitute a beginning for a world economy and may be evaluated as such. Most international trade is rational, in the sense that it is profitable to both sides, but there is much evidence that suboptimality exists. Trade is distorted by ideological conflicts and loyalties. There may be too much trade within a political bloc, while good opportunities to trade outside the bloc are ignored. Also, the more powerful world nations may be able to control prices to their own advantage, thus aggravating international differences in development. As well, most nations impose barriers against trade from their foreign competitors.

The main evidence of economic imbalance and inefficiency is the extreme inequality in the world

THE SPATIAL STRUCTURE OF ECONOMICS

distribution of income (see Figure 1.03). Variations in level of development and income among nations are of course far greater than within a nation. The technology available to a society and the organizational complexity, types of production, and consumption of nations vary greatly.

Although development in an earlier era could be defined by the achievement of a nation's few rich men, in the modern era, where a man's expectations are no longer bounded by his social position, development is better measured by the median income per consuming unit—usually the family. All the other measures of development—consumption of energy, literacy, health, quality of transport —are closely related to the typical family's income.

To account for these variations in national development would be a herculean task. We will just suggest some of the major factors.

1. The quality of a nation's land and its endowment of resources vary. Some areas are blessed with rich resources, land or mineral; the preeminent position of America is partly a function of such superiority.

2. Development and technology diffuse only gradually from more advanced areas. Areas with a head start in development have a great advantage over possible competitors; their existing educational, industrial, and research structures best generate new technology.

3. Nations vary in age, political stability, and damage from past wars. The development of countries that have stayed out of war and avoided subsequent destruction of property (such as Sweden and Switzerland) may be aided. Areas plagued by frequent political change and unrest with the resulting unstable currency and shifting economic leadership have difficulty developing.

4. Economic and social organization and attitudes toward development vary among nations. In many countries, the leadership has allowed or pursued deliberately antidevelopmental policies—maintaining a feudal land organization or engaging in futile wars against neighbors, for instance.

5. The size and population of countries differ. Naturally, a small country is at the disadvantage of having a small internal market and limited resources.

Barriers to Development

Economic development is the goal of most countries; most are concerned also with questions of security and ideology. The cost of the Cold War between the United States and its allies and the USSR, China, and their allies has been far in excess of one trillion dollars, a drain that obviously reduces the willingness—and ability—of the larger rich nations to aid the poorer ones. In the extreme case of the Vietnam War, although over 100 billion dollars has been spent, Vietnam has been severely damaged—a measure of the perceived superiority of ideological over economic values. Perhaps even more seriously, the Cold War has caused an aura of insecurity to pervade most nations, who therefore spend an unnecessarily high proportion of their limited capital on nonproductive armaments.

Population Imbalance Population imbalances are a basic developmental problem of many countries. Many nations have a very small population, so that both their markets and their labor force are too small to allow them to realize even modest scale and agglomeration economies, let alone accumulate enough capital to finance a variety of different industries. No other factor is so important in limiting their development.

There are three types of population imbalance: the ratio of population to arable land is too high, there are few alternate opportunities, and only a low level of technology exists; absolute population is too high to be supported by available land and resources; the rate of population increase is excessive. In countries where land is already used intensively, most of society's investment and labor is commonly required just to increase food production enough to feed the additional population. In spite of a large potential market and labor force for other kinds of production, not enough surplus food can be generated to provide capital for allocation to alternate activities. In these countries, a birth control program is needed to reduce the rate of population growth below that of economic expansion and capital formation; such a program is often difficult, however, in the face of little education, traditions of large families (so that the parents will be guaranteed care in their old age), inadequate nutrition, and, in some countries, religious and other kinds of barriers.

Tradition In many countries the means necessary for development conflict with existing attitudes and traditions. In some cases, religious practices and beliefs or traditional diets conflict with economic efficiency; for example, India's cattle population is under-utilized. More important is the lack of enthusiasm for development often shown in aristocratic social structures; if a ruling group has achieved extreme wealth through the small surpluses of many or through controlling the resources, it will gain little from development in the modern sense, which is based on the concept of a mass market. The aristocracy can gain more security and a greater return by investing funds in countries more successful than their own.

Competition with Wealthy Nations A powerful barrier to development is the superior position of already developed nations. In the short run, a new plant in a poor country will rarely—even with extreme savings on labor costs—be able to compete with a highly efficient plant in a wealthy country. Until the local labor force increases its productivity and local markets develop as well, such new industries will commonly require financial protection. Unfortunately, deciding whether to support such industries is another problem; it is difficult to know whether a given industry will eventually be competitive or whether it will always be cheaper to purchase a product from another country.

Colonial Trade Patterns An underdeveloped nation's existing trade patterns, often inherited from its colonial period, are frequently typified by too much dependence on a single or a few exports that are subject to severe price fluctuations. Hence, there are variations in capital formation that make developmental schedules and payments difficult to meet. Also, the colonial pattern of exporting primary goods and importing manufactured products leads to excessive emphasis on imports of consumption goods and thus a continuing conflict between importing materials for future gain and importing materials for consumption now. Democratic but uneducated societies are unlikely to restrict consumption sufficiently to encourage the high investment that will lead to sustained growth. Even dictatorial societies are often unwilling to invest in needed public works—transportation, roads, schools, and water systems—which create the basis for later productivity.

Forces Working toward Development

In spite of this catalog of barriers, development does occur. Strong motivation and a determination to industrialize are common to growing countries. They are aided in this process by the large body of technology, already created by the developed countries, available to them.

The most successful are nations with very strong governments dedicated to development and able to enforce an unpopular emphasis on investment to the neglect of present living standards; it is clear that austerity and very high reinvestment levels were common during the industrialization of all the now wealthy nations.

Totally "bootstrap" development seems to be almost impossible, but growth financed by exports, without outside aid, is possible. Less developed countries have also received loans and gifts, which can increase the speed and ease of development. Some aid, such as technical aid for health, agriculture, and water supplies, is channeled through the United Nations and related agencies; larger in scope are private investment—primarily to develop exports of desired commodities, such as petroleum and mineral deposits—and governmental loans and gifts.

THE SPATIAL STRUCTURE OF ECONOMICS

Governmental aid constitutes the most realistic source of general capital, although it is subject to severe political conflict. The donor nation, for example, must spread the available capital over far too many receivers, and the receiving nations resent any strings attached to the aid, even though such control might bring the greatest gain to the country.

Problems of Internal Efficiency and Capital Allocation

The richer nations are characterized by national economies in which virtually all the people participate commercially. In contrast, most poorer nations have dual economies—the smaller portion of the population participates in the commercial sector, which is often closely tied to exports, and the larger portion remains in the semisubsistence sector, mainly engaged in producing food crops. The distinction between the two groups in income, power, and education is great, and a major problem of less-developed nations is commercializing the subsistence sector of their economies.

Typically, the main sources of capital for such nations are fairly small exports of foods or minerals. As stated above, there is also a temptation to spend heavily on consumer goods and to invest in secure overseas markets, or, at best, to invest in urban services, ignoring the subsistence sector of the economy. This is spatially inefficient because resources are under-utilized and excessive income differences remain.

Given its desire for widespread development and less dependence on overseas markets, the nation is faced with the difficult task of finding the optimum allocation of resources within the country. Its alternatives are to disperse investment evenly over the entire territory; to concentrate investment in the one best place; or perhaps to distribute it to a set of growth points (Figure 10.05). Dispersal is a popular choice when political control is diffuse and all parts of the country wish to develop at

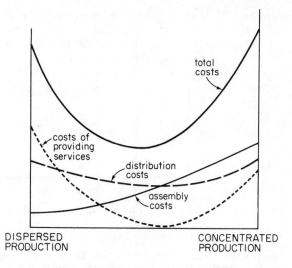

Figure 10.05 Balance between concentration and dispersion. Both extreme urban concentration and extreme rural dispersion are economically inefficient.

once. However, such a pattern is highly inefficient; the investment in each area will be on an uneconomically small scale and will probably do no more than enable food production to keep up with population growth.

In the short run, in a small country the most profitable use of capital is to concentrate industrial development in the one best place, usually the capital, where threshold markets can be found, and adequate labor is available (see Figure 10.06). Settlers should then migrate from the countryside to supply additional labor, and the surrounding agriculture will then commercialize in order to serve the urban market.

In a fairly large and populous country, however, extreme concentration of capital in one place will not lead to the most general development (Figure 10.06). Investment must rather be allocated to a set of regional centers, which may in turn commercialize their hinterlands.

Total concentration of investment in strategic growth centers—either one or a few—is, of course,

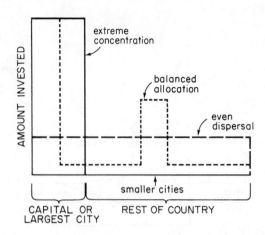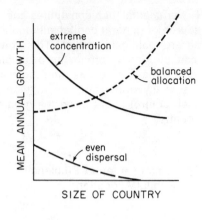

Figure 10.06 Internal allocation of capital for development. For a small country, concentration of investment in the largest city may be best, but in larger countries, some allocation to smaller cities and rural areas is best. Even dispersal of investment over the territory is always inefficient.

unrealistic. Some more diffuse small-scale investment in agriculture may be very beneficial; poor areas not selected for development cannot be ignored without risking social and economic unrest that may drag down the entire economy.

If the chosen strategy is successful, development will spread from the growth centers to their hinter-lands, until all the territory and population of the nation are brought into a unified economy. Such an orderly development should lead to a more even distribution of population, production, and income and perhaps even a closer approximation to the theoretical landscape outlined in preceding chapters than is presently true of most advanced countries.

THE SPATIAL STRUCTURE OF ECONOMICS

References

CHAPTER ONE

A. General References

Alexander, J. W. *Economic geography.* Englewood Cliffs, N.J.: Prentice-Hall, 1963.

Anderson, M. "A working bibliography of mathematical geography." Michigan Inter-University Community of Mathematical Geographers, Discussion Paper 2, 1963.

Berry, B. J. L., and D. Marble. *Spatial analysis: Readings in statistical analysis.* Evanston, Ill.: Northwestern University, 1966.

Bunge, W. "Theoretical geography." *Lund Studies in Geography,* Series C, 1, 1962.

Friedmann, J., and W. Alonso, eds. *Regional development and planning: A reader.* Cambridge, Mass.: The M.I.T. Press, 1964.

Haggett, P. *Locational analysis in human geography.* New York: St. Martin's, 1966.

Hawley, A. H. *Human ecology.* New York: Ronald Press, 1950.

Hoover, E. M. *Location of economic activity.* New York: McGraw-Hill, 1948.

Isard, Walter. *Location and space-economy,* New York: Technology Press, M.I.T., 1956.

Jones, E. *Human geography.* London: Chatto and Windus, 1964.

Lösch, A. *The economics of location,* translated by W. Stolper. New Haven, Conn.: Yale University, 1954.

Ponsard, C. *Economie et éspace.* Paris: Sedes, 1955.

Reichenbach, Hans. *Philosophy of space and time.* New York: Dover, 1958.

Stea, D. "Space, territory, and human movement." *Landscape* (September, 1965).

Thomas, W. L., Jr., ed. *Man's role in changing the face of the earth.* Chicago: University of Chicago Press, 1956.

B. Nature of Geography, Economic Geography

Ackerman, E. A. "Where is a research frontier?" *Annals of the Association of American Geographers* 53 (1963): 429–440.

Barrows, H. H. "Geography as human ecology." *Annals of the Association of American Geographers* 13 (1923): 1–14.

Boesch, Hans. *A geography of world economy.* Princeton: van Nostrand, 1964.

Bunge, W. "Spatial relations: The subject of theoretical geography." in *Voprosy Geografii,* edited by Y. G. Saushkin. Moscow: University of Moscow, 1964.

Burton, I. "The quantitative revolution and theoretical geography." *Canadian Geographer* 7 (1963): 151–162.

Dicken, S. N., and F. R. Pitts. *Introduction to human geography.* New York: Blaisdell, 1963.

Doxiadis, C. A. "Ekistics and regional science." *Papers and Proceedings of the Regional Science Association* 10 (1962): 9–46.

Fryer, D. W. *World economic development.* New York: McGraw-Hill, 1965.

Hartshorne, R. *The nature of geography; A critical survey of current thought in the light of the past.* Washington, D.C.: Association of American Geographers, 1949.

Hartshorne, R. *Perspective on the nature of geography,* edited by Andrew H. Clark (Association of American Geographers, monograph series, 1). Chicago: Rand McNally, 1959.

Hoffman, L. A. *Economic geography.* New York: Ronald Press, 1965.

Isard, W., et al. *Methods of regional analysis: An introduction to regional science.* New York: Technology Press, M.I.T., 1960.

Isard, W. "Regional science: The concept of region and regional structure." *Papers and Proceedings of the Regional Science Association* 2 (1956): 13–26.

James, P. E. and C. F. Jones, eds. *American geography: Inventory and prospect.* Syracuse, N.Y.: Syracuse University Press, 1954.

King, L. J. "A note on theory and reality." *Professional Geographer* 12 (1960)): 4–5.

Lukermann, F. "The role of theory in geographic enquiry." *Professional Geographer* 13 (1961): 1–6.

McCarty, H. H., and J. B. Lindberg. *A preface of economic geography.* Englewood Cliffs, N.J.: Prentice-Hall, 1966.

Morgan, W. B., and R. P. Moss. "Geography and ecology: Concept of the community and its relationship to environment." *Annals of the Association of American Geographers* 55 (1965): 339–350.

Philbrick, A. K. *This human world.* New York: Wiley, 1963.

Schaeffer, F. K. "Exceptionalism in geography: A methodological examination." *Annals of the Association of American Geographers* 43 (1953): 226–249.

Schnore, L. F. "Geography and human ecology." *Economic Geography* 37 (1961): 207–217.

Stewart, J. Q., and W. Warntz. "Macrogeography and social science." *Geographical Review* 48 (1958): 167–184.

Thoman, R. S. *The geography of economic activity.* New York: McGraw-Hill, 1962.

Wagner, P. *The human use of the earth.* New York: Free Press, 1960.

Warntz, W. "Contributions toward a macro-economic geography: A review. "*Geographical Review* 47 (1957): 420–424.

Watson, J. W. "Geography—A discipline in distance." *Scottish Geographical Magazine* 71 (1955): 1–13.

Woytinsky, W. S., and E. S. Woytinsky. *World population and production.* New York: Twentieth Century Fund, 1953.

C. Environmental Factors

Amiran, D. H. K. "Arid zone development: A reappraisal under modern technological conditions." *Economic Geography* 41 (1965): 189–210.

Branch, M. C. "Rome and Richmond: A case study in topographic determinism." *Journal of the American Institute of Planners* 28 (1962): 1–9.

Bridger, M. K., and B. Greer-Wooten. "Landscape components and residential urban growth in western Montreal Island." *Revue de Géographie de Montréal,* 1965.

Burghardt, A. F. "The location of river towns in the central lowland of the United States." *Annals of the Association of American Geographers* 49 (1959): 305–323.

Burton, I., and R. W. Kates. "The floodplain and the seashore: A comparative analysis of hazard-zone occupance." *Geographical Review* 54 (1964): 366–385.

Curry, L. "Climate and economic life: A new approach." *Geographical Review* 42 (1952): 367–383.

Gould, P. R. "Man against his environment: A game-theoretic framework." *Annals of the Association of American Geographers* 53 (1963): 290–297.

REFERENCES

Hansen, W. G. "How accessibility shapes land use." *Journal of the American Institute of Planners* 15 (1959): 73–76.

Hidore, J. J. "The relations between cash-grain farming and landforms." *Economic Geography* 39 (1963): 84–89.

Kates, R. W. "Industrial flood losses." University of Chicago Department of Geography, Research Paper 98, 1965.

Kollmorgen, W. M. "Settlement control beats flood control." *Economic Geography* 29 (1953): 208–215.

Murphey, R. "The city in the swamp: Aspects of the siting and early growth of Calcutta." *Geographical Journal* 130 (1964): 241–255.

Pepelasis, A. A., and K. Thompson. "Agriculture in a restrictive environment." *Economic Geography* 36 (1960): 145–157.

Semple, E. C. *Influences of geographic environment.* New York: American Geographical Society, 1911.

Taylor, G. "Environment, village, and city: A genetic approach to urban geography." *Annals of the Association of American Geographers* 32 (1942): 1–67.

Ullman, E. L. "Amenities as a factor in regional growth." *Geographical Review* 44 (1954): 119–132.

Webber, M. "Culture, territoriality, and the elastic mile." *Papers and Proceedings of the Regional Science Association* 13 (1964): 59–70.

Weigend, G. C. "Some elements in the study of port geography." *Geographical Review* 48 (1958): 185–200.

D. Other Factors, Abstract Geography

Bachi, R. "Standard distance measures and related methods for spatial analysis." *Papers and Proceedings of the Regional Science Association* 10 (1963): 83–132.

Boyce, R. B., and W. A. V. Clark. "The concept of shape in geography." *Geographical Review* 54 (1964): 561–572.

Bunge, W. "Patterns of locations." Michigan Inter-University Community of Mathematical Geographers, Discussion Paper 3, 1964.

Clark, P. J., and F. C. Evans. "Distance to nearest neighbor as a measure of spatial relationships in populations." *Ecology* 35 (1954): 445–453.

Court, A., and P. W. Porter. "The elusive point of minimum travel." *Annals of the Association of American Geographers* 54 (1964): 400–406.

Dacey, M. F. "Analysis of central place and point patterns by a nearest neighbor method." *Lund Studies in Geography,* Series B, 24, 1962.

Dacey, M. F. "Imperfections in the uniform plane." Michigan Inter-University Community of Mathematical Geographers, Discussion Paper 4, 1964.

Duncan, O. D., R. P. Cuzzort, and B. Duncan. *Statistical geography: Problems of analyzing areal data.* New York: Free Press, 1961.

Feder, E. "Feudalism and agricultural development." *Land Economics* 36 (1960): 92–108.

Hart, J. F. "Central tendency in areal distributions." *Economic Geography* 30 (1954): 48–59.

Hudson, J. C., and P. M. Fowler. "The concept of pattern in geography." University of Iowa Department of Geography, Discussion Paper 1, 1965.

Isard, W. "A general location principle of an optimum space-economy." *Econometrica* 20 (1952): 406–430.

Jones, S. B. "Boundary concepts in the setting of place and time." *Annals of the Association of American Geographers* 49 (1959): 241–255.

Kristof, L. K. D. "The nature of frontiers and boundaries." *Annals of the Association of American Geographers* 49 (1959): 269–282.

Mackay, J. R. "The interactance hypothesis and boundaries in Canada." *Canadian Geographer* 11 (1958): 1–8.

Mayer, H. M. "Politics and land use: The Indiana shoreline of Lake Michigan." *Annals of the Association of American Geographers* 54 (1964): 508–523.

McCleneghan, T. J. "Land use contrasts in a border economy." Bureau of Business Research, University of Arizona, Tucson, 1965.

Minghi, J. "Boundary studies in political geography." *Annals of the Association of American Geographers* 53 (1963): 407–428.

Nystuen, J. D. "Identification of some fundamental spatial concepts." *Papers of the Michigan Academy of Science, Arts, and Letters* 48 (1963): 373–384.

Richard, J. H. "Provincialism, regionalism, and federalism as seen in joint resource development projects." *Canadian Geographer* 9 (1965): 205–215.

Warntz, W., and D. Neft. "Contributions to a statistical methodology for areal distribution." *Journal of Regional Science* 2 (1960): 47–66.

Wolpert, J. "The decision process in spatial context." *Annals of the Association of American Geographers* 54 (1964): 537–558.

Zipf, G. K. *Human behavior and the principle of least effort.* Cambridge, Mass.: Harvard University Press, 1949.

E. Resources

Abrahamson, S. R. "The shifting geographic center of petroleum production and its effect on pricing systems." *Economic Geography* 28 (1952): 295–301.

Borchert, J. R. "The surface water supply of American municipalities." *Annals of the Association of American Geographers* 44 (1954): 15–32.

Brooks, D. "Supply of individually mined minor metals." *Land Economics* 40 (1964): 19–28.

Church, M. "The spatial organization of electric power territories in Massachusetts." University of Chicago Department of Geography, Research Paper 69, 1960.

Firey, W. *Man, mind, and land: A theory of resource use.* New York: Free Press, 1960.

Ginsburg, N. "Natural resources and economic development." *Annals of the Association of American Geographers* 47 (1957): 196–212.

Henderson, J. M. *The efficiency of the coal industry: An application of linear programming.* Cambridge, Mass.: Harvard University Press, 1958.

Karaska, G. "Pattern of settlements in the southern and middle anthracite region of Pennsylvania." Ph.D. dissertation, Pennsylvania State University, 1962.

Kohn, C. F., and R. E. Specht. "The mining of taconite, Lake Superior iron mining district." *Geographical Review* 48 (1958): 528–539.

Krutilla, J. V. "Water resources development: The regional incidence of costs and gains." *Papers and Proceedings of the Regional Science Association* 4 (1958): 273–312.

Linton, D. L. "The geography of energy." *Geography* 50 (1965): 197–228.

McNee, R. B. "Centrifugal-centripetal forces in international petroleum company regions." *Annals of the Association of American Geographers* 51 (1961): 124–138.

Manners, G. *The geography of energy.* London: Hutchinson University Library, 1964.

Melamid A. "Geography of the world petroleum price structure." *Economic Geography* 38 (1962): 283–298.

Murphy, R. E., and H. Spittal. "Movements of the center of coal mining in the Appalachian plateaus." *Geographical Review* 35 (1945): 624–633.

Parsons, J. "The geography of natural gas in the United States." *Economic Geography* 26 (1950): 162–178.

Raitt, W. L. "The changing pattern of Norwegian hydroelectric development." *Economic Geography* 34 (1958): 127–144.

Roepke, H. G. "Changing patterns of coal production in the eastern interior field. *Economic Geography* 31 (1955): 234–247.

Sewell, W. R. D. "The role of regional interties in postwar energy resource development. *Annals of the Association of American Geographers* 54 (1964): 566–581.

Van Burkalow, A. "The geography of New York City's water supply." *Geographical Review* 49 (1959): 369–386.

White, G. F. "Industrial water use; A review." *Geographical Review* 50 (1960): 412–430.

F. Conservation

Burton, I. and R. Kates. *Readings in resource management and conservation.* Chicago: University of Chicago Press, 1965.

Calef, W. "Land management policy." *Annals of the Association of American Geographers* 42 (1952): 327–331.

Ciriacy-Wantrup, S. V. *Resource conservation: Economics and policies.* Berkeley: University of California Press, 1965.

Duncan, C. "Resource utilization and the conservation concept." *Economic Geography* 38 (1962): 113–121.

Krutilla, J. V., and O. Eckstein. *Multiple purpose river development.* Baltimore: Johns Hopkins, 1958.

Udall, S. I. *The quiet crisis.* New York: Holt, 1963.

Zobler, L. "An economic-historical view of natural resource use and conservation. *Economic Geography* 38 (1962): 189–194.

CHAPTER TWO

A. Nomadism, Shifting Cultivation

Brookfield, H. C. "Local study and comparative method, central New Guinea." *Annals of the Association of American Geographers* 52 (1962): 242–254.

Clarke, J. I. "Summer nomadism in Tunisia." *Economic Geography* 31 (1955): 155–167.

Conklin, H. C. Hanunoo agriculture: A report on the integral system of shifting cultivation in the Philippines." Food and Agricultural Organization, 1957.

Hunter, J. M. "Ascertaining population carrying capacity under traditional systems of agriculture in developing countries." *Professional Geographer* 18 (1966): 151–154.

Melamid, A. "Political boundaries and nomadic grazing." *Geographical Review* 55 (1965): 287–289.

Pelzer, K. "The shifting cultivator," in *Pioneer settlement in the Asian tropics.* New York: American Geographical Society, 1945.

Rasmussen, T. F. "Population and land utilization in the Assam village." *Journal of Tropical Geography* 14 (1960): 51–74.

Salisbury, R. F. "Changes in land use and tenure among the Siane of the New Guinea highlands." *Pacific Viewpoint* 5 (1964): 1–10.

Sonnenfeld, J. "Changes in an Eskimo hunting technology." *Annals of the Association of American Geographers* 50 (1960): 172–186.

Vandermeer, C. "Corn cultivation on Cebu: an example of an advanced stage of migratory farming." *Journal of Tropical Geography* 17 (1963): 172–177.

Watters, R. F. "Some forms of shifting cultivation in the southwest Pacific." *Journal of Tropical Geography* 14 (1960): 35–50.

B. Intensive Subsistence Agriculture

Ahmad, N. "The pattern of rural settlement in East Pakistan." *Geographical Review* 46 (1956): 388–398.

Belshaw, C. S. *Traditional exchange and modern markets.* Englewood Cliffs, N.J.: Prentice-Hall, 1965.

Bhatia, S. S. "Patterns of crop concentration and diversification in India." *Economic Geography* 41 (1965): 39–56.

Clark, C., and M. Haswell. *Economics of subsistence agriculture.* New York: St. Martin's, 1954.

Dobby, E. H. G. "The north Kedah plain—A study in the environment of pioneering for rice cultivation." *Economic Geography* 27 (1951): 287–320.

Enke, S. "Labor supply, land rents, and agricultural output in backward countries." *Southern Economics Journal* 29 (1962): 82–87.

Eyre, J. D. "Water controls in a Japanese irrigation system." *Geographical Review* 45 (1955): 197–216.

Gamble, S. D. *North China villages.* Berkeley: University of California Press, 1963.

Hale, R. A. "The origin, nature, and distribution of agricultural terracing." *Pacific Viewpoint* 2 (1961): 1–40.

Henshall, J. D., and L. J. King. "Some structural characteristics of peasant agriculture in Barbados." *Economic Geography* 42 (1966): 74–84.

Ho, R. "Mixed farming and multiple cropping in Malaya." *Journal of Tropical Geography* 16 (1962): 1–17.

Hore, P. N. "Rainfall, rice yields, and irrigation needs in West Bengal." *Geography* 49 (1964): 114–121.

Kakiuchi, G. H. "Early season cultivation of wet-rice in southwest Japan." *Pacific Viewpoint* 5 (1964): 151–168.

Kakiuchi, G. H. "Recent development and trends in the cultivation of wet-rice in Japan." *Land Economics* 41 (1965): 69–73.

Matui, I. "Statistical study of the distribution of scattered villages in two regions of the Tonami plain." *Japanese Journal of Geology and Geography* 9 (1932): 251–256.

Nash, M. *Primitive and peasant economic systems.* San Francisco: Chandler, 1965.

Rutheford, J. "Double cropping of wet padi in Penang, Malaya." *Geographical Review* 56 (1966): 239–255.

Shafi, M. "Measurement of agricultural efficiency in Uttar Pradesh." *Economic Geography* 3 (1960): 296–305.

Sopher, D. E. "The Swidden wet-rice transition zone in the Chittagong Hills." *Annals of the Association of American Geographers* 54 (1964): 107–126.

Trewartha, G. T. "Land reform and land reclamation in Japan." *Geographic Review* 40 (1950): 376–396.

C. Estates

Brookfield, H. C. "Problems of monoculture and diversification in a sugar island, Mauritius." *Economic Geography* 35 (1959): 25–40.

Hill, P. *Migrant cocoa-farmers of Southern Ghana.* Cambridge, Eng.: Cambridge University Press, 1963.

Hodder, B. W. "Tin mining on the Jos plateau of Nigeria." *Economic Geography* 35 (1959): 109–122.

Robertson, C. J. "The integration of plantation agriculture in economic planning." *Pacific Viewpoint* 4 (1963): 1–8.

Ude, R. K. "Sixty years of plantation agriculture in Nigeria, 1902–1962." *Economic Geography* 41 (1965): 356–368.

Ward, R. G. "Cash cropping and the Fijian village." *Geographical Journal* 130 (1964): 484–506.

D. Development and Change

Augelli, J. P., and H. W. Taylor. "Race and population pattern in Trinidad." *Annals of the Association of American Geographers* 50 (1960): 123–138.

Coi, J. B. "Rural development in tropical areas." *Journal of Tropical Geography* 12 (1958): (entire issue).

Fryer, D. W. "Development of cottage and small scale industry in Malaya and Southeast Asia." *Journal of Tropical Geography* 17 (1963): 92–98.

Kolars, J. F. "Tradition, season, and change in a Turkish village." University of Chicago Department of Geography, Research Paper 82, 1963.

Murphey, R. E. "The economic geography of a micronesian atoll." *Annals of the Association of American Geographers* 40 (1950): 58–83.

Pirie, P., and W. Parrett. "Western Samoa—Population, production, and wealth." *Pacific Viewpoint* 3 (1962): 63–96.

Tosi, J. A., and R. F. Voertman. "Some environmental factors in the economic development of the tropics." *Economic Geography* 40 (1964): 189–205.

White, H. P. "Internal exchange of staple foods in the Gold Coast." *Economic Geography* 32 (1956): 115–125.

CHAPTER THREE

A. Agriculture: General and Regional

Black, J. D. *The rural economy of New England—A regional study.* Cambridge, Mass.: Harvard University Press, 1950.

Chisholm, M. *Rural settlement and land use: An essay in location.* London: Hutchinson University Press, 1962.

Chisholm, M. "Tendencies in agricultural specialization and regional concentration of industry." *Papers and Proceedings of the Regional Science Association* 10 (1963): 157–162.

Eder, G. J. "Urban concentration, agriculture, and agrarian reform." *Annals of the American Academy of Political and Social Science* (May 1965).

Gregor, H. F. "Regional hierarchies in California agricultural production." *Annals of the Association of American Geographers* 53 (1963): 27–37.

Hagood, M. J. "Statistical methods for delineation of regions applied to data on agriculture and population." *Social Forces* 21 (1943): 288–297.

Haystead, L., and G. Fite. *Agricultural regions of the United States.* Norman, Okla.: University of Oklahoma Press, 1955.

Higbee, E. C. *American agriculture: Geography, resources, conservation.* New York: Wiley, 1958.

Higbee, E. C. *Farms and farmers in an urban age.* New York: Twentieth Century Fund, 1963.

Highsmith, R. M. "Irrigated lands of the world." *Geographical Review* 55 (1965): 362–389.

Jaatinen, S., and W. R. Mead. "Intensification of Finnish farming." *Economic Geography* 33 (1957): 31–40.

Kendall, M. G. "The geographical distribution of crop productivity in England." *Journal, Royal Statistical Society* 102 (1939): 21–62.

Lambert, A. M. "Farm consolidation and improvement in the Netherlands." *Economic Geography* 37 (1961): 115–123.

Robinson, A. H., J. B. Lindberg, and L. W. Brinkman. "A correlation and regression analysis applied to rural farm population densities on the Great Plains." *Annals of the Association of American Geographers* 51 (1961): 211–221.

REFERENCES

Sauer, C. O. "Agricultural origins and dispersals." American Geographical Society, Bowman Memorial Lectures 2, 1952.

Spencer, J. E., and R. J. Horvath. "How does an agricultural region originate?" *Annals of the Association of American Geographers* 53 (1963): 74–92.

Van Valkenburg, S. "An evaluation of the standard of land use in Western Europe." *Economic Geography* 36 (1960): 283–295.

Weaver, J. C. "Crop combination regions in the Middle West." *Geographical Review* 44 (1954): 536–565.

Whittlesey, D. "Agricultural regions of North America." A series in *Economic Geography* I (1925)–9 (1933). (14 articles.)

Whittlesey, D. "Major agricultural regions of the earth." *Annals of the Association of American Geographers* 26 (1936): 199–240.

B. Location Factors in Agriculture

Baker, O. E. "Increasing importance of physical conditions in determining the utilization of land for agriculture and forest production in the United States." *Annals of the Association of American Geographers* 11 (1921): 17–46.

Chisholm, M. "Economies of scale in road good transport: Off-farm milk collection in England and Wales." *Oxford Economic Papers* II (1959): 282–290.

Fielding, G. J. "The role of government in New Zealand wheat growing." *Annals of the Association of American Geographers* 55 (1965): 87–97.

Fliegel, F. C. "Obstacles to change for the low-income farms." *Rural Sociology* 25 (1960): 347–351.

Grebler, L. "Mexican immigration to the United States: The record and implications." UCLA School of Business Administration, 1965.

Griff, D. "The geography of farm size: A preliminary survey." *Economic Geography* 42 (1966): 205–235.

Hart, J. F., and E. Mather. "The geography of manure." *Land Economics* 32 (1956): 25–30.

Heady, E. O., and A. C. Egbert. "Regional programming of efficient agricultural production patterns." *Econometrica* 32 (1964): 374–386.

Huddelston, H. F. "An inverted matrix approach for determining crop-weather relationships." *Biometrics* 2 (1955): 231–236.

Hudson, J. "Irrigation water in the Utah Valley." University of Chicago Department of Geography, Research Paper 79, 1962.

Johnson, V. W. "Significance of land ownership in land reform." *Land Economics* 42 (1966): 21–28.

Klingman, G. C. *Crop productivity in the South.* New York: Wiley, 1957.

Schuh, G. E., and J. R. Leeds. "A regional analysis of the demand for hired agricultural labor." *Papers and Proceedings of the Regional Science Association* 11 (1962): 295–308.

C. Agricultural Location Theory: Models

Birch, J. W. "Rural land use and location theory: A review." *Economic Geography* 39 (1963): 273–276.

Dunn, E. S. *The location of agricultural production.* Gainesville, Fla.: University of Florida, 1954.

Garrison, W. L., and D. F. Marble. "The spatial structure of agricultural activities." *Annals of the Association of American Geographers* 47 (1957): 137–144.

Grotewold, A. "Von Thünen in retrospect." *Economic Geography* 35 (1959): 346–355.

Harvey, D. W. "Theoretical concepts and the analysis of agricultural land use patterns in geography." *Annals of the Association of American Geographers* 56 (1966): 361–374.

Heady, E. O. *Economics of agricultural production and resource use.* Englewood Cliffs, N.J.: Prentice-Hall, 1952.

Henderson, J. M. "The utilization of agricultural land: A regional approach." *Papers and Proceedings of the Regional Science Association* 3 (1957): 99–117.

D. Extensive Agricultures: Ranching, Cash Grain

Beyer, J. "Integration of grazing and crop agriculture." University of Chicago Department of Geography, Research Paper 52, 1957.

Calef, W. *Private grazing and public lands: Studies of the local managements of the Taylor Grazing Act.* Chicago: University of Chicago Press, 1960.

Curry, L. "Regional variation in the seasonal programming of livestock farms in New Zealand." *Economic Geography* 39 (1963): 95–118.

Hewes, L. "Causes of wheat failure in the dry farming region, central great plains, 1939–1957." *Economic Geography* 41 (1965): 313–330.

Hoag, L. P. "Locational determinants for cash-grain farming in the corn belt." *Professional Geographer* 14 (1962): 1–7.

Jackson, W. A. D. "The virgin and idle lands program reappraised." *Annals of the Association of American Geographers* 52 (1962): 32–50.

James, P. E. "The process of pastoral and agricultural settlement on the Argentine humid pampas." *Geographical Review* 40 (1950): 121–137.

Kollmorgen, W. M., and Jenks, G. F. "Sidewalk farming in Toole County, Montana, and Traill County, North Dakota." *Annals of the Association of American Geographers* 48 (1958): 209–231.

Mather, E. "The production and marketing of Wyoming beef cattle." *Economic Geography* 26 (1950): 81–93.

Meinig, D. *On the margins of the good earth.* Chicago: University of Chicago Press, 1962.

Grotewold, A "Regional changes in corn production in the United States from 1909 to 1949." University of Chicago Department of Geography, Research Paper 40, 1955.

Henderson, D. A. " 'Corn belt' cattle feeding in eastern Colorado's irrigated valleys." *Economic Geography* 30 (1954): 364–372.

Mighell, R. L., and J. D. Black. *Interregional competition in agriculture with special reference to dairy farming in the lake states and New England.* Cambridge, Mass.: Harvard University Press, 1951.

Schrader, L. F., and G. A. King. "Regional location of beef cattle feeding." *Journal of Farm Economics* 44 (1962): 64–81.

Simpson, E. S. "Milk production in England and Wales: A study in the influence of collective marketing." *Geographical Review* 49 (1959): 95–111.

Snodgrass, M. M., and C. E. French. *Linear programming approach to interregional competition in dairying,* Lafayette, Ind.: Purdue University Agricultural Experiment Station, 1958.

Weaver, J. C., L. P. Hoag, and B. L. Fenton. "Livestock units and combinations regions in the Middle West." *Economic Geography* 32 (1956): 237–259.

E. Grain–Animal Agricultures: Dairying

Coppock, J. T. "Crop, livestock, and enterprise combinations in England and Wales." *Economic Geography* 40 (1964): 65–81.

Durand, L. "The major milksheds of the northeastern quarter of the United States." *Economic Geography* 40 (1964): 9–33.

Durand, L. "Recent market orientation of the American dairy regions." *Economic Geography* 23 (1947): 32–40.

Edmondson, M. S. "Hybrid corn and the economics of innovation." *Science* 132 (1960): 275–280.

Fielding, G. J. "Dairying in cities designed to keep people out." *Professional Geographer* (January 1962): 12–17.

Fielding, G. J. "The Los Angeles milkshed: A study of the political factor in agriculture." *Geographical Review* 44 (1964): 1–12.

Gibson, L. E. "Characteristics of a regional margin of the corn and dairy belts." *Annals of the Association of American Geographers* 38 (1948): 244–270.

F. Agricultural Specialties: Horticulture, Cotton

Gregor, H. F. "The local supply agriculture of California." *Annals of the Association of American Geographers* 47 (1957) 267–276.

Inui, K. "Truck gardening in the suburbs of great cities and related supply areas." *Human Geography* 2 (1950): 58–66.

Large, D. C. "Cotton in the San Joaquin Valley: A study in government in agriculture." *Geographical Review* 47 (1957): 365–380.

Loeffler, M. J. "Beet sugar production in the Colorado Piedmont." *Annals of the Association of American Geographers* 53 (1963): 364–390.

Martin, K. R. "An analysis of the broiler chicken industry on the Delmarva Peninsula." Ph.D. dissertation, University of Wisconsin, 1955.

Prunty, M. "Recent quantitative changes in the cotton regions of the southeastern states." *Economic Geography* 27 (1951): 189–208.

G. Rural Settlement

Christensen, D. E. *Rural occupance in transition: Sumter and Lee counties, Georgia.* University of Chicago Department of Geography, Research Paper 43, 1955.

Golledge, R., G. Rushton, and W. A. V. Clark. "Some spatial characteristics of Iowa's dispersed farm population and their implications for the grouping of central place functions." *Economic Geography* 42 (1966): 261–272.

Johnson, H. B. "Rational and ecological aspects of the quarter section: An example from Minnesota." *Geographical Review* 47 (1957): 330–348.

Zelinsky, W. "Changes in the geographic pattern of rural population in the United States, 1790–1960. *Geographical Review* 52 (1962): 492–524.

H. Forestry

American Geographical Society. *A world geography of forest resources.* New York: Ronald Press, 1956.

Haggett, P. "Regional and local components in the distribution of forested areas in southeast Brazil." *Geographical Journal* 130 (1964): 365–380.

Hardwick, W. G. "Log towing rates in coastal British Columbia." *Professional Geographer* (September 1961): 1–5.

CHAPTER FOUR

A. General and Theoretical

Berry, B. J. L. "Aggregate relations and elemental components of central place systems." *Journal of Regional Science* 4 (1962): 35–68.

Berry, B. J. L. "Cities as systems within systems of cities." *Papers and Proceedings of the Regional Science Association* 13 (1964): 147–164.

Berry, B. J. L. *A geography of market centers and retail distribution.* Englewood Cliffs, N.J.: Prentice-Hall, 1967.

Berry, B. J. L. "A note on central place theory and the range of a good." *Economic Geography* 34 (1958): 304–311.

Berry, B. J. L. "Functional bases of the central place hierarchy." *Economic Geography* 34 (1958): 145–154.

Berry, B. J. L., H. G. Barnum, and R. J. Tennant. "Retail location and consumer behavior." *Papers and Proceedings of the Regional Science Association* 9 (1962): 65–106.

Berry, B. J. L., and Pred, A. Central Place Studies: A Bibliography of Theories and Applications. Regional Science Institute, Bibliographic Series 1, 1961.

Christaller, W. "Central places in southern Germany." Translated by C. W. Baskin. Englewood Cliffs, N.J.: Prentice-Hall, 1966.

Dacey, M. F. "The geometry of central place theory." *Geografiska Annaler* 47B (1965): 111–124.

Dacey, M. F. "A probability model for central place locations." Northwestern University, Department of Geography, Discussion Paper 6, 1965.

Harris, C. D., and E. L. Ullmann. "The nature of cities." *Annals of the American Academy of Political and Social Science* 242 (1945): 7–17.

Herbert, D. T. "An approach to the study of the town as a central place." *Sociological Review* 9 (1961): 273–292.

Marshall, J. U. "Model and reality in central place studies." *Professional Geographer* 16 (1964): 5–8.

Morrill, R. L. "The development and spatial distribution of towns in Sweden: An historical—predictive approach." *Annals of the Association of American Geographers* 53 (1963): 1–14.

Morrill, R. L. "Migration and the spread and growth of urban settlement." *Lund Studies in Geography,* Series B, 26, 1965.

Rogers, A. "A stochastic analysis of the spatial clustering of retail establishments." *Journal of the American Statistical Association* December 1965.

Thijsse, J. "A rural pattern for the future in the Netherlands." *Papers and Proceedings of the Regional Science Association* 10 (1963): 183–192.

Ullman, E. L. "A theory of location for cities." *American Journal of Sociology* 19 (1946): 853–864.

B. Empirical Studies: Central Places and Hinterlands

Applebaum, W., and S. B. Cohen. "The dynamics of store trading areas and market equilibrium. *Annals of the Association of American Geographers* 51 (1961) 73–101.

Bohannon, P. J., and G. D. Dalton. "Markets in Africa." Northwestern University, African Studies 9, 1962.

Bracey, H. E. "Towns as rural service centers." *Transactions of the Institute of British Geographers* 19 (1953): 95–105.

Brush, J. E. "The hierarchy of central places in southwestern Wisconsin." *Geographical Review* 43 (1953): 380–402.

Carter, H. "The urban hierarchy and historical geography." *Geographical Studies* 3 (1956): 85–101.

Deshpande, C. D. "Market villages and periodic fairs of Bombay, Karnatak." *Indian Geographical Journal* 16 (1941): 327–339.

Dickinson, R. E. *City and Region.* New York: Humanities, 1964.

Green, H. L. "Hinterland boundaries of New York City and Boston in southern New England." *Economic Geography* 31 (1955): 283–300.

Haggett, P., and K. A. Gunawardena. "Determination of population thresholds for settlement functions by the Reed-Muench method." *Professional Geographer* 16 (1964): 6–9.

Hodgen, M. T. "Fairs of Elizabethan England." *Economic Geography* 18 (1942): 389–400.

King, L. "A multivariate analysis of the spacing of urban settlements in the United States." *Annals of the Association of American Geographers* 51 (1961): 222–233.

McCarty, H. H. "The market functions of villages in eastern Iowa." *Annals of the Association of American Geographers* 31 (1941): 63.

Olsson, G., and A. Persson. "The spacing of central places in Sweden." *Papers and Proceedings of the Regional Science Association* 12 (1964): 87–94.

Siddall, W. R. "Wholesale-retail trade ratios as indices of urban centrality." *Economic Geography* 37 (1961): 124–132.

Spencer, J. "The Szechwan village fair." *Economic Geography* 16 (1940): 48–58.

Stafford, H. A., Jr. "The functional bases of small towns." *Economic Geography* 39 (1963): 165–175.

Thomas, E. N., R. A. Mitchell, and D. Blome. "The spatial behavior of a dispersed non-farm population." *Papers and Proceedings of the Regional Science Association* 9 (1962): 107–133.

C. Retail Trade

Berry, B. J. L. "Ribbon developments in the urban business pattern." *Annals of the Association of American Geographers* 49 (1959): 145–155.

Cohen, S. B. "Location research programming for voluntary food chains." *Economic Geography* 37 (1961): 1–11.

Converse, P. D. "New laws of retail gravitation." *Journal of Marketing* 14 (1949): 379–384.

Friedly, P. "A note on the retail trade multiplier and residential mobility." *Journal of Regional Science* 6 (1965): 57–64.

Holdren, B. R. "Structure of a retail market and the market behavior of retail units." *Englewood Cliffs, N.J.: Prentice Hall,* 1960.

Holton, R. H. "Price discrimination at retail: The supermarket case." *Journal of Industrial Economics* 6 (1957): 13–32.

Huff, D. L. "Ecological characteristics of consumer behavior. *Papers and Proceedings of the Regional Science Association* 7 (1961): 19–28.

Kriebel, C. H. "Warehousing with transhipment under seasonal demand." *Journal of Regional Science* 3 (1961): 57–70.

Murdie, R. "Cultural differences in consumer travel." *Economic Geography* 41 (1965): 211–233.

Ratcliff, R. U. "Efficiency in the location of urban activities." in *Metropolis in modern life,* edited by R. M. Fisher. New York: Doubleday, 1955.

Reilly, W. J. *The law of retail gravitation.* New York: Knickerbocker, 1931.

Reynolds, R. B. "A test of the law of retail gravitation." *Journal of Marketing* 42 (1953): 276.

Simmons, J. "The changing pattern for retail location." *University of Chicago Department of Geography,* Research Paper 92, 1964.

Sparicio, F. J. "Trade area variations for different goods sold in the same store." *Professional Geographer* 18 (1966): 5–8.

D. Other Services

Duncan, O. D. "Service industries and the urban hierarchy." *Papers and Proceedings of the Regional Science Association* 5 (1959): 105–120.

REFERENCES

Godlund, S. "The function and growth of bus traffic within the sphere of urban influence." *Lund Studies in Geography Series* B, 18, 1956.

Godlund, S. "Population, regional hospitals, transport facilities, and regions: Planning the location of regional hospitals in Sweden." *Lund Studies in Geography,* Series B, 21, 1961.

Hoffer, C. R., et al. "Health needs and health care in Michigan." Michigan State College Agricultural Experiment Station, Bulletin 365, 1950.

Kerr, D. "Some aspects of the geography of finance in Canada." *Canadian Geographer,* 9, 1965; 175–192.

CHAPTER FIVE

A. Industrialization

Beesley, M. "The birth and death of industrial establishments: Experience in the West Midlands conurbation." *Journal of Industrial Economics* 4 (1955); 45–61.

Kerr, C., et al. *Industrialization and industrial man.* Cambridge, Mass.: Harvard University Press, 1960.

Pred, A. "Industrialization, initial advantage, and American metropolitan growth." *Geographic Review* 55 (1965): 158–189.

Pred, A. "Manufacturing in the American mercantile city, 1800–1840." *Annals of the Association of American Geographers* 56 (1966): 307–338.

B. Principles of Location: Manufacturing in General

Alampiyev, P. M. "New aspects of the location of production in the period of full-fledged construction of communism." *Soviet Geography: Review and Translation,* 3: 49–59.

Alderfer, E. B., and Michl, H. E. *Economics of American Industry,* New York: McGraw-Hill, 1957.

Alexander, J. "Location of Manufacturing: Methods of measurement." *Annals of the Association of American Geographers* 48 (1958): 20–26.

Alexander, J., and J. B. Lindberg. "Measurement of manufacturing: Coefficients of correlation." *Journal of Regional Science* 3 (1961): 71–81.

Bain, J. S. "Economies of scale, concentration, and the condition of entry in twenty manufacturing industries." *American Economic Review* 44 (1954): 15–39.

Bain, J. S. *Barriers to new competition.* Cambridge, Mass.: Harvard University Press, 1956.

Barloon, M. J. "The interrelationship of the changing structure of American transportation and changes in industrial location." *Land Economics* 41 (1966): 169–182.

Dunn, E. S. "The market potential concept and the analysis of location." *Papers and Proceedings of the Regional Science Association* 2 (1956): 183–194.

Florence, P. S. *Investment, location, and size of plant.* Cambridge, Eng.: Cambridge University Press, 1948.

Fulton, M., and L. C. Hoch. "Transportation factors affecting locational decisions." *Economic Geography* 35 (1959): 51–59.

Goldman, T. A. "Efficient transportation and industrial location." *Papers and Proceedings of the Regional Science Association* 4 (1958): 91–106.

Greenhut, M. C. "When is the demand factor of location important?" *Land Economics* 40 (1964): 175–184.

Harris, C. D. "The market as a factor in the localization of industry in the United States." *Annals of the Association of American Geographers* 44 (1954): 315–348.

Isard, W., and E. W. Schooler. "Industrial complex analysis, agglomeration economies, and regional development." *Journal of Regional Science* 1: 19–33.

Kadas, C. "The impact of the development of transportation on the optimal size of plants and on optimal regional location." *Papers and Proceedings of the Regional Science Association* 12 (1963): 193–206.

McCarty, H. G., J. C. Hook, and D. B. Knos. "The measurement of association in industrial geography. State University of Iowa Department of Geography, Report 1, 1956.

McLaughlin, G. E., and S. Robock. "Why industry moves south." National Planning Association, 1949.

McMillan, T. E. "Why manufacturers choose plant locations vs. determinants of plant location." *Land Economies* 41 (1965): 239–246.

Manners, G. "Regional protection: A factor in economic geography." *Economic Geography* 38 (1962): 122–129.

Mehta, M. M. "Interrelationship between size, location and integration." *Indian Economic Journal* 2 (1955): 311–322.

Miller, E. W. *A geography of manufacturing.* Englewood Cliffs, N.J.: Prentice Hall, 1962.

Needleman, L., and B. Scott. "Regional problems and location of industry problems in Britain." *Urban Studies* 1 (1964): 153–173.

Pred, A. "The intrametropolitan location of American manufacturing." *Annals of the Association of American Geographers* 54 (1964): 165–180.

Smith, W. "The location of industry." *Institute of British Geographers* 21 (1955): 1–18.

Soffer, E., and E. Korenich. " 'Right to work' laws as a location factor." *Journal of Regional Science* 3 (1961): 41–56.

Tiebout, C. M. "Location theory, empirical evidence, and economic evolution." *Papers and Proceedings of the Regional Science Association* 3 (1957): 74–86.

Tornqvist, G. "Transport costs as a location factor for manufacturing industries." *Lund, Studies in Geography,* Series B, 23, 1962.

Wallace, L. T., and V. W. Ruttan. "The role of the community as a factor in industrial location." *Papers and Proceedings of the Regional Science Association* 7 (1961): 133–142.

Will, R. T. "Federal influences on industrial location. How extensive?" *Land Economics* 40 (1964): 49–58.

Winsborough, H. H. "Variations in industrial composition with city size." *Papers and Proceedings of the Regional Science Association* 5 (1959): 121–132.

Wonnacott, R. J. "Manufacturing costs and the comparative advantage of United States regions." Upper Midwest Economic Study Paper 9, 1963.

Yaseen, L. C. *Plant location.* New York: American Research Council, 1960.

Zelinsky, W. "A method for measuring change in the distribution of manufacturing activity: The United States, 1939–1947." *Economic Geography* 34 (1958): 95–126.

C. Theory of Industrial Location

Ackley, G. "Spatial competition in a discontinuous market." *Quarterly Journal of Economics* 56 (1942): 212–230.

Chamberlin, E. *The Theory of monopolistic competition."* Cambridge, Mass.: Harvard University Press, 1933.

Dean, W. H. *The theory of the geographic location of economic activities.* Ann Arbor, Mich.: Edward Brothers, 1938.

Fetter, F. A. "The economic law of market areas." *Quarterly Journal of Economics* 38 (1924): 520–523.

Friedrich, C. J. *Alfred Weber's theory of the location of industries.* Chicago: University of Chicago Press, 1929.

Greenhut, M. L. *Microeconomics and the space economy.* Chicago: Scott-Foresman, 1963.

Greenhut, M. L. *Plant location in theory and practice; The economics of space.* Chapel Hill, N.C.: University of North Carolina Press, 1956.

Hoover, E. M. *Location theory and the shoe and leather industries.* Cambridge, Mass.: Harvard University Press, 1937.

Hotelling, H. "Stability in competition." *Economic Journal* 39 (1929): 41–57.

Isard, W. "Game theory, and industrial agglomeration." *Papers and Proceedings of the Regional Science Association* 18 (1967): 1–12.

Isard, W. "Location theory and trade theory: Short-run analysis." *Quarterly Journal of Economics* 68 (1954): 305–320.

Kuhn, H. W., and R. L. Kuenne. "An efficient algorithm for the numerical solution of the generalized Weber problem." *Journal of Regional Science* 4 (1962): 21–34.

Lerner, A. P., and H. W. Singer. "Some notes on duopoly and spatial competition." *Journal of Political Economy* 45 (1937): 145–186.

Orr, E. W. "A synthesis of theories of location, of transport rates, and of spatial price equilibrium." *Papers and Proceedings of the Regional Science Association* 3 (1957): 61–73.

Palander, R. *Beitrage zu Standortstheorie.* Uppsala: Almqvist and Wiksells, 1935.

Predohl, A. "Das standortsproblem in der wirtschaftstheorie." *Weltwirtschaftsliches Archiv* 21 (1925): 294–331.

Quinn, J. A. "The hypothesis of median location." *American Sociological Review* 8: 148–156.

Smith, D. M. "A theoretical framework for geographical studies of industrial location." *Economic Geography* 42 (1966): 95–113.

Smithies, A. "Optimum location in spatial competition." *Journal of Political Economy* 44: (1941): 423–439.

Stevens, B. H. "An application of game theory to a problem in locational strategy." *Papers and Proceedings of the Regional Science Association* 7: (1957), 143–157.

D. Resource Orientation

Airov, J. *The location of the synthetic fiber industry.* Cambridge, Mass.: Harvard University Press, 1959.

Cotterill, C. H. "Industrial plant location: Its application to zinc smelting." American Zinc, Lead, and Smelting Co., 1950.

Dinsdale, E. M. "Spatial patterns of technological change: The lumber industry of northern New York." *Economic Geography* 41 (1965): 252–274.

Hunters, H. "Innovation, competition, and locational change in the pulp and paper industry." *Land Economics* 31 (1955): 314–327.

Lindbergh, O. "An economic geographic study of the Swedish paper industry." *Geografiska Annaler* 35 (1953): 27–40.

E. Complex Transport Orientation

Alexandersson, G. "Changes in the location pattern of the Anglo-American steel industry, 1948–1959." *Economic Geography* 37 (1961): 95–114.

Casetti, E. "Optimum location of steel mills serving the Quebec and southern Ontario steel markets." *Canadian Geographer* 10 (1966): 27–39.

Craig, P. G. "Location factors in the development of steel centers." *Papers and Proceedings of the Regional Science Association* 3 (1957): 249–265.

Isard, W. "Some locational factors in the iron and steel industry since the early nineteenth century." *Journal of Political Economy* 56 (1948): 203–217.

Isard, W., and J. H. Cumberland. "New England as a possible location for an integrated iron and steel works. *Economic Geography* 26 (1950): 245–259.

Kerr, D. "The geography of the Canadian iron and steel industry." *Economic Geography* 35 (1959): 151–163.

McNee, R. B. "Functional geography of the firm, with an illustrative case study from the petroleum industry." *Economic Geography* 34 (1958): 321–337.

Marschak, T. "A spatial model of United States petroleum refining." Rand Corporation Publication 2205.

Melamid, A. "Geographical distribution of petroleum refining capacity (Europe)." *Economic Geography* 31 (1955): 168–178.

Pounds, N. J. G. "World production and use of steel scrap." *Economic Geography* 35 (1959): 247–258.

F. General Market Orientation

Beesley, M. "Changing locational advantages in the British motor car industry." *Journal of Industrial Economics* 6 (1957): 47–57.

Boas, C. W. "Locational patterns of American automobile assembly plants, 1895–1958." *Economic Geography* 37 (1961): 218–230.

Cunningham, W. G. *The aircraft industry: A study in industrial location.* Los Angeles: L. L. Morrison, 1961.

Estall, R. C. "The electronic products industry of New England." *Economic Geography* 39 (1963): 189–216.

Hurley, N. P. "The automotive industry: A study in industrial location." *Land Economics* 35 (1959): 1–14.

Pred, A. "The concentration of high value-added manufacturing." *Economic Geography* 41 (1965): 108–132.

G. Processing Cost Operations

Hague, D. C., and J. H. Dunning. "Costs in alternative locations: The radio industry." *Review of Economic Studies* 22 (1955): 203–213.

Krutilla, J. V. "Locational factors influencing recent aluminum expansion." *Southern Economic Journal* 21 (1955): 273–288.

Rodgers, H. B. "The changing geography of the Lancashire cotton industry." *Economic Geography* 38 (1962): 299–314.

Rydberg, H. "The location of the English shoe industry." *Geografiska Annaler* 47B (1965): 44–55.

H. Manufacturing Regions

Conkling, E. C. "South Wales: A study in industrial diversification." *Economic Geography* 39 (1963): 258–272.

Fuchs, V. R. *Changes in the location of manufacturing in the United States since 1929*. New Haven: Yale University Press, 1962.

Funck, R. "Some aspects of an optimum pattern of industry location in the European Economic Community. *Papers and Proceedings of the Regional Science Association* 14 (1965): 43–52.

Kitigawa, E. M., and D. J. Bogue. *Suburbanization of manufacturing within standard metropolitan areas*. Chicago: University of Chicago Press, 1955.

Linge, J. R. "The concentration and dispersion of manufacturing in New Zealand." *Economic Geography* 36 (1960): 326–343.

Lonsdale, R. E. "Industrial location planning in the Soviet Union." *Professional Geographer* November 1961, 11–15.

Nicholson, R. J. "The regional location of industry." *Economic Journal* 66 (1956): 467–481.

Robinson, I. R. "New industrial towns on Canada's resource frontier." University of Chicago Department of Geography, Research Paper 73, 1963.

Rodgers, A. "Some aspects of industrial diversification in the United States." *Economic Geography* 33 (1957): 16–30.

I. Specialized Settlement

Deasy, G. F., and P. R. Griess. "Impact of a tourist facility on its hinterland." *Annals of the Association of American Geographers* 56 (1966): 290–306.

Guthrie, H. W. "Demand for tourists' goods and services in the world market." *Papers and Proceedings of the Regional Science Association* 7 (1961): 159–176.

CHAPTER SIX

A. General Transportation and Trade

Beckmann, M. J., C. B. McGuire, and C. B. Winston. *Studies in the economics of transportation*. New Haven, Conn.: Yale University Press, 1956.

Cooley, C. H. "The theory of transportation. "American Economic Association 1894.

Fogel, R. W. *Railroads and American economic growth: Essays in economic history*. Baltimore, Md., Johns Hopkins, 1964.

Fulton, M., and J. C. Hoch. "Transportation factors affecting locational decisions." *Economic Geography* 35 (1959): 51–59.

Garrison, W. L., and D. F. Marble. "A prolegomenon to the forecasting of transportation development, Final report to the U.S. Army aviation material laboratories, Northwestern University Transportation Center, 1965.

Garrison, W. L., et al. *Studies of highway development and geographic change*. Seattle: University of Washington Press, 1959.

Huff, D. L., and D. F. Marble. "Economic impact of highway improvements." *University of Washington Business Review* 19 (1959): 3–20.

Perle, E. D. "Estimation of transportation demand." *Papers and Proceedings of the Regional Science Association* 15 (1965): 203–215.

Smith, P. E. "A note on comparative advantage, trade, and the turnpike." *Journal of Regional Science* 5 (1964): 57–62.

Tattersall, J. N. "Exports and economic growth; The Pacific Northwest, 1880–1960." *Papers and Proceedings of the Regional Science Association* 9 (1962): 215–234.

Troxel, E. *Economics of transport*. New York: Rinehart, 1955.

Voorhees, A. M. "A general theory of traffic movement." *Proceedings of the Institute of Traffic Engineers* (1955): 46–56.

Warntz, W. "Transatlantic flights and pressure patterns." *Geographical Review* 51 (1961): 187–212.

Wolfe, R. I., and B. Hickok. "An annotated bibliography of the geography of transportation." University of California Institute of Transportation and Traffic Engineering, 1961.

Woytinsky, W. S., and E. S. Woytinsky. *World commerce and government*. New York: Twentieth Century Fund, 1955.

B. Theory of Trade

Alexander, J. W., E. S. Brown, and R. E. Dahlberg. "Freight rates: selected aspects of uniform and nodal regions." *Economic Geography* 34 (1958): 1–18.

Berry, B. J. L. "Recent studies concerning the role of transportation in the space-economy." *Annals of the Association of American Geographers* 49 (1959): 328–342.

Boudeville, J. R. "An operational model of regional trade in France." *Papers and Proceedings of the Regional Science Association* 7 (1961): 177–190.

Boye, Y. "Collecting and distributing commodities: Approaches to appropriate systems." *Papers and Proceedings of the Regional Science Association* 12 (1963): 221–224.

Enke, S. "Equilibrium among spatially separated markets; Solution by electric analogue." *Econometrika* 19 (1951): 40–47.

Fox, K. A., and R. C. Taeuber. "Spatial equilibrium models of the livestock-feed economy." *American Economic Review* 45 (1955): 584–608.

Graham, F. *The theory of international values.* Princeton, N.J.: Princeton University Press, 1940.

Henderson, J. M. *The efficiency of the coal industry: An application of linear programming.* Cambridge, Mass.: Harvard University Press, 1958.

Isard, W., and M. J. Peck. "Location theory and international and interregional trade theory." *Quarterly Journal of Economics* 68 (1954): 97–114.

Mackay, J. R. "The interactance hypothesis and boundaries in Canada." *Canadian Geography* 38 (1962): 122–129.

Mohring, H. D., and M. Harwitz. *Highway benefits: An analytical framework.* Evanston, Ill.: Northwestern University Press, 1962.

Morrill, R. L., and W. L. Garrison. "Projection of interregional patterns of trade in wheat and flour." *Economic Geography* 36 (1960): 116–126.

Porter, H. "Models of flow: Of people, commodities, and messages." Ph.D. dissertation, Northwestern University, 1963.

Richards, P. I. "Shock waves on the highway." *Journal of Operations Research* 4 (1956): 42–51.

Samuelson, P. A. "Spatial price equilibrium and linear programming." *American Economic Review* 42 (1952): 283–303.

Takayama, T., and G. G. Judge. "Spatial equilibrium and quadratic programming." *Journal of Farm Economics* 46 (1964): 67–93.

Vidale, M. L. "A graphic solution of the transportation problem." *Journal of Operation Research* 4 (1956): 193–203.

Warntz, W. "Transportation, social physics and the law of refraction." *Professional Geographer* 10 (1958): 6–10.

C. Transport Networks and Systems

Boyce, D. E. "The description and generation of transportation networks." Department of Regional Science (mimeographed), 1963.

Garrison, W. L. "Connectivity of the interstate highway system." *Papers and Proceedings of the Regional Science Association* 6 (1960): 121–137.

Garrison, W. L. and D. F. Marble. "Analysis of highway networks." *Highway Research Board Proceedings* 37 (1958): 1–17.

Garrison, W. L., and D. F. Marble. "Factor analytic study of the connectivity of the transportation network." *Papers and Proceedings of the Regional Science Association* 12 (1964): 231–234.

Kalaba, R. E., and M. L. Juncosa. "Optimal design and utilization of communication networks." *Management Science* 3 (1956): 33–44.

Kansky, K. "Structure of transport networks." University of Chicago Department of Geography, Research Paper 84, 1963.

Koopmans, T. C. "Optimum utilization of the transportation system." *Econometrica* 17 (1949): 136–146.

Lachene, R. "Networks and the location of economic activities." *Papers and Proceedings of the Regional Science Association* 14 (1965): 197–202.

Meinig, D. "A comparative historical geography of two railnets: Columbia basin and southern Australia." *Annals of the Association of American Geographers* 52 (1962): 394–413.

Pitts, F. R. "A graph theoretic approach to historical geography." *Professional Geographer* 17 (1965): 15–20.

Quant, R. E. "Models of transportation and optimal network construction." *Journal of Regional Science* 2 (1960): 27–45.

Smith, R. H. T. "Transport competition in Australian border areas." *Economic Geography* 39 (1963): 1–13.

Taaffe, E. J., R. L. Morrill, and P. R. Gould. "Transport expansion in underdeveloped countries: A comparative analysis." *Geographical Review* 53 (1963): 502–529.

Ullmann, E. L. "The railroad pattern of the United States." *Geographical Review* 39 (1949): 242–256.

D. International Trade, Ports

Alexander, J. W. "International trade: Selected types of world regions." *Economic Geography* 36 (1960): 95–115.

Alexandersson, G., and G. Norstrom. *World shipping.* New York: Wiley, 1963.

Carter, R. E. "A comparative analysis of United States ports and their traffic characteristics." *Economic Geography* 38 (1962): 162–175.

Grotewold, A. "Some aspects of the geography of international trade." *Economic Geography* 37 (1961): 309–319.

Hochwald, W. "Dependence of local economies upon foreign trade." *Papers and Proceedings of the Regional Science Association* 4 (1958): 259–272.

Mayer, H. M. "Great Lakes overseas: An expanding trade route." *Economic Geography* 30 (1954): 117–143.

Rice, J. "Patterns of Swedish foreign trade in the late eighteenth century." *Geografiska Annaler* 47B (1965): 86–99.

Smith, H. R., and J. F. Hart. "American tariff map." *Geographical Review* 45 (1955): 327–346.

Thorbecke, E. "European economic integration and the patterns of world trade." *American Economic Association Papers* 53 (1963): 147–174.

Verburg, M. C. "Location analysis of the common frontier in the EEC." *Papers and Proceedings of the Regional Science Association* 12 (1963): 61–78.

Weigend, G. C. "Some elements in the study of port geography." *Geographical Review* 48 (1958): 185–200.

E. Internal Trade

Beckerman, W. "Distance and the pattern of intra-European trade." *Review of Economics and Statistics* 38 (1956): 31–40.

Chinitz, B. *Freight and the metropolis.* Cambridge, Mass.: Harvard University Press, 1960.

Helvig, M. "Chicago's external truck movements: Spatial interactions between the Chicago area and its hinterland." University of Chicago Department of Geography, Research Paper 90, 1964.

Isard, W. "Regional commodity balances and interregional commodity flows." *American Economic Review* 43 (1953): 167–180.

Moses, L. "The stability of interregional trading patterns and input-output analysis." *American Economic Review* 45 (1955): 803–832.

Olsson, R. "Commodity flows and regional interdependence." *Papers and Proceedings of the Regional Science Association* 12 (1963): 25–230.

Patton, D. "The traffic pattern on American inland waterways." *Economic Geography* 32 (1956): 29–37.

Pfister, R. L. "The commodity balance of trade of the Pacific Northwest for selected years, 1929–1955." *Papers and Proceedings of the Regional Science Association* 5 (1959): 253–266.

Pfister, R. L. "The terms of trade as a tool for regional analysis." *Journal of Regional Science* 3 (1961): 57–66.

Richmond, S. B. "Interspatial relationships affecting air travel." *Land Economics* 33 (1957): 67–73.

Smith, S. A. "Interaction within a fragmented state: The example of Hawaii." *Economic Geography* 39 (1963): 234–244.

Spiegelglass, S. "Some aspects of state-to-state commodity flows in the United States." *Journal of Regional Science* 2 (1960): 71–80.

Ullmann, E. L. *American commodity flow.* Seattle: University of Washington Press, 1957.

Wallace, W. H.: "Freight traffic functions of Anglo-American railways." *Annals of the Association of American Geographers* 53 (1963): 312–331.

Wallace, W. H. "Railroad traffic densities and patterns." *Annals of the Association of American Geographers* 48 (1958): 352–374.

Wise, M. "The impact of a Channel tunnel on planning of southeast England." *Geographical Journal* 131 (1965): 167–185.

CHAPTER SEVEN

A. Population Redistribution

Anderson, T. R. "Potential models and the spatial distribution of population." *Papers and Proceedings of the Regional Science Association* 2 (1956): 175–182.

Barbour, K. M., and R. M. Prothero. *Essays on African population.* London: Kegan Paul, 1961.

Beale, C. L. "Rural depopulation in the United States." *Demography* 1 (1964): 264–272.

Bogue, D. J. "The geography of recent population trends in the United States." *Annals of the Association of American Geographers* 44 (1954): 124–134.

Carrothers, G. A. P. "Population projection by means of income potential models." *Papers and Proceedings of the Regional Science Association* 4 (1958): 121–152.

Duncan, O. D. "Measurement of population distributions." *Population Studies* 2 (1957-8): 27–45.

Geddes, A. "Variability in change of population in the United States and Canada." *Geographical Review* 44 (1954): 88–100.

Gibbs, J. "Evolution of population concentration." *Economic Geography* 39 (1963): 119–129.

Gregor, H. "Spatial disharmonies in California population growth." *Geographical Review* 53 (1963): 100–122.

Hart, J. F. "The changing distribution of the American Negro." *Annals of the Association of American Geographers* 50 (1960): 242–265.

Hauser, P. M., and O. D. Duncan. *The study of population: An inventory and appraisal.* Chicago: University of Chicago Press, 1959.

Isard, W., and D. Bramhall. "Regional employment and population forecasts via relative income potential models." *Papers and Proceedings of the Regional Science Association* 5 (1959): 25–48.

Keyfitz, N. "On the interaction of populations." *Demography* 2 (1965): 276–288.

Lee, E. S. et al. *Population redistribution and economic growth, 1870–1950.* Philadelphia: American Philosophical Society, 1957.

Loeffler, M. J. "The population syndromes on the Colorado piedmont." *Annals of the Association of American Geographers* 55 (1965): 26–66.

Lowenthal, D., and L. Comitas. "Emigration and depopulation: Some neglected aspects of population geography." *Geographical Review* 52 (1962): 195–210.

Murray, M. "The geography of death in England and Wales." *Annals of the Association of American Geographers* 52 (1962): 130–149.

Northam, R. "Declining urban centers in the United States, 1940–1960." *Annals of the Association of American Geographers* 53 (1953): 50–59.

Schwartzberg, J. E. "The distribution of selected castes in the North Indian plain." *Geographical Review* 55 (1965): 477–495.

Stewart, J. Q. "Empirical mathematical rules concerning the distribution and equilibrium of population." *Geographical Review* 37 (1947): 461–485.

Stewart, J. Q., and W. Warntz. "Physics of population distribution." *Journal of Regional Science* 1 (1958): 99–123.

Trewartha, G. T., and W. Zelinsky. "Population distribution and change in Korea, 1925–1949." *Geographical Review* 45 (1955): 1–26.

Webb, J. W. "Natural migrational components of population change in England and Wales, 1921–1931." *Economic Geography* 39 (1963): 130–148.

Zelinsky, W. "A bibliographic guide to population geography." University of Chicago Department of Geography, Research Paper 80, 1962.

Zelinsky, W. *A prologue to population geography.* Englewood Cliffs, N.J.: Prentice-Hall, 1966.

Zelinsky, W. "An approach to the religious geography of the United States: Patterns of church membership, 1952." *Annals of the Association of American Geographers* 51 (1961): 139–193.

B. Temporary Person Movements

Ajo, R. "Contributions to social-physics." *Lund Studies in Geography* B, 11, 1953.

Ajo, R. "An approach to demographical system analysis." *Economic Geography* 38 (1962): 359–371.

Boyce, D. E. "The effect of direction and length of person trips on urban travel patterns." *Journal of Regional Science* 6 (1965): 65–80.

Carroll, J. D., and H. B. Bevis. "Predicting local travel in urban regions." *Papers and Proceedings of the Regional Science Association* 3 (1957): 183–197.

Carrothers, G. A. P. "An historical review of the gravity and potential concepts of human interaction." *Journal of the American Institute of Planners* 22 (1956): 94–102.

Chisholm, M. D. "The geography of commuting." *Annals of the Association of American Geographers* 50 (1960): 187–8, 491–2.

Dickinson, R. E. "The geography of commuting: Netherlands and Belgium." *Geographical Review* 47 (1957): 521–538.

Dodd, S. C. "The interactance hypothesis." *American Sociological Review* 15 (1950): 245–256.

Ellis, J. B., and C. S. Van Doren. "A comparative evaluation of gravity and systems theory models for statewide recreational traffic flows." *Journal of Regional Science* 6 (1965): 57–70.

Hart, J. F., and B. H. Luebke. "Migration from a southern Appalachian community." *Land Economics* 34 (1958): 44–53.

Ikle, F. C. "Sociological relationship of traffic to population and distance." *Traffic Quarterly* 8 (1954): 123–136.

Isard, W., and M. F. Dacey. "On the projection of individual behavior in regional analysis." Part 1, *Journal of Regional Science* 4 (1962): 1–35; Part 2, *Journal of Regional Science* 4 (1962): 51–83.

Lukermann, F., and P. Porter. "Gravity and potential models in economic geography." *Annals of the Association of American Geographers* 50 (1960): 493–504.

Moses, L. "Toward a theory of intra-urban wage differentials and their influence on travel patterns." *Papers and Proceedings of the Regional Science Association* 9 (1962): 53–64.

Olsson, G. "Distance and human interaction." *Geografiska Annaler* 47B: 3–43.

Schneider, M. "Gravity models and trip distribution theory." *Papers and Proceedings of the Regional Science Association* 5 (1959): 51–56.

Sealy, K. R. *The geography of air transport.* London: Hutchinson, 1957.

Taaffe, E. J. "A map analysis of United States airline competition." *Journal of Air Law and Commerce* (1958).

Taaffe, E. J. "The urban hierarchy: An airline passenger definition." *Economic Geography* 38 (1962): 1–14.

Taaffe, E. J., B. Garner, and M. H. Yeates. *The peripheral journey to work.* Evanston, Ill.: Northwestern University Press, 1963.

Wolfe, R. I. "Recreation travel: The new migration." *Canadian Geographer* 10 (1966): 1–14.

C. Migration

Anderson, T. R. "Intermetropolitan migration: A comparison of the hypotheses of Zipf and Stouffer." *American Sociological Review* 20 (1955): 287–291.

Blanco, C. "The determinants of interstate population movements." *Journal of Regional Science* 5 (1963): 77–84.

Bogue, D. J., and W. S. Thompson. "Migration and distance." *American Sociological Review* 14 (1949): 236–244.

Bright, M. L., and D. S. Thomas. "Interstate migration and intervening opportunities." *American Sociological Review* 6 (1941): 773–783.

Duncan, O. D. "Occupation trends and patterns of net mobility." *Demography* 3 (1966): 1–18.

Eldridge, H. T. "Primary, secondary, and return migration in the United States" *Demography* 2 (1965): 444–455.

Goldstein, S. "Repeated migration as a factor in high mobility rates." *American Sociological Review* 19 (1954): 536–541.

Goldstein, S., and K. B. Mayer. "The impact of migration on the socioeconomic structure of cities and suburbs." *Sociology and Social Research* 50 (1965): 5–23.

Goodrich, C. *Migration and economic opportunity.* Philadelphia: University of Pennsylvania Press, 1936.

Hägerstrand, T. "A Monte Carlo approach to diffusion." *Archives Europeennes de Sociologie* 6 (1965): 43–67.

Hannerberg, D., ed. "Migration in Sweden: A symposium." *Lund Series in Geography,* B, 13, 1957.

Hitt, H. L. "The role of migration in population change among the aged." *American Sociological Review* 19 (1954): 194–200.

Isaac, J. *Economics of migration,* London: Kegan Paul, 1947.

Kitagawa, E. M. "The Negro leaves the South." *Demography* 1 (1964): 273–295.

Kulldorff, G. "Migration probabilities." *Lund Studies in Geography,* B, 15, 1955.

Lee, E. S. "A theory of migration." *Demography* 3 (1966): 7–57.

Lövgren, E. "The geographic mobility of labor." *Geografiska Annaler* 38 (1956): 344–394.

REFERENCES

Morrill, R. L. "The distribution of migration distances." *Papers and Proceedings of the Regional Science Association* 11 (1962): 75–84.

Morrill, R. L., and F. R. Pitts. "Marriage, migration, and the mean information." *Annals of the Association of American Geographers* 57 (1967): 402–422.

Nelson, P. "Migration, real income, and information." *Journal of Regional Science* 1 (1959): 43–74.

Pearson, J. E. "The significance of urban housing in rural-urban migration." *Land Economics* 39 (1963): 231–239.

Porter, R. "Approach to migration through its mechanism." *Geografiska Annaler* 38 (1956): 317–343.

Price, D. O. "Distance and direction as vectors of internal migration." *Social Forces* 27 (1948): 48–53.

Raimon, R. L. "Interstate migration and wage theory." *Review of Economics and Statistics* 54 (1962): 428–438.

Rashevsky, N. *Mathematical theory of human relations.* Bloomington: Principia Press, 1947.

Ravenstein, E. G. "The laws of migration." *Journal of the Royal Statistical Society* 48 (1885): 167–235; 52 (1889): 241–305.

Rogers, E. M. *Diffusion of innovations.* New York: Macmillan, 1962.

Shryock, H. S. "The efficiency of internal migration in the United States." *Proceedings of the International Population Conference,* Wien, 1959, 685–694.

Sjaastad, L. A. "Costs and returns of human migration." *Journal of Political Economy* 70 (1962): 80–93.

Sjaastad, L. "The relationship between migration and income in the United States." *Papers and Proceedings of the Regional Science Association* 6 (1960): 37–64.

Stouffer, S. "Intervening opportunities and competing migrants." *Journal of Regional Science* 2 (1960): 1–26.

Thomas, B. *Migration and economic growth.* Cambridge, Eng.: Cambridge University Press, 1954.

Velikonja, J.: "Post-war population movements in Europe." *Annals of the Association of American Geographers* 48 (1958): 458–472.

Wolpert, J. "Behavioral aspects of the decision to migrate." *Papers and Proceedings of the Regional Science Association* 15 (1966): 159–172.

D. Diffusion of Settlement and Innovation

Bowden, L. W. "Diffusion of the decision to irrigate: Colorado High Plains simulation of the spread of a new resource management practice." University of Chicago Department of Geography, Research Paper 97, 1965.

Coleman, J. "The diffusion of an innovation." *Sociometry* 20 (1957): 253–270.

Coleman, J. *Introduction to mathematical sociology.* New York: Free Press, 1964.

Dodd, S. C. "Diffusion is predictable: Testing probability models for laws of interaction." *American Sociological Review.* 20 (1955): 392–401.

Edmonson, M. S.: "Neolithic diffusion rates." *Current Anthropology.* 2 (1961): 71–102.

Hägerstrand, T. *Innovation diffusion as a spatial process,"* translated by A. Pred. Chicago: University of Chicago Press. 1968.

Hägerstrand, T. "On Monte Carlo simulation of diffusion." in *Quantitative geography,* W. L. Garrison. Evanston, Ill.; Northwestern University Press, 1967.

Karlsson, G. *Social mechanisms.* Stockholm: Almqvist and Wiksell, 1958.

Katz, E. *The diffusion of innovation.* New York: Wiley, 1964.

Kniffen, F. "Folk housing: Key to diffusion." *Annals of the Association of American Geographers* 55 (1965): 549–577.

Lionberger, H. F. *Adoption of new ideas and practices.* Ames, Iowa: Iowa State University Press, 1960.

Marble, D. F., and J. D. Nystuen. "An approach to the direct measurement of community mean information fields." *Papers and Proceedings of the Regional Science Asociation* 11 (1963): 99–110.

Pemberton, H. E. "Spatial order of cultural diffusion." *Sociology and Social Research* 22 (1938): 246–251.

Scoville, W. C. "Minority migrations and the diffusion of technology." *Journal of Economic History* 11 (1951): 347–360.

Sommer, R. "Leadership and group geography." *Sociometry* 24 (1961): 99–110.

Turner, F. J. *The frontier in American history.* New York: H. Holt, 1920.

Yuill, R. S. "A simulation study of barrier effects in spatial diffusion problems." Michigan inter-University Community of Mathematical Geographers, Discussion Papers 5, 1965.

Zipf, G. K. "Some determinations of the circulation of information." *American Journal of Psychology* 59 (1946): 401–421.

CHAPTER EIGHT

A. Urbanization, Growth, and Decline

Borchert, J. R., and R. B. Adams. "Projected urban growth in the upper midwest, 1960–1975." University of Minnesota Upper Midwest Economic Study, 1964.

Chang, S. D. "The historical trend of Chinese urbanization." *Annals of the Association of American Geographers* 53 (1963): 109–143.

Dickinson, R. E. *City and region.* New York: Humanities, 1964.

Gallion, A. B., and S. Eisner. *The urban pattern.* New York: Van Nostrand, 1950.

Hauser, P. M., and L. F. Schnore. *The study of urbanization.* New York: Wiley, 1965.

Lampard, E. E. "The history of cities in the economically advanced areas." *Economic Development and Cultural Change* 3 (1955): 81–136.

Lean, W. "Economics of new town size." *Journal of the Town Planning Institute* 52 (1966): 262–264.

Madden, C. H. "Some spatial aspects of urban growth in the United States." *Economic Development and Cultural Change* 4 (1956): 371–387.

Mayer, H., and C. Kohn. *Readings in urban geography.* Chicago: University of Chicago, 1959.

Morris, S. S. "Impact of the motor car on urban evolution." *Traffic Quarterly,* July 1966.

Murphey, R. "The city as a center of change: Western Europe and China." *Annals of the Association of American Geographers* 44 (1954): 349–362.

Perlman, M., ed. *Human resources in the urban economy.* Baltimore, Md.: Resources for the Future, Johns Hopkins Press, 1963.

Rapkin, C. "Some effects of economic growth on the character of cities." *Papers and Proceedings of the Regional Science Association* 2 (1956): 126–132.

Sjoberg, G. *The pre-industrial city.* New York: Free Press, 1960.

Smailes, A. E. *The geography of towns.* London, Hutchinson University Library, 1960.

Smailes, A. E. "The urban mesh of England and Wales." *Institute of British Geographers* 11 (1946): 87–101.

Taylor, G. *Urban geography.* New York: Dutton, 1949

Vance, R. N. B., and N. J. Demerath. *The urban south.* Chapel Hill, N.C.: University of North Carolina Press, 1954.

B. Variation among Cities: Economic Base

Alexander, J. W. "The basic-nonbasic concept of urban economic functions." *Economic Geography* 30 (1954): 246–261.

Alexandersson, G. *The industrial structure of American cities.* Lincoln, Nebr.: University of Nebraska Press, 1956.

Alonso, W. "The form of cities in developing countries." *Papers and Proceedings of the Regional Science Association* 13 (1964): 165–176.

Beckman, M. J. "City hierarchies and the distribution of city size." *Economic Development and Cultural Change* 6 (1958): 243–248.

Burton, I. "A restatement of the dispersed city hypothesis." *Annals of the Association of American Geographers* 53 (1963): 285–289.

Daly, M. C. "An approximation to a geographic multiplier." *Economic Journal* 50 (1940): 198–199.

Dickinson, R. E. "Distribution and functions of the smaller urban settlements of East Anglia," *Geography* 17 (1932): 19–31.

Harris, C. D., and E. L. Ullman. "The nature of cities," *Annals of the American Academy of Political and Social Science* 242 (1945): 7–17.

Leven, C. L. "Measuring the economic base." *Papers and Proceedings of the Regional Science Association* 2 (1956): 250–258.

Mayer, H. M. "Urban nodality and the economic base." *Journal of the American Institute of Planners* 20 (1964): 117–121.

Mehta, S. K. "Some demographic and economic correlates of primate cities." *Demography* 1 (1964): 136–147.

Moore, F. T. "A note on city size distributions." *Economic Development and Cultural Changes* (1959): 465–466.

Morrissett, I. "The economic structure of American cities." *Papers and Proceedings of the Regional Science Association* 4 (1958): 239–258.

Nelson, H. "Some characteristics of the population of cities in similar service classifications." *Economic Geography* 33 (1957): 95–108.

Smith, R. H. T. "Method and purpose in functional town classification." *Annals of the Association of American Geographers* 55 (1965): 539–548.

Stafford, H. "The dispersed city." *Professional Geographer* July 1962: 8–10.

Stewart, C. T. "The size and spacing of cities." *Geographical Review* 48 (1958): 222–245.

Stone, R. "A comparison of the economic structure of regions based on the concept of distance." *Journal of Regional Science* 2 (1960): 1–20.

Ullman, E. L., and M. F. Dacey. "The minimum requirements approach to the urban economic base." *Papers and Proceedings of the Regional Science Association* 6 (1960): 175–194.

C. Urban-Rural Relations

Anderson, T. R., and J. Collier. "Metropolitan dominance and the rural hinterland." *Rural Sociology* 21 (1956): 152–157.

Ashby, A. W. "The effects of urban growth on the countryside." *Sociological Review* 31 (1939): 345–369.

Griffin, P. F., and R. Chatham, "Urban impact on agriculture in Santa Clara County, California." *Annals of the Association of American Geographers* 48 (1958): 195–208.

McGee, T. G. "The rural urban continuum debate; The pre-industrial city and rural-urban migration." *Pacific Viewpoint* 5 (1964): 159–182.

Muth, R. F. "Economic change and rural-urban land use conversion." *Econometrica* 29 (1961): 1–23.

Schaffer, A. "A rural community at the urban fringe." *Rural Sociology* 23 (1958): 277–285.

Thomas, W., ed. "Man, time, and space in Southern California." *Annals of the Association of American Geographers* 49 (1959).

D. Settlement History and Patterns

Curry, L. "The random spatial economy: An exploration in settlement theory." *Annals of the Association of American Geographers* 54 (1964): 138–146.

Harris, B. "Some problems in the theory of inter-urban location." *Operations Research* 9 (1961): 695–721.

Hodge, G. "The prediction of trade center viability on the Great Plains." *Papers and Proceedings of the Regional Science Association* 15 (1965): 87–118.

Lively, C. E. "The appearance and disappearance of minor trade centers in Minnesota." *Social Forces* 10 (1931): 71–75.

McKenzie, R. D. "Spatial disturbance and community organization pattern." *Social Forces* 5 (1927): 623–627.

Morrill, R. L. "Migration and the spread and growth of urban settlement." *Lund Studies in Geography,* Series B., 26, 1965.

Northam, R. M. "Declining urban centers in the United States, 1940–1960." *Annals of the Association of American Geographers* 53 (1963) 50–59.

Salisbury, N. E., and G. Rushton. "Growth and decline of Iowa villages." State University of Iowa Department of Geography, 1963.

Trewartha, G. T. "The unincorporated hamlet: One element in the American settlement fabric." *Annals of the Association of American Geographers* 33 (1943): 32–81.

Webb, J. W. "Basic concepts in the analysis of small urban centers in Minnesota." *Annals of the Association of American Geographers* 49 (1959): 55–72.

E. The Metropolis

Bogue, D. J. *The structure of the metropolitan community: A study of dominance and subdominance.* Ann Arbor, Mich.: University of Michigan Press, 1949.

Borchert, J. R. "The twin cities urbanized area; Past, present, and future." *Geographical Review* 51 (1961): 47–70.

Duncan, O. D., et al. *Metropolis and region.* Baltimore, Md.: Johns Hopkins Press, 1960.

Goldner, W. "Spatial and locational aspects of metropolitan labor markets." *American Economic Review* 45 (1955): 113–128.

Gottman, J. *Megalopolis: The urbanized northeastern seaboard of the United States.* New York: Twentieth Century Fund, 1961.

Gregor, H. "Urbanization and water in Southern California." *Geographical Review* 44 (1954): 422–423.

Hall, Max, ed. *New York: Metropolitan region study.* Cambridge, Mass.: Harvard University Press, 1959.

Hawley, A. H. *The changing shape of metropolitan America.* New York: Free Press, 1956.

Hoover, E. M., and R. Vernon. *Anatomy of a metropolis.* Cambridge, Mass.: Harvard University Press, 1959.

Park, R. E., E. W. Burgess, and R. D. McKenzie. *The city.* Chicago: University of Chicago Press, 1925.

Schnore, L. F., and D. W. Varley. "Some concomitants of metropolitan size." *American Sociological Review* 20 (1955): 408–413.

F. Theory of Urban Structure

Alonso, W. *Location and land use: Toward a general theory of land rent.* Cambridge, Mass.: Harvard University Press, 1964.

Berkman, H. G. "The game theory of land use determination." *Land Economics* 41 (1965): 11–20.

Blumenfeld, H. "Are land use patterns predictable?" *Journal of the American Institute of Planners* 25 (1959): 61–66.

Blumenfeld, H. "On the concentric-circle theory of urban growth." *Land Economics* 25 (1949): 209–212.

von Boventer, E. "The relationship between transportation costs and location rent." *Journal of Regional Science* 3 (1961): 27–40.

Brigham, E. F. "The determinants of residential land values." *Land Economics* 41 (1965): 324–334.

Burgess, E. W. "The determination of gradients in the growth of the city." *American Sociological Society Publications* 21 (1927): 178–84.

Carroll, J. D. "Spatial interaction and the urban-metropolitan regional description." *Papers and Proceedings of the Regional Science Association* 1 (1955): D1–D14.

Clark, C. "Urban population densities." *Journal of the Royal Statistical Society* 114: 490–496.

Colby, C. C. "Centrifugal and centripetal forces in urban geography." *Annals of the Association of American Geographers* 23 (1933): 1–20.

Friedmann, J., and J. Miller. "The urban field." *Journal of the American Institute of Planners* 31 (1965): 312–319.

Guttenburg, A. Z. "Urban structure and urban growth." *Journal of the American Institute of Planners* 26 (1960): 104–110.

Hatt, P. K., and J. Reiss, eds. *Cities and society.* New York: Free Press, 1957.

Herbert, J. D., and B. Stevens. "A model for the distribution of residential activity in urban areas." *Journal of Regional Science* 2 (1960): 21–36.

Huff, D. L. "A topographic model of consumer space preferences." *Papers and Proceedings of the Regional Science Association* 6 (1960): 159–173.

Kain, J. F. "An economic model of urban residential and travel behavior." *Review of Economics and Statistics* 46 (1964): 55–64.

Lakshmanan, T. R. "An approach to the analysis of intra-urban location applied to the Baltimore region." *Economic Geography* 40 (1964): 348–370.

Loewenstein, L. C. "Location of urban land uses." *Land Economics* 39 (1963): 407–420.

Lynch, K., and L. Rodwin. "A theory of urban form." *Journal of the American Institute of Planners* 24 (1958): 201–214.

Meier, R. L. "Gaming simulation for urban planning." *Journal of the American Institute of Planners* 32 (1966): 3–16.

Newling, B. E. "Urban growth and spatial structure." *Geographic Review* 56 (1966): 213–225.

Ratcliff, R. U. *Urban land economics.* New York: McGraw-Hill, 1949.

Stevens, B. H. "Linear programming and location rent." *Journal of Regional Science* 3 (1961): 15–26.

Webber, M. M., et al. *Explorations into urban structure.* Philadelphia: University of Pennsylvania Press, 1964.

Weimar, A. M., and H. Hoyt. *Principles of urban real estate.* New York: Ronald Press, 1954.

Wendt, F. "Theory of urban land values." *Land Economics* 33 (1957): 228–240.

G. Studies of Land Use and Urban Structure

Anderson, T. R. "Scale and economic factors affecting the location of residential neighborhods. *Papers and Proceedings of the Regional Science Association* 9 (1962): 161–172.

Bartholemew, H. *Land use in American cities.* Cambridge, Mass.: Harvard University Press, 1955.

Berkman, H. G. "Decentralization and blighted vacant land." *Land Economics* 32 (1956): 270–280.

Carroll, J. D. "Relation of homes to work place and the spatial patterns of cities." *Social Forces* 30 (1952): 272–282.

Carroll, J. D. "Spatial interaction and urban-metropolitan regional description." *Papers and Proceedings of the Regional Science Association* 1 (1955): D1–D14.

Chapin, F. S. and H. C. Hightower. "Household activity patterns and land use." *Journal of American Institute of Planners* 31 (1965): 222-231.

Clark, W. A. V. "Markov chain analysis in geography: an application to the movement of rental housing areas." *Annals of the Association of American Geographers* 55 (1965): 351–359.

Duncan, B. "Factors in work-residence separation." *American Sociological Review* 21 (1956): 48–56.

Fellman, J. D. "Prebuilding growth patterns of Chicago." *Annals of the Association of American Geoographers* 47 (1957): 59–82.

Firey, W. *Land use in central Boston.* Cambridge, Mass.: Harvard University Press, 1947.

Foley, D. L. "Urban daytime population: A field for demographic-ecological analysis." *Social Forces* 32 (1954): 323–330.

Fuches, R. J. "Intraurban variations in residential quality." *Economic Geography* 36 (1960): 313–325.

Getis, A. "Temporal land-use pattern analysis with the use of nearest neighbor and quadrant methods." *Annals of the Association of American Geographers* 54 (1964): 391–399.

Gottlieb, M. "Influences on value in urban land markets." *Journal of Regional Science* 6 (1965): 1–16.

Hansen, W. G. "How accessibility shapes land use." *Journal of the American Institute of Planners* 15 (1959): 73–76.

Hartman, G. W., and J. C. Hook. "Substandard urban housing in the United States." *Economic Geography* 32 (1956): 95–114.

Hoyt, H. *One hundred years of land values in Chicago.* Chicago: University of Chicago Press, 1933.

Hoyt, H. "Recent distortions of classical models of urban structure." *Land Economics* 40 (1964): 194–212.

Kain, J. F. "The journey to work as a determinant of residential location." *Papers and Proceedings of the Regional Science Association* 9 (1962): 137–160.

Marble, D. F. "Transport inputs at urban residential sites." *Papers and Proceedings of the Regional Science Association* 5 (1960): 253–266.

Muth, R. F. "The spatial structure of the housing market." *Papers and Proceedings of the Regional Science Association* 7 (1961): 207–220.

Powers, M. E. "Age and space aspects of city and suburban housing." *Land Economics* 40 (1964): 383–387.

Schnore, L. F. "Urban structure and suburban selectivity." *Demography* 15 (1964): 164–176.

Seyfried, W. R. "The centrality of urban land values." *Land Economics* 39 (1963): 275–284.

Vance, J. E. "Laborshed, employment field, and dynamic analysis in urban geography." *Economic Geography* 36 (1960): 189–220.

Yeates, M. H. "Some factors affecting the spatial distribution of Chicago land values." *Economic Geography* 41 (1965): 57–70.

H. Urban Transportation

Felman, J. D. "Truck transportation patterns of Chicago." University of Chicago Department of Geography, Research Paper 12, 1956.

Hoover, R. "Policy growth and transportation planning in the Detroit metropolitan area." *Papers and Proceedings of the Regional Science Association* 7 (1961): 223–240.

Jurkat, E. H. "Land use analysis and forecasting in traffic planning." *Traffic Quarterly* 11 (1957): 151–163.

Kain, J. F. "The development of urban transportation models. *Papers and Proceedings of the Regional Science Association* 14 (1965): 147–174.

Meyer, J. R., J. F. Kain, and M. Wohl. *The urban transportation problem.* Cambridge, Mass.: Harvard University Press, 1965.

Mitchell, R. B., and C. Rapkin. *Urban traffic: A function of land use.* New York: Columbia University Press, 1954.

I. Retail Business Centers

Berry, B. J. L. "Commercial structure and commercial blight." University of Chicago Department of Geography, Research Paper 85, 1963.

Boyce, R. R., and W. A. V. Clark. "Selected spatial variables and central business district sales." *Papers and Proceedings of the Regional Science Association* 11 (1963): 167–194.

Breese, G. *Daytime population of the central business district.* Chicago: University of Chicago Press, 1949.

Durden, D. and D. F. Marble. "The rise of theory in central business district planning." *Journal of American Institute of Planners* 27 (1961): 10–16.

Griffin, D. W., and R. E. Preston. "A restatement of the 'Transition Zone' concept." *Annals of the Association of American Geographers* 56 (1966): 339–350.

Horwood, E. M., and R. R. Boyce. *Studies of the central business district and urban freeway development.* Seattle: University of Washington Press, 1959.

Hoyt, H. "Classification and significant characteristics of shopping centers." *Appraisal Journal* 26 (1958): 214–222.

Huff, D. L. "A note on the limitations of intra-urban gravity models." *Land Economics* 38 (1962): 64–66.

Murphy R. "A comparative study of nine central business districts." *Economic Geography* 30 (1954): 301–336.

Proudfoot, M. S. "The outlying business centers of Chicago." *Journal of Land and Public Utility Economics* 13 (1937): 57–70.

Seyfried, W. R., and B. Appelo. "Land tenure in the central business district." *Land Economics* 42 (1966): 171–178.

Ward, D. "The industrial revolution and the emergence of Boston's central business district." *Economic Geography* 42 (1963): 152–171.

J. Urban Growth: Political Structure

Andrews, R. B. "Elements in the urban-fringe pattern." *Journal of Land and Public Utility Economics* 13 (1942): 169–183.

Blumenfeld, H. "The tidal wave of metropolitan expansion." *Journal of the American Institute of Planners* 20 (1954): 3–14.

Chapin, F. S. "A model for simulating residential development, in urban development models: New tools in planning." *Journal of American Institute of Planners* 32 (1965): 120–125.

Chapin, F. S., and S. F. Weiss, eds. *Urban growth dynamics in a regional cluster of cities.* New York: Wiley, 1962.

Chapin, F. S. *Urban land use planning.* New York: Harper, 1957.

Chinitz, B. *City and suburb.* Englewood Cliffs, N.J.: Prentice Hall, 1965.

Clawson, M. "Urban sprawl and speculation in suburban land." *Land Economics* 38 (1962): 99–111.

Czamanski, S. "A model of urban growth." *Papers and Proceedings of the Regional Science Association* 13 (1964): 177–200.

Hansen, W. B. "An approach to the analysis of metropolitan residential extension." *Journal of Regional Science* 3 (1961): 37–55.

Harvey, R. C., and W. A. V. Clark. "The nature and economics of urban sprawl." *Land Economics* 41 (1965): 1–10.

Morrill, R. L. "Expansion of the urban fringe; A simulation experiment." *Papers and Proceedings of the Regional Science Association* 15 (1965): 185–202.

Nelson, H. "The spread of an artificial landscape over Southern California." *Annals of the Association of American Geographers* 48 (1959): 80–99.

Niedercorn, J. H., and J. F. Kain. "An econometric model of metropolitan development." *Papers and Proceedings of the Regional Science Association* 11 (1963): 123–144.

Nourse, H. O. "The Economics of urban renewal." *Land Economics* 42 (1966): 65–74.

Thomas, E. N. "Area association between population growth and selected factors in the Chicago urbanized area." *Economic Geography* 36 (1960): 158–170.

Ward, D. "A comparative historical geography of streetcar suburbs in Boston and Leeds, 1850–1920." *Annals of the Association of American Geographers* 54 (1964): 477–489.

Winsborough, H. "City growth and city structure." *Journal of Regional Science* 4 (1962): 25–50.

K. Social Structure

Anderson, T. R., and J. A. Egeland. "Spatial aspects of social area analysis." *American Sociological Review* 26 (1961): 392–398.

Brookfield, H. C. "The redistribution of racial groups in Durban." *Geographical Review* 47 (1957): 44–65.

Case, F. E. "Prediction of the incidence of urban blight." *Papers and Proceedings of the Regional Science Association* 11 (1963): 211–216.

Hawley, A. H., and C. D. Duncan. "Social area analysis; A critical appraisal." *Land Economics* 33 (1957): 337–344.

Issacs, R. R. "The neighborhood theory: An analysis of its adequacy." *Journal of the American Institute of Planners* 14 (1948): 15–23.

Morrill, R. L. "The Negro ghetto: Problems and alternatives." *Geographical Review* 55 (1965): 339–361.

Seeley, J. R. "The slum: Its nature, use and users." *Journal of American Institute of Planners* 25 (1959): 7–14.

Stokes, C. L. "The theory of slums." *Land Economics* 38 (1962): 187–197.

Taeuber, K. E., and A. F. Taeuber. *Negroes in cities.* Chicago: Aldine, 1965.

CHAPTER NINE

A. Spatial Organization

Bos, H. C. *Spatial dispersion of economic activity.* Rotterdam: Rotterdam University Press, 1965.

Boustedt, O., and H. Ranz. *Regionale Struktur und Wirtschaftsforschung.* Bremen: Walter Dorn Verlag, 1957.

von Boventer, E. "Spatial organization theory as a basis for regional planning." *Journal of American Institute of Planners* 30 (1964): 90–100.

von Boventer, E. "Toward a united theory of spatial economic structure." *Papers and Proceedings of the Regional Science Association* 10 (1963): 163–188.

Chisholm, M. "Toward a geography of price." *Professional Geographer* 16 (1964): 10–12.

Curry, L. "Landscape as system." *Geographical Review* 54 (1964): 121–124.

Friedmann, J. "The spatial structure of economic development in the Tennessee Valley." University of Chicago Department of Geography, Research Paper 39, 1955.

Garrison, W. L. "Spatial structure of the economy." *Annals of the Association of American Geographers* 49 (1959): 232–239, 471–482; 50 (1960): 357–373.

Isard, W., and T. Tung. "Some concepts for the analysis of spatial organization." *Papers and Proceedings of the Regional Science Association* 12 (1964): 1–27.

Moore, F. T., and Peterson, J. W. "Regional analysis: an inter-industry model of Utah." *Review of Economics and Statistics* 37 (1955): 368–383.

North, D. C. "The spatial and interregional framework of the United States' economy." *Papers and Proceedings of the Regional Science Association* 2 (1956): 201–209.

Philbrick, A. K. "Principles of area functional organization in regional human geography." *Economic Geography* 33 (1957): 299–336.

Ullman, E. L. "Regional development and the geography of concentration." *Papers and Proceedings of the Regional Science Association* 4 (1958): 179–200.

Vining, R. "1955 description of certain spatial aspects of an economic system." *Economic Development and Cultural Change* 3 (1955): 147–195.

Warntz, W. *Toward a geography of price.* Philadelphia: University of Pennsylvania Press, 1959.

B. Regional Economics

Baumol, W. J. *Economic theory and operations analysis.* Englewood Cliffs, N. J.: Prentice-Hall, 1961.

Beckmann, M. J. "The economics of location." *Kyklos* 8 (1955): 416–421.

Beckmann, M. J. and T. C. Koopmans. "Assignment problems and the location of economic activities." *Econometrica* 25 (1957): 53–76.

Bramhall, D. F. "Projecting regional accounts and industrial locations." *Papers and Proceedings of the Regional Science Association* 7 (1961): 89–118.

Chenery, H. B., and P. G. Clark. *Interindustry economics.* New York: Wiley, 1964.

Duncan, O. D., and R. Cuzzort. "Regional differentiation and socio-economic change." *Papers and Proceedings of the Regional Science Association* 4 (1958): 163–178.

Harris, S. *International and interregional economics.* New York: McGraw-Hill, 1957.

Hurter, A. P., and L. Moses. "Regional investment and interregional programming." *Papers and Proceedings of the Regional Science Association* 13 (1964): 105–120.

Isard, W., et al. *Methods of regional analysis: An introduction to regional science.* New York: Minnesota Institute of Technology Press, 1960.

Isard, W., and P. Isard. "General social, political, and economic equilibrium for a system of regions." Part 1, *Papers and Proceedings of the Regional Science Association* 14 (1965): 1–34; Part 2, *Papers and Proceedings of the Regional Science Association* 15 (1965): 7–28.

Kavesh, R. A., and J. B. Jones. "Differential regional impacts of federal expenditures." *Papers and Proceedings of the Regional Science Association* 2 (1956): 152–173.

Leven, C. L. "Regional and interregional accounts in perspective. *Papers and Proceedings of the Regional Science Association* 13 (1964): 127–146.

Moore, F. T. "Regional economic reaction paths." *American Economic Review* 45 (1955): 133–148.

Moses, L. "A general equilibrium model of production, interregional trade and location of industry." *Review of Economics and Statistics* 42 (1960): 376–397.

North, D. C. "Location theory and regional economic growth." *Journal of Political Economy* 63 (1955): 243–258.

Peters, W. S. "Measures of regional interchange. *Papers and Proceedings of the Regional Science Association* 11 (1962): 285–294.

Stevens, B. H. "An interregional linear programming model. "*Journal of Regional Science* 1 (1958): 60–98.

C. Regions and Regionalization

Berry, B. L. J. "Approaches to regional analysis; A synthesis. *Annals of the Association of American Geographers* 54 (1964): 2–11.

Berry, B. J. L. "A method for deriving multi-factor uniform regions." *Przeglad Geograficzny* 33 (1961): 263–282.

Bogue, D. L., and C. L. Beale. *Economic areas of the United States.* New York: Free Press, 1961.

Bunge, W. "Gerrymandering, geography, and grouping." *Geographical Review* 56 (1966): 256–263.

Dziewonski, K. "Theoretical problems in the development of economic regions." Part 1, *Papers and Proceedings of the Regional Science Association* 8 (1961); Part 2, *Papers and Proceedings of the Regional Science Association* 10 (1962): 51–60.

Fox, F. A., and T. K. Kumar. "The functional economic area." *Papers and Proceedings of the Regional Science Association* 15 (1965): 57–86.

Green, F. H. W. "Community of interest areas in Western Europe." *Economic Geography* 29 (1953): 283–298.

Grigg, D. "The logic of regional systems." *Annals of the Association of American Geographers* 55 (1965): 465–491.

Harris, C. D. "Salt Lake City." *Economic Geography* 17 (1941): 204–212.

Jensen, M., ed. *Regionalism in America.* Madison: University of Wisconsin Press, 1951.

Lösch, A. "The nature of economic regions." *Southern Economic Journal* 5 (1938): 71–78.

Meinig, D. W. "The Mormon culture region: Strategies and patterns in the geography of the American West, 1847–1964." *Annals of the Association of American Geographers* 55 (1965): 191–220.

Nystuen, J. D., and M. F. Dacey. "A graph theory interpretation of nodal regions." *Papers and Proceedings of the Regional Science Association* 7 (1961): 29–42.

Perloff, H. S. *Regions, resources, and economic growth.* Baltimore: Johns Hopkins, 1960.

Teitz, M. B. "Regional theory and regional models." *Papers and Proceedings of the Regional Science Association* 9 (1962): 35–52.

Vining, R. "Delimitation of economic areas." *Journal of the American Statistical Association* 18 (1953): 44–64.

Wrobel, W. "Regional analysis of the geographic concept of region." *Papers and Proceedings of the Regional Science Association* 8 (1961): 37–42.

Zobler, L. "Decision making in regional construction." *Annals of the Association of American Geographers* 48 (1958): 140–48.

CHAPTER TEN

A. Regional Planning and Development

Booth, E. J. R. "Interregional income differentials." *Southern Economic Journal* 31 (1964): 44–51.

Easterlin, R. A. "Long term regional income changes." *Papers and Proceedings of the Regional Science Association* 4 (1958): 313–328.

Fisher, J. L. "Concepts in regional economic development." *Papers and Proceedings of the Regional Science Association* 1 (1955): W1–W20.

Friedmann, J. "Regional economic policy for developing areas." *Papers and Proceedings of the Regional Science Association* 11 (1963): 41–62.

Gilmore, D. R. "Development of the little economies." Committee for Economic Development, 1960.

Guthrie, J. A. "Economies of scale in regional development." *Papers and Proceedings of the Regional Science Association* 1 (1955): J1–J10.

Hanna, F. A. "Contribution of manufacturing wages to regional difference in per capital income." *Review of Economics and Statistics* 33 (1951): 18–28.

Hansen, N. M. "Regional planning in a mixed economy." *Southern Economic Journal* 32 (1965): 176–190.

Harper, R. A., T. H. Schmudde, and F. H. Thomas. "Recreation-based economic development and the growth point concept." *Land Economics* 43 (1966): 95–102.

Leighton, P. A. "Geographical aspects of air pollution." *Geographical Review* 56 (1966): 151–174.

Maki., W. R., and Y. Tu. "Regional growth models for rural areas development." *Papers and Proceedings of the Regional Science Association* 9 (1962): 235–244.

Miernyk, W. H. "Labor mobility and regional growth." *Economic Geography* 31 (1955): 321–330.

Osborn, F. J., and A. Whittick. *The new towns: Answer to megalopolis.* New York: McGraw-Hill, 1963.

Parr, J. B. "Out migration and the depressed area problem." *Land Economics* 42 (1966): 149–160.

Parr, J. B. "Specialization, diversification, and regional development." *Professional Geographer* 17 (1965): 21–25.

Reiner, T. A. "Sub-national and national planning: Decision criteria." *Papers and Proceedings of the Regional Science Association* 14 (1965): 107–136.

Roterus, V. "Suitability of economic activities in relation to the local economy." *Journal of the American Institute of Planners* 13 (1947): 29–31.

Smolensky, E. "Industrialization and income inequality: Recent United States experience." *Papers and Proceedings of the Regional Science Association* 7 (1961): 67–88.

Thomas, M. D. "Regional economic growth and industrial development." *Papers and Proceedings of the Regional Science Association* 10 (1962): 61–67.

Tiebout, C. M. "Exports and regional economic growth." *Journal of Political Economy* 64 (1956): 160–164.

White, G. F. "Contribution of geographic analysis to river basin development." *Geographical Journal* 129 (1963): 412–436.

B. Studies of Regional Economic Development

Hansen, N. M. "Some neglected factors in American regional development policy: The case of Appalachia." *Land Economics* 42 (1966): 1–10.

Klimm, L. "The empty areas of the northeastern United States." *Geographical Review* 44 (1954): 325–345.

Thompson, J. H., et al. "Toward a geography of economic health: The case of New York State." *Annals of Association of American Geographers* 52 (1962): 1–20.

C. Problems of World Economic Development

Chandrasekhar, S. *Hungry people and empty lands.* London: Allen and Unwin, 1954.

Clark, C. *The conditions of economic progress.* London: Macmillan, 1940.

Friedman, J. "Poor regions and poor nations." *Southern Economic Journal* 32 (1966): 465–473.

Fryer, D. W. "World income and types of economies." *Economic Geography* 34 (1958): 282–303.

Ginsburg, N. "Essays on geography and economic development." University of Chicago Department of Geography, Research Paper 62, 1960.

Lewis, W. A. *The theory of economic growth.* London: Allen and Unwin, 1955.

Melamid, A. "Regional aspects of economic development in multi-national states." *Papers and Proceedings of the Regional Science Association* 3 (1957): 301–306.

Rostow, W. W. *The economics of take-off into sustained growth.* New York: St. Martin's, 1963.

Rostow, W. W. *The stages of economic growth.* Cambridge, Mass.: Harvard University Press, 1960.

Schwartzberg, J. E. "Three approaches to the mapping of economic development in India." *Annals of the Association of American Geographers* 52 (1962): 455–468.

Sebestyen, J. "Some thoughts on a spatial model for development purposes." *Papers and Proceedings of the Regional Science Association* 12 (1963): 119–124.

Zaidi, I. H. "Toward a measure of the functional effectiveness of a state: The case of West Pakistan." *Annals of the Association of American Geographers* 56 (1966): 52–57.

MOST RECENT REFERENCES: 1967 THROUGH 1969

Chapter One

Brown, R. C. "Use and misuse of distance variables in land-use analysis." *Professional Geographer* 20 (1968): 337–341.

Burton, I., R. Kates, and R. Snead, *Human ecology of coastal flood hazard in Megalopolis.* University of Chicago Department of Geography, Research Paper 115, 1969.

Buttimer, A. "Social space in interdisciplinary perspective." *Geographical Review* 59 (1969): 417–426.

Chorley, R., and P. Haggett. *Models in Geography.* London: Methuen, 1967.

Cole, J. P., and C. A. M. King, *Quantitative Geography.* New York: Wiley, 1968.

Dacey, M. "Some properties of order distance for random point distributions." *Geografiska Annaler* 49B (1967): 25–32.

Dale, E. "Some geographical aspects of African landlocked states." *Annals of the Association of American Geographers* 58 (1968): 485–505.

Golledge, R., and L. Brown. "Search, learning, and the market decision process." *Geografiska Annaler* 49B (1967): 117–124.

Gould, P. "Problems of space preference measures and relationships." *Geographical Analysis* 1 (1969): 31–44.

Gould, P. "Structuring information on spacio-temporal preferences." *Journal of Regional Science* 7 (1967): 259–274.

Hudson, J. "A model of spatial relations." *Geographical Analysis* 1 (1969): 260–271.

Hudson, J. C. "Pattern recognition in empirical map analysis." *Journal of Regional Science* 9 (1969): 189–200.

Karaska, G., and D. Bramhall. *Location analysis for manufacturing.* Cambridge, Mass.: MIT Press, 1969.

King, L. J. "Analysis of spatial form and its relation to geographic theory." *Annals of the Association of American Geographers* 59 (1969): 573–595.

Nourse, H. *Regional Economics.* New York: McGraw-Hill, 1968.

Olsson, G. "Trends in spatial model building." *Geographical Analysis* 1 (1969): 219–229.

Olsson, G., and S. Gale. "Spatial theory and human behavior." *Papers and Proceedings of the Regional Science Association* 21 (1969): 229–241.

Pred, A. *Behavior and location.* Lund Studies in Geography, Series B, 27, 1967; and 28, 1969.

Quinn, F. "Water transfers: Must the West be won again?" *Geographical Review* 58Z (1968): 108–132.

Rushton, G. "Analysis of spatial behavior by revealed space preference." *Annals of the Association of American Geographers* 59 (1969): 391–402.

Smith, R. H. T., E. Taaffe, and L. J. King, *Readings in Economic Geography.* Chicago: Rand McNally, 1967.

Taylor, P. J. "Location variables in taxonomy." *Geographical Analysis* 1 (1969): 181–195.

Törnqvist, G. *Flows of information and the location of economic activities.* Lund Studies in Geography, Series B, 30, 1968.

Warntz, W. "Global science and the tyranny of space." *Papers and Proceedings of the Regional Science Association* 19 (1967): 7–22.

Chapter Two

Clark, R. J. "Land reform and peasant market participation (Bolivia)." *Land Economics* 44 (1968): 153–172.

Floyd, B. "Toward a more specific geography of traditional agriculture in the tropics." *Professional Geographer* 21 (1969): 248–251.

Freebairn, D. K. "Dichotomy of prosperity and poverty in Mexican agriculture." *Land Economics* 45 (1969): 31–42.

Johnson, D. *Nature of nomadism.* University of Chicago Department of Geography, Research Paper 118, 1969.

Lentnek, B. "Economic transition to commercial agriculture: El Llano, Mexico." *Annals of the Association of American Geographers* 59 (1969): 65–84.

Smith, R. H. T., and A. M. Hay. "Theory of the spatial structure of internal trade in underdeveloped countries." *Geographical Analysis* 1 (1969): 121–136.

Street, J. M. "Evaluation of the concept of carrying capacity." *Professional Geographer* 21 (1969): 104–107.

Chapter Three

Brown, R. W. "Upsala community; A case study in rural dynamics." *Annals of the Association of American Geographers* 57 (1967): 277–300.

Day, R. H., and E. H. Tinney. "A dynamic von Thünen model." *Geographical Analysis* 1 (1969): 137–151.

Gregor, H. F. "Farm structure in regional comparison: California and New Jersey vegetable farms." *Economic Geography* 45 (1969): 209–225.

Grigg, D. "Agricultural regions of the world." *Economic Geography* 45 (1969): 95–132.

Horvath, R. "Von Thünen's isolated state and the area around Addis Ababa, Ethiopia." *Annals of the Association of American Geographers* 59 (1969): 308–323.

Howes, R. "Test of the linear programming model of agriculture." *Papers and Proceedings of the Regional Science Association* 19 (1967): 123–140.

Hudson, J. C. "A location theory for rural settlement." *Annals of the Association of American Geographers* 59 (1969): 365–381.

Jensen, R. "Regionalism and price zonation in Soviet agricultural planning." *Annals of the Association of American Geographers* 59 (1969): 324–347.

Peet, J. R. "Spatial expansion of commercial agriculture in the 19th century." *Economic Geography* 45 (1969): 283–301.

Stevens, B. H. "Location theory and programming models: The von Thünen case." *Papers and Proceedings of the Regional Science Association* 21 (1968): 19–34.

Chapter Four

Boventer, E. von. "Christaller's central places and peripheral areas." *Journal of Regional Science* 9 (1969): 117–124.

Brush, J. E., and H. L. Gauthier. *Service centers and consumer trips: Studies on the Philadelphia metropolitan fringe.* University of Chicago Department of Geography, Research Paper 113, 1968.

Clark, W. A. V. "Consumer travel patterns and the concept of range." *Annals of the Association of American Geographers* 58 (1968): 386–396.

Curry, L. "Central places in the random spatial economy." *Journal of Regional Science* 7 (1967): 217–238.

Curry, L. "Classical approach to central place dynamics." *Geographical Analysis* 1 (1969): 272–282.

Dacey, M. F., and A. Sen. "Central place hexagonal lattice." *Journal of Regional Science* 8 (1968): 209–213.

Gruen, N. J., and C. Gruen. "Behavioral approach to determining optimal locations for the retail firm." *Land Economics* 43 (1967): 320–327.

Hurst, M. E. E., and J. Sellers. "Analysis of the spatial distribution of customers around two grocery retailer operations." *Professional Geographer* 21 (1969): 184–191.

Illeris, S., and P. O. Pedersen. *Central places and functional regions of Denmark.* Lund Studies in Geography, Series B, 31, 1968.

Janelle, D. G. "Central place development in a time—space framework." *Professional Geographer* 20 (1968): 5–10.

Johnston, R. L., and P. J. Rimmer. "Consumer behavior in an urban hierarchy." *Journal of Regional Science* 7 (1967): 161–166.

Kenyon, J. "On the relation between central function and size of place." *Annals of the Association of American Geographers* 57 (1967): 736–750.

Medvedkov, Y. V. "Application of topology in central place analysis." *Papers and Proceedings of the Regional Science Association* 20 (1968): 77–84.

Morrill, R. L., and R. Earickson. "Variation in the character and use of Chicago hospitals." *Health Services Research* 3 (1968): 224–238.

Morrill, R. L., and P. Kelley. "Optimal allocation of services." *Annals of Regional Science* 3 (1969): 55–66.

Parr, J. B. "City hierarchies and the distribution of city sizes." *Journal of Regional Science* 9 (1969): 239–254.

Roder, W. "Genesis of the central place system: Rhodesian example." *Professional Geographer* 21 (1969): 333–336.

Rushton, G., and R. Golledge. "Formulation and test of a normative model for the spatial allocation of grocery expenditures." *Annals of the Association of American Geographers* 57 (1967): 389–400.

Tarrant, J. R. "Note concerning affinities of groups of settlements for a central place hierarchy." *Economic Geography* 44 (1968): 144–151.

Teitz, M. B. "Toward a theory of urban public facilities location." *Papers and Proceedings of the Regional Science Association* 21 (1968): 35–52.

Thijsse, J. "Second thoughts about a rural pattern for the future in the Netherlands." *Papers and Proceedings of the Regional Science Association* 20 (1968): 69–76.

Tinbergen, J. "Hierarchical model of the size distribution of cities." *Papers and Proceedings of the Regional Science Association* 20 (1968): 65–68.

Woldenberg, M. J. "Energy flow and spatial order: Mixed hexagonal hierarchies of central places." *Geographical Review* 58 (1968): 552–574.

Woldenberg, M. L., and B. J. L. Berry. "Rivers and central places, analogous systems?" *Journal of Regional Science* 7 (1967): 129–139.

Yuill, R. S. "Spatial behavior of retail customers." *Geografiska Annaler* 49B (1967): 105–116.

Zaidi, I. H. "Measuring the locational complementarity of central places in West Pakistan." *Economic Geography* 44 (1968): 218–239.

Chapter Five

Albert, L. D., and J. H. Kellow. "Decision-makers' reactions to plant location factors." *Land Economics* 45 (1969): 376–380.

Alonso, W. "Reformulation of classical location theory and its relation to rent theory." *Papers and Proceedings of the Regional Science Association* 19 (1967): 23–44.

Carrier, R. E., and W. R. Schriver. "Location theory: Empirical models and selected findings." *Land Economics* 44 (1968): 450–460.

Cooper, L. "Generalized Weber problem." *Journal of Regional Science* 8 (1968): 181–197.

Cooper, L. "Locational equilibrium models." *Journal of Regional Science* 7 (1967): 1–18.

Deasy, G. F., and P. R. Griess. "Local and regional differences in long-term bituminous coal production in the eastern U.S." *Annals of the Association of American Geographers* 57 (1967): 519–533.

Diones, L. "Locational factors and locational developments in the Soviet chemical industry." University of Chicago Department of Geography, Research Paper 119, 1969.

Faden, A. M. "Inefficiency of the regular hexagon in industrial location." *Geographical Analysis* 1 (1969): 321–328.

Golledge, R. "Conceptualizing the market decision process." *Journal of Regional Science* 7 (1967): 239–258.

Greenhut, M. L. "Interregional programming and the demand factor of location." *Journal of Regional Science* 7 (1967): 151–160.

Hayes, C. R., and N. W. Schul. "Why do manufacturers locate in the southern Piedmont?" *Land Economics* 44 (1968): 117–120.

Hoover, E. M. "Some programming models of industry location." *Land Economics* 43 (1967): 303–311.

Isard, W., and T. Smith. *"Location games." Papers and Proceedings of the Regional Science Association* 19 (1967): 45–82.

Karaska, G. "Manufacturing linkages in the Philadelphia economy." *Geographical Analysis* 1 (1969): 354–369.

Karaska, G., and D. Bramhall. *Locational analysis for manufacturing.* Cambridge, Mass.: MIT Press, 1969.

Krumme, G. "Note on locational adjustment patterns in industrial geography." *Geografiska Annaler* 51B (1969): 15–19.

Krumme, G. "Toward a geography of enterprise." *Economic Geography* 45 (1969): 30–40.

Leamer, E. E. "Locational equilibria." *Journal of Regional Science* 8 (1968): 229–242.

Little, W. I. "Location solutions through integrated systems management." *Land Economics* 45 (1969): 97–102.

Mason, P. F. "Some changes in domestic iron mining as a result of pelletization." *Annals of the Association of American Geographers* 58 (1968): 535–551.

Melamid, A. "Geography of the Nigerian petroleum industry." *Economic Geography* 44 (1968): 37–56.

Morrison, J. L., M. Scripter, and R. H. T. Smith. "Basic measures of manufacturing in the U.S." *Economic Geography* 44 (1968): 296–311.

Patni, R. L. "A new method for measuring location changes in a manufacturing industry." *Economic Geography* 44 (1968): 210–217.

Richter, C. E. "Impact of industrial linkages on geographic association." *Journal of Regional Science* 9 (1969): 19–28.

Rydell, C. P. "Location principle between the median and the mode." *Journal of Regional Science* 7 (1967): 185–192.

Sakashita, N. "Production and demand function and location theory of the firm." *Papers and Proceedings of the Regional Science Association* 20 (1968): 109–122.

Schultz, G. "Facility planning for a public service system: Solid waste collection." *Journal of Regional Science* 9 (1969): 291–308.

Seymour, D. "Polygon of forces and the Weber problem." *Journal of Regional Science* 8 (1968): 243–246.

Steed, G. "Changing milieu of the firm: A study in manufacturing geography." *Annals of the Association of American Geographers* 58 (1968): 506–525.

Streit, M. E. "Spatial association and economic linkages between industries." *Journal of Regional Science* 9 (1969): 177–188.

Teitz, M. "Locational strategies for competitive systems." *Journal of Regional Science* 8 (1968): 135–148.

Webb, G. W. "Factors affecting location of coal-burning steam electric generating plants." *Professional Geographer* 19 (1967): 171–174.

Williams, W. "Impact of state and local taxes on industry location." *Journal of Regional Science* 7 (1967): 49–59.

Chapter Six

Burghardt, A. F. "Origin and development of the rail network of the Niagara peninsula." *Annals of the Association of American Geographers* 59 (1969): 417–440.

Casetti, E. "Optimal interregional investment transfers." *Journal of Regional Science* 8 (1968): 101–107.

Dayal, E. "Changing patterns of India's international trade." *Economic Geography* 44 (1968): 240–261.

Fleming, D. K. "Independent transport carriers in ocean transportation." *Economic Geography* 44 (1968): 21–36.

Gauthier, H. "Transportation and the growth of the San Paulo economy." *Journal of Regional Science* 8 (1968): 77–94.

Haggett, P. "Horton combinatorial model and regional highway networks." *Journal of Regional Science* 7 (1967): 281–290.

Johnson, J. F. "Influence of cost—distance factors on overseas exports of corn from the U.S. Midwest." *Economic Geography* 45 (1969): 170–179.

Kuenne, R. "Dynamic combinatorial problem in space." *Journal of Regional Science* 8 (1968): 165–180.

Lewis, J. E. "Changes in highway mobility in the U.S. South, 1940–1960." *Professional Geographer* 20 (1968): 382–387.

Morawski, W. "Balance of interregional commodity flows in Poland." *Papers and Proceedings of the Regional Science Association* 20 (1968): 29–42.

Munro, J. M. "Planning the Appalachian Development Highway System." *Land Economics* 45 (1969): 149–161.

Scott, A. J. "Programming models of an integrated transport network." *Papers and Proceedings of the Regional Science Association* 19 (1967): 215–222.

Siddall, W. "Railroad gauges and spatial interaction." *Geographical Review* 59 (1969): 29–57.

Werner, C. "Role of topology and geometry in optimum network design." *Papers and Proceedings of the Regional Science Association* 21 (1968): 173–190.

Wohl, M. "Transient queuing behavior, capacity restraints, and travel forecasting." *Papers and Proceedings of the Regional Science Association* 21 (1968): 191–204.

Yeates, M. "A note concerning the development of a geographic model of international trade." *Geographical Analysis* 1 (1969): 399–403.

Chapter Seven

Adams, J. "Directional bias in intra-urban migration." *Economic Geography* 45 (1969): 302–323.

Alcaly, R. E. "Aggregation and gravity models." *Journal of Regional Science* 7 (1967): 61–73.

Berry, B. J. L., and P. Schwind. "Information and entropy in migrant flows." *Geographical Analysis* 1 (1969): 5–14.

Brown, L. *Diffusion dynamics.* Lund Studies in Geography, Series B, 29, 1968.

Casetti, E., and R. K. Semple. "Concerning the testing of spatial diffusion hypotheses." *Geographical Analysis* 1 (1969): 254–259.

Claeson, C. F. "Distance and human interaction." *Geografiska Annaler* 50B (1968): 143–169.

Claeson, C. F. "Zone preference in intra-regional population movement." *Geografiska Annaler* 50B (1968): 133–143.

Gerger, T. "Investigations into migrations of manpower." *Geografiska Annaler* 50B (1968): 27–31.

Hägerstrand, T. *Innovation diffusion as a spatial process.* Chicago: University of Chicago Press, 1967.

Horton, F. E., and R. I. Witticks. "Spatial model for examining the journey to work." *Professional Geographer* 21 (1969): 223–226.

Howrey, E. O. "On the choice of forecasting models for air travel." *Journal of Regional Science* 9 (1969): 215–224.

Hudson, J. C. "Diffusion in a central place system." *Geographical Analysis* 1 (1969): 45–58.

Huff, D. L., and G. F. Jenks. "Graphic interpretation of the friction of distance in gravity models." *Annals of the Association of American Geographers* 58 (1968): 814–824.

Jayawardena, C. "Migration and social change: Survey of Indian communities overseas." *Geographical Review* 58 (1968): 426–449.

Johnsson, B. "Utilizing telegrams for describing contact patterns and spatial interaction." *Geografiska Annaler* 50B (1968): 38–51.

Jordan, T. G. "Origin of Anglo-American cattle ranching in Texas: A documentation of diffusion from the rural South." *Economic Geography* 45 (1969): 63–87.

Jordan, T. G. "Population origins in Texas, 1850." *Geographical Review* 59 (1969): 83–103.

Katzman, M. "Ethnic geography and regional economies." *Economic Geography* 45 (1969): 45–52.

Laber, G. "Determinants of international travel between Canada and the U.S." *Geographical Analysis* 1 (1969): 329–336.

Long, W. H. "City characteristics and the demand for international air travel." *Land Economics* 44 (1968): 197–204.

McDonald, J. R. "Labor immigration in France, 1946–1965." *Annals of the Association of American Geographers* 59 (1969): 116–134.

Mazek, W. F. "Unemployment and the efficiency of migration." *Journal of Regional Science* 9 (1969): 101–108.

Morrill, R. L. "Waves of spatial diffusion." *Journal of Regional Science* 8 (1968): 1–18.

Morrill, R. L. and F. Pitts. "Marriage, migration, and the mean information field." *Annals of the Association of American Geographers* 57 (1967): 401–422.

Murray, M. A. "Geography of death in the U.S. and the U.K." *Annals of the Association of American Geographers* 57 (1967): 301–314.

Niedercorn, J. H., and B. V. Bechdolt. "Economic derivation of the gravity law of spatial interaction." *Journal of Regional Science* 9 (1969): 273–282.

Olsson, G. "Complementary models: A study of colonization maps." *Geografiska Annaler* 50B (1968): 115–132.

Pyle, G. F. "Diffusion of cholera in the U.S. in the 19th century." *Geographical Analysis* 1 (1969): 59–75.

Rogers, A. *Matrix analysis of interregional population growth and distribution.* Berkeley: University of California Press, 1968.

Wheeler, J. "Work-trip length and the ghetto." *Land Economics* 44 (1968): 107–111.

Wheeler, J. O. "Some effects of occupational status on work trips." *Journal of Regional Science* 9 (1969): 69–78.

Wheeler, J. O., and S. Brunn. "Negro migration into rural southwestern Michigan." *Geographical Review* 58 (1968): 214–230.

Wolpert, J. "Basis for stability of interregional transactions." *Geographical Analysis* 1 (1969): 152–180.

Wolpert, J. "Distance and directional bias in inter-urban migratory streams." *Annals of the Association of American Geographers* 57 (1967): 605–616.

Chapter Eight

Amato, P. "Population density, land value and socioeconomic class in Bogotá." *Land Economics* 45 (1969): 66–73.

Bahl, R. W. "A land speculation model: Urban sprawl." *Journal of Regional Science* 8 (1968): 199–208.

Borchert, J. R. "American metropolitan evolution." *Geographical Review* 57 (1967): 301–332.

Bourne, L. "Location factors in the redevelopment process." *Land Economics* 45 (1969): 183–193.

Bourne, L. *Private redevelopment of the central city.* University of Chicago Department of Geography, Research Paper 112, 1967.

Bourne, L. "Spatial allocation: Land-use conversion model of urban growth." *Journal of Regional Science* 9 (1969): 261–272.

Breese, G., ed. *Cities in newly developed countries.* Englewood Cliffs, N.J.: Prentice-Hall, 1969.

Breger, G. E. "Concept and causes of urban blight." *Land Economics* 43 (1967): 369–376.

Brush, J. E. "Spatial patterns of population in Indian cities." *Geographical Review* 58 (1968): 362–391.

Carey, G. W., L. Macomber, and M. Greenberg. "Educational and demographic factors in the urban geography of Washington, D.C." *Geographical Review* 58 (1968): 515–537.

Chapin, F. S. "Activity system and urban structure." *Journal of the American Institute of Planners* 34 (1968): 11–18.

"Cities, the black and the poor." *Journal of the American Institute of Planners* 35 (1969), entire issue.

Clark, W. A. V. "Spacing models in intra-city studies." *Geographical Analysis* 1 (1969): 391–398.

Coulson, M. R. L. "Distribution of population age structure in Kansas City." *Annals of the Association of American Geographers* 58 (1968): 155–176.

Cox, K. R. "Suburbia and voting behavior in a London metropolitan area." *Annals of the Association of American Geographers* 58 (1968): 111–127.

Deskins, D., and R. S. Yuill. "A new functional urban boundary?" *Professional Geographer* 19 (1967): 330–338.

Doeppers, D. F. "Globeville neighborhood in Denver." *Geographical Review* 57 (1967): 506–522.

Dott, A. K. "Intra-city hierarchy of central places, Calcutta." *Professional Geographer* 21 (1969): 18–22.

Harris, B. "City of the future." *Papers and Proceedings of the Regional Science Association* 19 (1967): 185–198.

Harris, C. "Stochastic process model of residential development." *Journal of Regional Science* 8 (1968): 29–39.

Hart, J. F., N. Salisbury, and E. Smith. "Dying village and some notions about urban growth." *Economic Geography* 44 (1968): 343–349.

Hewings, G. J. D. "A note on forecasting the economic base." *Professional Geographer* 21 (1969): 315–318.

Holzner, L., E. Domisse, and J. Mueller. "Toward a theory of cultural-genetic city classification." *Annals of the Association of American Geographers* 57 (1967): 367–381.

Jakle, J. A., and K. Wheeler. "Changing residential structure of the Dutch population in Kalamazoo." *Annals of the Association of American Geographers* 59 (1969): 441–460.

Kaiser, E. "Location decision factors in a producer's model of residential development." *Land Economics* 44 (1968): 351–362.

Kersten, E., and D. Ross. "Clayton: A new metropolitan focus in the St. Louis area." *Annals of the Association of American Geographers* 58 (1968): 637–649.

Kikkinen, K. "Change in village and rural population with distance from Duluth." *Economic Geography* 44 (1968): 312–325.

King, L. "Discriminatory analysis of urban growth patterns in Ontario and Quebec, 1951–1961." *Annals of the Association of American Geographers* 57 (1967): 566–578.

Lo, C. P. "Changing population distribution in Hong Kong." *Annals of the Association of American Geographers* 58 (1968): 273–289.

Lubove, R. "Urbanization process." *Journal of the American Institute of Planners* 33 (1967): 33–38.

Murdie, R. *Factorial ecology of Metropolitan Toronto, 1951–1961.* University of Chicago Department of Geography, Research Paper 116, 1969.

Murray, B. "Metropolitan interpersonal income inequality." *Land Economics* 45 (1969): 121–124.

Newling, B. "Spatial variation of urban population densities." *Geographical Review* 59 (1969): 242–252.

Northam, R. "Population size, relative location, and declining urban centers in the U.S." *Land Economics* 45 (1969): 313–322.

Pratt, R. T. "Appraisal of minimum requirements techniques." *Economic Geography* 44 (1968): 117–124.

Preston, R. "Detailed comparison of land use in three transition zones." *Annals of the Association of American Geographers* 58 (1968): 461–484.

Putnam, S. H. "Intra-urban industry location design and implementation." *Papers and Proceedings of the Regional Science Association* 19 (1967): 199–214.

Schenker, E., and J. Wilson. "Use of public mass transportation in major metropolitan areas of the U.S." *Land Economics* 43 (1967): 361–367.

Scott, A. "Spatial equilibrium of the central city." *Journal of Regional Science* 9 (1969): 29–46.

Simmons, J. W. "Changing residence in the city: A review of intra-urban mobility." *Geographical Review* 58 (1968): 622–651.

Sinclair, R. "Von Thünen and urban sprawl." *Annals of the Association of American Geographers* 57 (1967): 72–87.

Smolensky, E., S. Becker, and H. Molotch. "Prisoner's dilemma and ghetto expansion." *Land Economics* 44 (1968): 419–430.

Solomon, R. J. "Property values as a structural element of urban evolution." *Economic Geography* 45 (1969): 1–29.

Stegner, M. "Accessibility models and residential location." *Journal of the American Institute of Planners* 35 (1969): 30–34.

Sternlieb, G., and B. Inkik. "Housing vacancy analysis." *Land Economics* 45 (1969): 117–120.

Stoner, G. E. "Comparative analysis of urban economic base: Employment structure of Indian cities." *Economic Geography* 44 (1968): 71–82.

Ullman, E. "Minimum requirements after a decade." *Economic Geography* 44 (1968): 364–369.

Ward, D. "Emergence of central immigrant ghettos in American cities." *Annals of the Association of American Geographers* 58 (1968): 343–359.

Ward, D. "Spatial structure of immigrant residential districts in the late 19th century." *Geographical Analysis* 1 (1969): 337–353.

Wheeler, J. "Transportation models and changing home—work location." *Professional Geographer* 19 (1967): 144–148.

Wolf, L. "Metropolitan tidal wave in Ohio, 1900–2000." *Economic Geography* 45 (1969): 133–154.

Chapter Nine

Airov, J. "Fiscal policy theory in interregional economy." *Papers and Proceedings of the Regional Science Association* 19 (1967): 83–110.

Berry, B. J. L. *Essays on commodity flows and the spatial structure of the Indian economy.* University of Chicago Department of Geography, Research Paper 111, 1966.

Berry, B. J. L. "Interdependence of spatial structure and spatial behavior." *Papers and Proceedings of the Regional Science Association* 21 (1968): 205–228.

Brown, S. E., and C. E. Trott. "Grouping tendencies in an economic regionalization of Poland." *Annals of the Association of American Geographers* 58 (1968): 327–342.

Garnick, D. H. "Disaggregated basic-service model and regional projections." *Journal of Regional Science* 9 (1969): 87–100.

Haggett, P. "Trend surface mapping in the interregional comparison of intra-regional structure." *Papers and Proceedings of the Regional Science Association* 20 (1968): 19–28.

Hamilton, H. R., et al. *System simulation for regional analysis: River basin planning.* Cambridge, Mass.: MIT Press, 1969.

Hartman, L. M., and D. Seckler. "Application of dynamic growth theory to regions." *Journal of Regional Science* 7 (1967): 167–173.

Hodge, G. "Urban structure and regional development." *Papers and Proceedings of the Regional Science Association* 21 (1968): 101–124.

Isard, W., et. al. "On the linkage of socioeconomic and ecologic systems." *Papers and Proceedings of the Regional Science Association* 21 (1968): 79–100.

Janelle, D. G. "Spatial reorganization: A model and concept." *Annals of the Association of American Geographers* 59 (1969): 348–364.

Karaska, G. "Input-output coefficients for different levels of aggregation." *Journal of Regional Science* 8 (1968): 215–227.

Lankford, P. M. "Regionalization: Theory and alternative algorithms." *Geographical Analysis* 1 (1969): 196–212.

Lees, F. A. "Interregional flows of funds through state and local government securities." *Journal of Regional Science* 9 (1969): 77–86.

Levin, M. R. "The big regions." *Journal of the American Institute of Planners* 34 (1968): 66–79.

Melezin, A. "Soviet regionalization." *Geographical Review* 58 (1968): 593–621.

Neutze, G. M. "Major determinants of location patterns." *Land Economics* 43 (1967): 222–232.

Pratt, R. "Regional production inputs and income generation." *Journal of Regional Science* 7 (1967): 141–149.

Sabbagh, M. E. "Some geographic characteristics of a plural society: Apartheid in South Africa." *Geographical Review* 58 (1968): 1–28.

Stabler, J. C. "Exports and evolution: Process of regional change." *Land Economics* 44 (1968): 11–23.

Weiss, S., and E. Gooding. "Estimates of different employment multipliers in a small regional economy." *Land Economics* 44 (1968): 235–244.

Whebell, C. F. J. "Corridors: A theory of urban systems." *Annals of the Association of American Geographers* 59 (1969): 1–26.

Chapter Ten

Bahl, R. W., and R. H. Saunders. "Role of state and local government in the economic development of Appalachia." *Land Economics* 44 (1968): 50–58.

Brown, H. "Shift and share projections of regional economic growth." *Journal of Regional Science* 9 (1969): 1–18.

Brunn, S., and W. Hoffman. "Geography of federal grants-in-aid to states." *Economic Geography* 45 (1969): 226–238.

Buchanan, R. "Towards the Netherlands 2000: Dutch national plan." *Economic Geography* 45 (1969): 258–274.

Church, R. J. "Some problems of regional economic development in West Africa." *Economic Geography* 45 (1969): 53–62.

Cole, L. M. "Transport investment strategies and economic development." *Land Economics* 44 (1968): 307–318.

Cumberland, J. H., and F. van Beek. "Regional economic development objective and subsidies of local industry." *Land Economics* 43 (1967): 253–264.

Dutt, A. K. "Levels of planning in the Netherlands with particular reference to regional planning." *Annals of the Association of American Geographers* 58 (1968): 670–685.

Hale, C. "Mechanics of the spread effect in regional development." *Land Economics* 43 (1967): 434–445.

Hampton, P. "Regional economic development in New Zealand." *Journal of Regional Science* 8 (1968): 41–55.

Hultman, C. "Exports and economic growth: A survey." *Land Economics* 43 (1967): 148–157.

Mash, V. A. "Problems of optimum economic development models." *Papers and Proceedings of the Regional Science Association* 20 (1968): 123–134.

Olsen, E. "Regional economic differences." *Papers and Proceedings of the Regional Science Association* 20 (1968): 7–18.

Parsons, K. "Poverty as an issue on developmental policy." *Land Economics* 45 (1969): 52–65.

Perloff, H. "Key features of regional planning." *Journal of the American Institute of Planners* 34 (1968): 153–159.

Rodwin, L., et al. *Planning urban growth and regional development: Guayana, Venezuela.* Cambridge, Mass.: MIT Press, 1969.

Sakashita, N. "Regional allocation of public investment." *Papers and Proceedings of the Regional Science Association* 19 (1967): 161–184.

Spitz, J. V. "Relative wage trends in nine southern states." *Journal of Regional Science* 9 (1969): 319–324.

Stewart, C. T. "Regional allocation of public funds for economic development." *Land Economics* 43 (1967): 421–433.

Thomas, M. D. "Regional economic growth." *Land Economics* 45 (1969): 43–51.

REFERENCES

Glossary

Accessibility The relative degree of ease with which a location may be reached from other locations.

Administrative principle In central place theory, the principle which states that a higher-order service area wholly includes seven service areas of the next lower order.

Agglomeration Spatial grouping together of activities or people for mutual benefit. Particular savings, or economies, accrue to such groupings of retailers and industries.

Amenities Features of the environment—natural or human—which are perceived as pleasant and attractive.

Assembly costs A manufacturer's transport costs on raw material inputs.

Basic activities Economic activities, the products of which are exported out of the region; the opposite of nonbasic or service activities which are produced and consumed internally.

Break-of-bulk A shipment's division into parts—typically at ports—upon transfer from water to land transport.

Central place function Activity offered from a place to the surrounding hinterland (countryside).

Centrality A state of high accessibility; the quality of being at the center of a transportation system.

Cluster A close spatial proximity of settlements.

Colonial Used here in the limited sense of dependence of a less developed area upon a more developed area.

Comparative advantage The variation of an area's or location's suitability for different activities; based on the idea that all locations have certain activities which are most profitable.

Competition Refers here to more than one place or enterprise seeking the same customers, resources, or whatever; it results in a division of territory.

Complementarity A state that exists if the varying advantages of two or more locations or areas permit a mutually beneficial linkage, usually by trade.

Concentration Used here to mean the tendency of people or activities to congregate, or cluster, in space.

Congestion On a transport link, the condition of retarded flow, resulting in increased costs.

Connectivity The degree of direct linkage from one location to other locations on a transport network.

Contact field Refers to the spatial distribution of acquaintances of an individual or group.

Convenience goods Goods used very frequently, such as groceries or gasoline.

Demand in space   The value of goods and/or services desired by customers; this may be expressed for unit areas or per capita.

Diseconomies   The diminishing returns or profitability that sometimes results from greater size (as of a city) or output (as of a plant).

Dispersed city   A term some authors apply to a cluster of towns with some specialization of function; other authors apply it to a built-up urban area together with its surrounding rural nonfarm population.

Diversification   For firms, refers to a variety of outputs, usually in more than one industrial sector; for cities, indicates there is no unusual dependence on or specialization in particular industries.

Economic margin   In agricultural location theory, refers to the farthest locations from which goods can be profitably shipped to commercial markets.

Efficiency   Best use of territory; inefficiency in space means less-than-optimal use of territory.

Environment   The natural and cultural setting within which people and firms exist; used here mainly to treat variations in natural conditions, such as landforms, or climate.

Equilibrium   A theoretical state of stability. Any deviation from this state would decrease efficiency or profitability; equilibrium prices are values (for goods, labor, capital, or land) corresponding to these conditions.

Extensive   Refers here to a relatively low level of inputs or outputs per unit area.

External economies   Benefits (higher sales, profits; lower costs) at a location, due to characteristics of the location (as size of city and its labor and capital supply) and of other firms (as spin-off of ideas from competitors).

Exurban   The zone beyond the urban built-up area, but within which commuters to the urban area are dominant.

Functional region   Area under the economic and social domination of a center; nodal region is a better term.

Ghetto   An area of the city distinguished by ethnic, racial, or religious character; usually, but not necessarily, a low income area.

Gravity model   A particular mathematical description of reduced interaction with increasing distance.

Hierarchy   The concept that urban places, together with their trade areas, may be grouped into distinctive levels of functional importance, and that the individual con-sumer will travel to smaller, closer places for everyday purchases and to larger, more distant places for less-demanded goods.

Industrial complex   A set of specific industries which are closely related, usually because each industry makes significant purchases from the others.

Information   Knowledge about the environment, technology, and other conditions that would be necessary for optimal decisions.

Information field   The geographical distribution (around an individual group) of knowledge about other people or areas.

Innovation   Using an idea to lead to change, often beneficial, in individual behavior or in a production process.

Input-output   Refers to the pattern of purchases and sales among sectors of the economy; especially useful in tracing the effects of change in one sector on the behavior of other sectors.

Intensive   Refers here to a relatively high level of inputs and/or outputs per unit area.

Interdependence   Used here to indicate that because of specialization and trade, what occurs at one location affects what happens at many other locations.

Intervening opportunity   In migration theory or shopping behavior, the presence of closer, better opportunities which greatly diminish the attractiveness of even slightly farther ones.

Isodapane   In industrial location theory, a line or contour of constant total cost (assembly, production, and distribution).

Labor productivity   The relative cost or labor per unit of output.

Laborshed   The zone from which workers commute to a plant or city.

Landscape   Refers here to the systematic human pattern of occupance.

Linkages   The pattern of interdependence among industries.

Location   An area which may be treated as a point at the scale of observation used; given meaning by its specialized use.

Location freedom   The notion that an activity is free to locate anywhere; probably only a theoretical freedom.

Location rent See Rent gradient.

Location triangle In location theory, a simple diagram of optimum location in the case of three markets and/or material sources.

Marginal farmer The farm entrepreneur with very low net return per man/hour.

Marginal productivity The additional output or return from the last added unit of inputs.

Market A place or location where goods and services are demanded and exchanged.

Market penetration A firm's share of a market (usually nonspatial).

Market principle In central place theory, that arrangement of the hierarchy of places which will minimize aggregate distance traveled to centers; service areas of larger, higher-order places include one-third of the service areas of each of the six neighboring lower-order places.

Milkshed The zone of an urban market's fluid milk supply.

Movements Refers to trips by people. These may be temporary (going to work or shopping), transient (going on vacation), or "permanent" (changing residence).

Nesting In central place theory, refers to the tendency for service areas of lower-order places to be wholly included in the service areas of larger, higher-order places.

Network, transport The actual physical system of links and nodes on which movement can take place.

Nodal region The area which is dependent on or is dominated by a nodal center; a nodal center is the center of a transport network.

Nonoptimal behavior Any decision making, whether intentional or by default, which results in a less-than-maximum profit outcome.

Oligopoly, spatial Refers to a fairly stable shared regional market, usually with a common price structure.

Orientation The tendency for various kinds of industries to locate at markets (market orientation), at resources (resource or raw-material orientation), or because transport costs are decisive (transport orientation).

Peripherality The state of being at the edge of a communication system, far from the controlling centers of the culture or economy.

Primacy An unusually high proportion of population and economic activity in the single largest city of a country, usually the capital.

Primary industry Manufacturing which specializes in basic processing or conversion of raw materials, as distinguished from secondary industry, which utilizes the outputs of primary manufacturers.

Processing activity Using a technological process to transform inputs to some demanded output.

Processing or production costs The actual costs— mainly capital and labor—incurred in the conversion process, not including transport costs.

Queuing The state in which demanders of a good or service must wait for its delivery, because it is already being provided at the limit of capacity (as right-of-way is being provided in rush-hour traffic).

Randomness Used here to indicate that locational uncertainty or imprecision which one may be expected to result from many small and unknown factors.

Range In central place theory, the maximum distance over which a seller will offer a good or service; or from which a purchaser will travel for it.

Rank-size rule Notes the empirical tendency for the product obtained by multiplying a city's rank times its size to equal a constant, the population of the country's largest city.

Region A portion of space which, according to specified criteria, possesses meaningful unity; see Uniform region and Nodal region.

Regional convergence Implies that as an economy tends to reach an equilibrium state, prices, incomes, and other measures of value will tend to equalize.

Regional planning The conscious attempt of government to influence the course of economic and social development; usually it is a result of welfare considerations, more rational use of resources, or alleviation of poverty.

Regionalism The existence of a regional or sectional identification and loyalty, often resulting in particular kinds of behavior.

Relative location The advantages or disadvantages of a particular location measured with reference to all competing locations.

Rent gradient In agricultural and urban structure theory, is a measure of the value to the landowner of the relative accessibility of a certain location; as a result of competition for more accessible locations, a distance-decay gradient in location rent will develop outward from the central point of greatest accessibility.

Residential farm   A farm occupied at low productivity by an urban commuter.

Resources   In an economic sense, any valued aspect of the environment; as used here, demanded natural materials, such as water, minerals, or soil.

Retail gravitation   The notion that the attractiveness of a seller to a customer varies inversely with the distance between them.

Scale, returns to   The concept used to measure the tendency for marginal costs (those of the next unit) and average costs (those of all units) to decrease with increasing volume of output; diminishing returns or diseconomies may set in at excess volumes.

Sector theory   The tendency for sectors or wedges projecting outward from a city's center to be devoted to different uses and social classes.

Self-sufficiency   The attempt of the local economy to provide by itself for all its needs and demands.

Service area (or trade area)   The territory from which most of a seller's customers originate.

Shifting cultivation   An agricultural economy in which fields must be abandoned, and hamlets must often migrate, due to exhaustion of soil fertility.

Social distance   Distance as perceived by individuals or small groups from themselves to other individuals or social groups.

Social space   The territory within which a social group carries on most of its interrelations.

Spatial adjustment   Implies changes in the location of a firm or of its suppliers' markets in the face of external change (perhaps change in resources or markets).

Spatial behavior   Refers to the decisions individuals make about their use of and action in space.

Spatial diffusion   The process of the gradual spread over space of people or ideas from critical centers of origin.

Spatial equilibrium   *see* Equilibrium.

Spatial error   Used here to indicate that individuals or firms make mistakes in their location decisions; *see* Nonoptimal behavior.

Spatial experience   Refers to the extent and intensity of knowledge of territory and travel through it.

Spatial interaction   The interrelation of locations usually in terms of movement of people or communications; the level of interaction varies inversely with distance between locations.

Spatial monopoly   Used here to mean that a given central place's sellers supply most of certain goods and services to its trade area; a processor (for example, of crops or minerals) may similarly have a spatial monopoly over surrounding suppliers.

Spatial organization   The aggregate pattern of use of space by a society.

Spatial relations   The ways in which space and distance influence behavior and location decisions.

Spatially-restricted society   A culture in which the experience of most members is limited to a small territory and in which local self-sufficiency is required.

Specialization   A particular location's or area's devotion to producing one or very few products.

Stress   In analysis of networks, refers to the degree to which nodes or links must be used in interaction between locations.

Subsistence   The condition of a local economy's ability to provide only for its basic food and shelter needs without significant surplus.

Substitution   In seeking maximum profitability at a location or for a firm, it may be possible to exchange more labor for less capital, or more fertilizer for less land, depending on which is scarcer.

Suitcase farmer   Urban worker who farms only part of the year, often using inadequate methods.

Technological unemployment   Refers to increasing productivity of labor (such as that due to mechanization of agriculture) displacing workers from activities which are no longer productive relative to other activities.

Threshold   In central place theory, the minimum level of sales needed to attain marginal profitability.

Transferability   The degree to which a good or service may be transported.

Transhumance   The practice of shifting herds between upland summer pasture and lowland winter pasture.

GLOSSARY

Transport principle In central place theory, that arrangement of the hierarchy of places which results in the most efficient transport network; *see* Network, transport.

Underemployment A case of individuals working either part time or part of the year, but seeking full-time work; or, particularly in agriculture, may refer to full-time occupation which inefficiently uses time and labor.

Uniform region A territory or space for which the internal variation of specified criteria is appreciably less than the variation between this area and other areas.

Index